TARYN BRUMFITT is an internationally recognised keynote speaker and the fiercely passionate thought leader behind the Body Image Movement. A bestselling author and director of the inspiring social-change documentaries *Embrace* and *Embrace Kids*, Taryn's global crusade to end the body dissatisfaction epidemic has seen her recognised by UN Women, Amy Poehler's Smart Girls and the Geena Davis Institute. Her talk at Google HQ in Silicon Valley was live-streamed to every Google office in the world. She was a finalist in the 2019 Australian of the Year and 2018 Australian Financial Review 100 Women of Influence awards, and was crowned the 2018 SA winner for Excellence in Women's Leadership and winner of the EY Entrepreneur of the Year, South Australia.

A two-time marathon runner, lover of life and people, and mum to three children, Taryn remains humble, proud and eager to make the biggest impact on body image and self-love the world has ever seen.

DR ZALI YAGER is the Executive Director of the Body Confident Collective and Honorary Associate Professor in the Institute for Health and Sport at Victoria University. Zali has a health and physical education background, and is an internationally recognised expert in the body image space, known for figuring out 'what works' to build body image in school and community settings and for her work in the Body Confident Mums project. A 2021 Westpac Social Change Fellow who has presented her work around the world, Zali is ridiculously passionate and driven by the desire to make this research matter and create a safer body image environment for the next generation. Zali is also a mum of three, and when she's not at her computer, you will usually find her at the beach.

embrace
kids

How you can help your kids to
love and celebrate their bodies

TARYN BRUMFITT
and DR ZALI YAGER

PENGUIN BOOKS

UK | USA | Canada | Ireland | Australia
India | New Zealand | South Africa | China

Penguin is part of the Penguin Random House group of companies whose
addresses can be found at global.penguinrandomhouse.com

Penguin
Random House
Australia

First published by Penguin Books in 2022

Cover design by Alex Ross © Penguin Random House Australia Pty Ltd
'1890s UK Curve of Youth Magazine Advert' (p. 44)
courtesy of Retro AdArchives/Alamy Stock Photo
Back cover photograph of Zali Yager courtesy of Fire & Fly Media
Internal design by Post Pre-Press Group, Australia
Typeset in 12/18 pt Freight Text Pro by Post Pre-Press Group, Australia

Printed and bound in Australia by Griffin Press, part of Ovato, an accredited
ISO AS/NZS 14001 Environmental Management Systems printer

 A catalogue record for this
book is available from the
National Library of Australia

ISBN 978 1 76104 657 5

penguin.com.au

We at Penguin Random House Australia acknowledge that Aboriginal and Torres Strait Islander
peoples are the Traditional Custodians and the first storytellers of the lands on which we live
and work. We honour Aboriginal and Torres Strait Islander peoples' continuous connection
to Country, waters, skies and communities. We celebrate Aboriginal and Torres Strait Islander
stories, traditions and living cultures; and we pay our respects to Elders past and present.

To all the kids (and the parents!)
who need to know that they are amazing,
just the way they are

Contents

Introduction

'I have no idea how to manage the impact
of social media on my kids' body image.'

'My daughter asked how she can chop off
her stomach – what should I say?'

'My kids have gained weight over lockdown.
What should I do?'

'I'm so scared that they will feel the same
way about their body that I do.'

These comments make you just want to run for the hills, don't
they? The curly questions our kids ask can be challenging to
answer, and it often feels like what we say to our kids is contradic-
tory to the way we live. How do we give our children confidence
about their tummies and wobbly bits if we'd like to 'chop off'
our own too? How do we assure our kids that it's okay to put
some weight on without 'promoting obesity'? How do we manage
our kids' social media use when most of us don't know how to
manage our own?

Body image, and the associated issues of weight, food and physical activity, are hot topics in our homes and families. The majority of us would like to change something about our bodies – around 50 per cent of children, and at least 70 per cent of adolescents and adults. While body image dissatisfaction can often be dismissed as 'superficial' and 'just a silly teenage problem', that couldn't be further from the truth. Body image is related to every other mental and physical health issue you can think of, including the big, scary ones like depression, eating disorders, self-harm and suicide. And it's a problem that doesn't just go away when puberty is over. Women – in particular – and men continue to be dissatisfied with their bodies throughout their whole lives.

By the time we've become parents, many of us are conscious of the huge impact that our battle with our bodies has had on our lives. Our confidence, our careers, our relationships, and the impact we could have on the world have all been affected by how we feel about the way we look. By now, we have realised we don't want our kids to feel this way. And we'll do just about anything *not* to pass this burden on to them. We don't want our kids to miss out, step down, or be held back by their body image. We don't want them to feel like they don't fit in, shouldn't go for opportunities, or can't be loved because of the way they look. We don't want them to waste their time, money and energy trying to make their bodies smaller, bigger, harder, tighter, more of this and less of that. We don't want this to rule their lives like it did ours.

After people had seen the *Embrace* film, hundreds of thousands of people all over the world said one thing – 'I wish I'd had this earlier' – and then they asked one question: How can we help our kids not to turn out like this?' And so, after eight long years of fundraising, creating, filming and editing, and significant amounts of Taryn's blood and sweat (and yes there were tears), the *Embrace Kids* documentary was born. We know it's going to inspire kids all around the world to embrace their bodies and create the change we need in the world to help *everyone* feel good about their bodies. We also think it passes the baton to you, the parents. While *Embrace Kids* is for young people, the parents and grown-ups watching it with them get to be a little inspired to support them through these changes, inside and out.

But while being inspired to change is one thing, knowing how to go about it is another. We hope that the *Embrace Kids* film inspires kids, parents, grandparents and everyone in between, but we've written this book to try to make sure everyone is informed to turn their inspiration into action. Most of us parents feel a little out of our depth at some point (or all points!). It's impossible to know how to do everything, particularly with issues as complex as bodies, weight and health. We know, because every time we've given a talk, parents have shared with us the very challenging body image problems that are present in their homes. They've come to us with so many heartbreaking questions, many of which can't be answered in a five-minute chat. All around us we see parents struggling with how to help their kids love their bodies in today's environment. They don't know what to say when their child says 'Am I fat?' or 'I want to lose weight' or 'I'm thinking of going on a diet' or 'I want to get a six-pack'.

We love quick fixes, and if you're a time-poor parent (never met a time-rich one!) we suspect you'll be tempted to jump around to chapters that interest you most, to skip to the 'how-to' part.

Please don't. We want you to get the most out of this book and implement meaningful change within your family. To do that, it is best to read this book from start to finish. You need to start with *you*.

This is a 'read it and swish it around in your head for a while' book. It's an unlearning of the way you might have lived your life until now. An important unlearning, so you can make sure that your kids grow up loving their bodies, liking their bodies, or even just not caring as much about what their bodies look like as we did.

We're aware that we are two middle-aged, able-bodied, white women in similarly sized bodies, and acknowledge the privileges we hold, and our intention to continue learning about lived experiences and identities that are different from our own. We write from our own lived and learned experiences, but this book wouldn't be what it is without the many important contributions from the diverse, talented, open and generous people who offered their wealth of experiences, stories and expertise. We encourage you to take what you need from our book, but to also support and read widely where other identities are represented, particularly those voices that have been marginalised. Some of the individuals who contributed here wanted to remain anonymous, so we have created pseudonyms for them – as indicated wherever we use the first name only for an adult. We also spoke to the kids – their insights from the *Embrace Kids* documentary are included throughout. It was wonderful to hear such strong, clear thoughts from our young voices. Change is possible.

SOME IMPORTANT CAVEATS

There are some things you need to know as you read and digest the material in this book.

Gender

Most of the research on this topic depicts gender as binary. We hope that researchers in the future will start to capture gender on the beautiful spectrum that it is, and understand more about non-binary attitudes and behaviours in relation to bodies and weight.

Size

In a book about accepting your body, we had to use some words to talk about body size.

1. **Obesity.** We don't use 'obesity' or 'overweight' in our regular life, in our writing, and in our talks as much as we can possibly avoid it. These words relating to weight categories are medicalised, and stigmatising. However, other people do use these words, and the research often refers to these terms, and we needed to use them at times for clarity and accuracy. We have used them as little as we can, often in inverted commas so you can tell we don't like them.

2. **BMI.** There is so much that is wrong with using the Body Mass Index. So, so, much. But it's used in pretty much every research study, so we have to keep using it until someone comes up with something else. We've explained more about the issues with BMI on p. 57.

Intentions

We have come to this book open, vulnerable and in pursuit of constant learning. Our intention is always to make everyone feel safe and welcome in our collaborative pursuit of making the world a better place.

BEFORE WE START

You can take a deep breath now. This book won't make you feel bad for things you've done (or not done). It won't be a whole bunch of things you have to remember. It's not another thing to add to your never-ending list.

This is not another parenting book.

It is a book for parents.

This is a book for every parent who wants to do everything they can to help their kids to be confident in who they are and how they look.

This is a book for every parent who falls into bed feeling like a failure each night, and still gets up to keep going the next day.

This is a book for every parent who was made to hate their body as a child, still carries a sense of shame around their body, and wants to make sure their kids don't feel the same way.

This is a book for every parent who wants to do the work on themselves – and in the world – to change the body image environment our kids are exposed to every day.

This is a book that will empower you with information for action.

part one

---

it starts with you

1

Our stories

TARYN'S STORY

NEVER SAY NEVER.

If you had said to me a few years back I'd be authoring a parenting book with a highly regarded Associate Professor, I would have said 'Get out of here' and given you a shove. I shouldn't be too surprised, though, because writing this book is just another thing on the 'didn't see that coming' list. I've had many of these moments over the past decade. In many ways, my life didn't end up how I thought it would.

When a photograph I posted online went viral back in 2013, everything changed. At the time I was a mum to three young children (seven, five and four years old), working as a photographer, living in suburbia, making half-hearted costumes for Book Week and trying not to run out of milk more than twice a week. Life was lovely and predictable; I was content.

If you're not familiar with the photo I posted, it's basically a reverse of the traditional 'Before' and 'After' shot. The 'Before' picture shows me with the 'perfect' body, at a bodybuilding competition, and the 'After' picture shows me bigger, with soft round curves, but much happier.

When I decided that I wanted to transform my body and be like the yummy mummies I'd seen, I dropped a bunch of weight by training myself into the ground and eating a restricted diet. I arrived in a body that was, according to society, 'hot'. I could go clothes shopping and everything would fit, I could wear sleeveless dresses and not be afraid of my 'tuckshop' arms wobbling around, and you could even crack a coconut on my tight butt. I was thin – oh, so blissfully thin (or so I thought).

But my new body was not sustainable, and after the short-lived weight loss, it returned to what it was before – curvy in parts, a wobbly tummy, and with arms so friendly they continue to wave well after I've finished waving. Sure, I was softer and curvier, but there was an undeniable difference in who I was. I was happy.

It was this happiness that led to much confusion among my friends. Many of them asked me, 'Taryn, your body is back to what it was before when you hated it, but you seem to be content and happy with how it looks. How?' The subtext being, how could I possibly be happy with this body? It's what led me to post the photo and tell a different narrative about how our bodies are not ornaments for display, but rather the vehicles to our dreams. It turns out that I found my peace in losing what I thought I wanted.

My non-traditional 'Before' and 'After' photos made news headlines across the world. It broke people's brains that a woman could love her body 'after' gaining weight. A friend even got off a Qantas flight and rang to tell me my story had made the *inflight* news. But I resented the fact that some parts of the media treated my story like a fluffy feel-good moment, and I resented the four-minute TV interviews that never allowed me to get to the depth and seriousness of the problem that people were experiencing – crippling relationships with their body.

I'll tell you what I resented more, though. The asshats who attacked me with such vitriol on social media, calling me a fat pig, a bad mother, and an all-round bad person for 'promoting obesity'. You see, even though 95 per cent of comments were overwhelmingly positive, my natural default was to only read the nasty ones.

Comments like:

> Fatso, put your clothes back on.

> This is just enabling fat people to stay fat and lazy. You want to truly love your body?? Get a fucking treadmill!

> Her body is gross either way.

> Just because you have had children doesn't give you an excuse to let yourself go and be out of shape – it's laziness!

And my personal fave:

> I'd bang her sober in the before pic. I'd need a few stiff drinks for the after.

How could people be so cruel? I attempted to defend myself as best as I could, but there were too many comments. It was the beginning of the end of my private life. A few days later I did my first TV interview on the *Today* show – the first of more than a thousand interviews I've given since that day.

I never intended to have a public profile, but this message needed a champion, and if my stepping up could help people have the same freeing and joyful relationship with their body that I had developed with mine, then sign me up, I thought. But it didn't come naturally. I had to work really hard at being comfortable in front of the spotlight. My new public life was quite a whirlwind of activity; an endless rollercoaster of steep learning curves, highs and lows. The highs were always the feedback I got from people letting me know that my story had changed their lives. The low was the sheer exhaustion. At times I felt like I had bitten off more than I could chew.

Later in 2013 I started the Body Image Campaign, which quickly turned into the Body Image Movement ('campaign' felt like it was going to end sometime soon, and I just knew I was in for the long haul). I realised this problem wasn't going away anytime soon, and that was made evident when I received over seven thousand emails and messages in response to my post. Every night, for months on end, I'd put the kids to bed, grab a coffee and respond to people's messages until 3 am. I didn't even make a dent in the volume. It was a futile mission, and I was exhausted.

So I decided it would make more sense to write a book rather than trying to get back to everyone individually. That book was my first, *Embrace*. Ricki Lake even wrote the foreword.

Around this time I decided to make a film, because I thought that being a photographer + enjoying telling stories (mostly when I've had too many mojitos) = a film. If I had known what I know now about the stamina it takes to get a feature doco on the big screen, would I have still gone down that path? Absolutely. With as much confidence and cockiness as I did? No way!

I raised the initial funds to make *Embrace* on Kickstarter. I set out to raise $200,000 in sixty days, and we hit that on day twelve, going on to raise a total of $331,000. (When I say 'we', I mean me and my three young kids at Home HQ surrounded by washing.) During this time I connected with celebrities far and wide; people like Ashton Kutcher who said, 'this is good for the world' and wrote about my story.

If you've not seen *Embrace*, ~~what is even wrong with you?~~ please do so as quickly as you can. Millions of people have watched it, and it's had a really big impact on how people view their body. It's through the film that Dr Zali Yager and I connected. After watching *Embrace*, Zali and her colleague Dr Ivanka Prichard approached the Body Image Movement to propose they conduct a global study on the impact of the film. They did, and in 2019 the study was published in a medical journal, which I hear in the academic world is kind of a big deal. Oh, and by the way, the findings of the study were overwhelmingly positive. *Embrace* the doco will make you 'embrace' your body.

I want you to know that this is the edge that embracing your body will give you and your child. Both of you will get off the sidelines, say yes, put your hand up, back yourself and get it done. When you embrace your body, you'll do things you never thought possible.

So that's a little bit about me. I'm the high school dropout who hated English and has written four bestselling books. I wasn't a filmmaker, yet I directed one of the world's most successful documentaries. I was paralysed by public speaking for most of my life and now find myself at Google HQ in Silicon Valley addressing leadership teams and having my keynote speech live streamed to every Google office in the world.

Never say never, huh?

ZALI'S STORY

I'm nine. I'm naked. I'm in the bath with my best friend. I look down and I see bulges and rolls and bits on my belly that she doesn't have. The water is lukewarm but I feel a shameful heat creep up on me, and a slow realisation. I am so much bigger than her, I am taking up her space, crowding the bath. I am fat. This is bad.

My earliest memories of my body were that it was bigger than everyone else's. I swallowed those feelings down and internalised the shame, but it seemed to be reinforced everywhere. None of the clothes at the shops fitted my body shape, and none of the popstars on TV looked like me.

I don't remember anyone saying anything about my body until one Christmas, when I must have been ten or eleven, joyfully choreographing dances with my sister, when my great-grandfather walked in, patted me on the stomach with his walking stick and pronounced 'You're getting fat, aren't you?'– words that are still imprinted in my brain thirty years later.

As I moved through adolescence, the messages I received got louder. At age thirteen, I took my mother's pocket calorie-counting book from the bookshelf, and got to work. A determined (read: stubborn) child, I worked hard, and by age fourteen, people were giving me compliments. 'How did you do it?' jealous friends would exclaim. I lapped up the attention and praise and kept going – why would I stop? I was still very far from popular, but at least my body looked more like the cool girls' now.

I now know that my 'healthy eating' was actually 'disordered eating'. As I moved through university, I became fascinated by body image and eating disorders, and obsessed with figuring out why I might have had the experiences that I had. My first degree in teaching meant that I came to the body image research space armed and ready to figure out what school-based programs we could implement to help prevent body image concerns and eating disorders.

And then I had kids. Given my research background, I tried not to panic about my post-baby body. As the midwife walked into my room the day after I'd given birth, I was prodding the wobbling mess that was now my stomach.

'Soooo, when does this go away?' I asked playfully.

She patted her own belly and responded, 'Oh, never,' before moving on to take my blood pressure. No-one had actually prepared me for the extent of the change that would happen in such a short time, and it seemed like none of the other new mothers had been told either.

As I sat in playgroups and mothers' groups, and women described the hatred and loathing they had for their post-baby bodies and the things they were trying to do to get their old bodies back, I looked at our kids, happily tottering around, and realised that this was where it all began. That I, and many women before me, had all picked up the messages about our bodies – that they should be small, and neat, and controlled – from the messages that the world fed our parents, as they did from their parents. And if we wanted anything to change, *we* needed to change.

I don't share my story because I think it's unique, but because it is universal. So many women struggle with their body image when they are young and believe they are only valuable to the world based on what they look like. So many women experience disordered eating in ways that aren't captured in statistics and prevalence rates, but in ways that impact the voices in their head for a lifetime. So many women think that they are fine with how they look, but unravel when they see a photo of themselves. Men can get away with joking about their 'dad bod', but the feelings of shame and being 'less of a man' because they are softer or smaller are often still there. And none of us want our kids to feel these feelings. So many parents desperately want to create a safer, kinder body image environment for our children, but have no idea how.

Imagine a world where children don't feel held back by their bodies. Where we judge each other by who we are and what we do rather than what we look like. Where we see images around us of people who inspire us, but look like us. Where girls don't feel like they have to be small, and boys to be big, to be loved and valued. This is the world we can create, together.

The aim of this book is to help us all to work together towards creating a safer body image environment for our kids than we had, and our parents had. We now know better, so we can do better.

Taryn on Zali

In the beginning, Zali was reluctant to write this book with me (as she explains below). Thank goodness she did, because her experience and wisdom in the area of body image are first class. She has been my go-to and right-hand ~~legend~~ support person right from the start. When I'm feeling challenged by curly media questions, it's Zali I'll call to workshop responses. When I need evidence-based data to substantiate a point I'm making, I call Zali. When making the *Embrace Kids* documentary, every creative decision was run past Zali first. She is exceptional and brilliant in every way. And just by association, working with Zali makes me look smarter. Thanks, Dr Yager!

The point I'm making is: she knows her stuff and you're in really good hands. We're going to provide you with evidence-based suggestions and practical offerings, all while patting you on the back. Just being here and reading this book makes you a great parent.

In this book we share the insights we've learned from the thirty-plus years of combined experience we have in the body image space. Sure, we both have the fancy-sounding bios with our qualifications and our speaking at all of the big and fancy places like Harvard and Google. But we also have six kids between us and we know how hard this whole parenting thing is. We have our own lived experiences of body image concerns and our own pretty messed-up relationships with eating and exercise at different times of our lives. We've both emerged from those times to be body confident ourselves, and want to encourage everyone else to be the same.

One of the main things we have learned, and one of the reasons why responding to those questions asked by parents with an Instagram-reel-worthy three-step process doesn't work is this: you have to heal yourself first to be able to help your kids. Reflecting, learning, *unlearning* and processing your own experiences are necessary so that you can help your kids with these challenges.

Zali on Taryn

Now, what Taryn's not telling you is that despite not having letters after her name, she is absolutely brilliant, and has changed people's lives because of her courage, vulnerability and tenacity. Millions of people across the world watched Taryn's documentary *Embrace* after its release in 2016. Millions of lives have been made better by their time with Taryn.

Watching *Embrace* was a huge moment for me too. At the time, I thought I was doing my research to help people. But seeing this film made me realise that it wasn't enough for me to do the research, develop and evaluate programs, and write in academic journals for other researchers to read. The *Embrace* film did more, and reached more people, than I could ever dream of doing in my little office locked away in my university. I had to start getting more public, speak up and put things out in the 'real world' instead of staying safely nestled in academia.

When I first saw the film, I had three kids under four and was drowning in my own expectations, at work and at home. I had a stack of parenting books on my bedside table to read, as I was sure that there was a magical 'right answer' – something I wasn't getting, or didn't know, that would help my toddler to behave like a human instead of an animal or create a perfect sleep routine for my twins. Most of those books made me feel like even more of a failure, though. Hence my initial reluctance to write a parenting book when Taryn asked.

I also wasn't sure that anyone would want to read about the sorts of things I knew that could be, well, a little dry at times. But Taryn has waved her wand here too. There is something genuinely sparkly and magical about her. She turns dry pieces of information and theories into something compelling, and finds a way to share this information in an emotional and engaging way that changes people. We knew making this film and writing this book would inspire our young ones to develop healthy and happy relationships with their bodies and to celebrate diversity in others. How could we not do it?

2

How we feel about our bodies (and why)

IN 1984 SOME RESEARCHERS REFERRED to women's dissatisfaction with their body weight as 'normative discontent' because they found so many women were unhappy with their weight. Not much has changed.

Although body image issues are usually associated with adolescents, more recent research that investigates body image across the lifespan has shown that there really is no improvement in women's body image until they hit age sixty-five. Yep, retirement age. According to different studies among large numbers of adult women, 91 per cent of women want to be thinner, 70 per cent are 'dissatisfied' with their bodies, and 51 per cent have 'moderate' or 'marked' shape and weight concerns. The men don't escape either: almost 40 per cent report some level of body image distress or preoccupation.

This dissatisfaction is not just some trivial, superficial thing. Hating our bodies means we treat them pretty badly. Women with higher levels of body dissatisfaction have poorer diet quality, engage in less physical activity and avoid healthcare, such as not having regular cervical screening or wearing sunscreen. The way you feel about the way you look impacts every other aspect of your physical and mental health and wellbeing, and the way you interact with the world.

Although typically thought to be unique to women, research has found that men do experience body dissatisfaction, in different ways. In general, men have lower levels of body dissatisfaction and higher levels of body appreciation than women, but these findings are complicated by the fact that the measures used to determine body dissatisfaction and body appreciation were developed for women and may not capture the extent of male body image concerns. New research does show that men's body appreciation takes a dip in midlife, whereas women's body appreciation increases in a very slow and steady way from adolescence onwards. However, motherhood can change all of that.

BODY IMAGE IN MOTHERHOOD

Some women assume that motherhood is another achievement to be ticked off or added to the list: study (tick), career (tick), car (tick), house (tick), partner (tick), babies (tick). We plan our pregnancies and maternity leave and assume that we can resume our normal lives afterwards; get our 'pre-baby body back', go to work as usual, see the same friends and do the same activities we did before having kids, except that we will have a cute little sidekick dressed up in adorable mini-me matching outfits.

Matrescence describes the transition to motherhood, and the complete transformation of a woman – physically, emotionally, socially, and financially. A woman will never actually return to who she was, or what she looked like before having children.

AMY TAYLOR-KABBAZ, *MAMA RISING*

The word 'matrescence', which was initially coined in the 1970s, was revived recently by Amy Taylor-Kabbaz in her book *Mama Rising*. When Amy first described this term on social media, it went viral. Women everywhere had an emotional reaction to finally having a word to describe the fact that they had been split in two (or more) pieces by motherhood, and needed a way to move forward.

A woman's body, identity and whole world changes so much as she transitions to motherhood. The extent of the changes is similar to what happens in puberty, just in a shorter time frame. Until now, we've never had a word for it. Just as 'adolescence' describes our transition from childhood to adulthood, 'matrescence' describes women's transition to motherhood. Having a word for this transition, and viewing this change as a transition, is important. Reconceptualising motherhood as an emergence of a new identity, rather than a temporary time-out from your past self, could be critical in ensuring that we survive and thrive through the gruelling years of early motherhood.

Many women tell us that the only time they loved their bellies was when they had a baby bump. Although pregnancy is a time of weight gain – something which most women typically avoid – many women do feel better about the way they look once they start to 'look' pregnant at around eighteen to twenty weeks. Pregnancy is one of the only times in our lives when we get a free pass from the pressure to be thin. We listen to our bodies and eat that second helping we are craving 'for the baby'. Instead of just being objects to be admired, our bodies are growing new organs, creating life, being functional and purposeful.

And then the baby comes out.

As soon as those babies leave our bodies, the pressure to 'get your pre-baby body back' comes crashing on in. The nice round bump that you patted gently and sang to so sweetly is now a saggy, wobbly mess. Your body no longer works like it used to or looks like it used to. No-one ever told you what to expect and what your belly or body might look like after birth, and you don't recognise what you see in the mirror. Women tell us: 'I was horrified', 'I was shocked', 'I was so disgusted with myself'.

The reality is that the postpartum body is not one that we see in the public sphere until we see our own. Instagram and tabloid magazines are full of women holding tiny babies, having 'bounced back'. This affects so many things about the way women feel about themselves, and the way they treat themselves in the first year of motherhood. Being unhappy with our bodies affects everything, and the research now shows a very clear and consistent relationship between body dissatisfaction and post-partum depression.

The pressure is huge. You bear children, your body feeds them. It's a miracle – and then you feel like you need to look like a teenager again afterwards. It's insulting and ridiculous. One of the reasons I've gone into this body image work is because of this unfair amount of pressure on women – the social norms that have been created and have imprisoned us in a way.

DENISE HAMBURGER

FOUNDER AND EXECUTIVE DIRECTOR, BE REAL USA

Similarly, adoptive mothers experience hormonal and physiological changes to their bodies and identities, additional stress, and constraints on their time to feed and move their bodies. There is much less research in this area, but there are physical and mental health impacts for all women who identify as mothers, and changes to the expectations of father's bodies too. The rise of the 'dad bod' – a body that looks active, but not the product of hours in the gym – might be just as unrealistic as the expectations of mother's bodies. Men experience hormonal and role shifts in the transition to parenthood too, and their bodies can change in this process. Muscularity and masculinity are linked in really complex ways, and the decline in body satisfaction we see in men at midlife reflects these concerns.

WHY DO WE FEEL BAD ABOUT THE WAY WE LOOK?

How did we get to this body-hating place? People often go straight to blaming magazines, supermodels and, now, social media. Media does have an influence, but it is only one of three broad areas that influence body image:

1. **Biological influences** like gender and genetics (that determine, for example, our height or eye colour) which affect our body size, shape and composition. These things are hard to change.
2. **Psychological influences** such as a person's tendency towards depression, anxiety, perfectionism and how much you compare yourself to others. These can also be hard to change (but it's possible).
3. **Social influences** like family, friends and the media. Technically, these are the easiest to change, but they require some work.

So why do we – and particularly women – care so much about the way we look?

Social and evolutionary psychologist Dr Danielle Wagstaff explains this as something hanging around from our caveman and cavewoman days, suggesting that much of it comes down to competition for resources and for mating partners.

Despite a lot of things changing in the way our social groups operate, our brains are still wired with some of the same mechanisms. We still compare ourselves to our community and we are still driven to fit in. Apparently, we mostly have the same network of around 150 close friends and family that would have been the size of the average caveperson tribe. There are still some leftover evolutionary ideas of how women and men are valued, based on their contributions to furthering the species. Women are still largely valued for their appearance and so they try to adapt their bodies to emphasise their highly prized features, such as large breasts and shapely hips, thought to represent fertility. Men are still valued for their strength, and ability to 'provide' for their families.

Evolutionary psychologists have studied the way men and women present themselves on online dating profiles. Men are more likely to depict themselves as strong, demonstrating their access to resources by holding a big fish. Women typically emphasise attractiveness and are more likely to upload full body shots and mirror selfies with more revealing clothing.

So in caveperson times we had to do two things: emphasise our valued features, but also know that we were fitting in. Fitting in with the group was critical, because if you weren't performing well and fell behind, or did things that they didn't like, you would be kicked out on your own, and would then become more susceptible to predators.

The tendency towards social comparison is still one of the major contributors to the way we feel about our bodies today. Alongside our internalised ideas about thinness being good, and the conversations that we have with others about weight and bodies, it is one of the main processes that influence the way we feel about our bodies.

COMPARING OUR BODIES

We are constantly comparing ourselves. It's an automatic thing that our brains do on a number of different levels: our skills and abilities, our 'successes', how clean our houses are, and of course, our appearance. Whenever we see another person, or an image of another person, our brains do a quick comparison in order to determine our own value. Our brains automatically compare how we think we look with the image or person in front of us. If we feel like they are closer to the societal 'ideals' for thinness and attractiveness, then we feel bad as a result.

Decades of research confirms that looking at images of thin or idealised models does us harm. Through hundreds of studies, researchers have confirmed that the female participants who view pictures of thin models feel depressed, and worse about themselves. Viewing idealised muscular bodies makes men feel dissatisfied with themselves too.

As we get older, we also have our younger selves to compare to. Much of women's dissatisfaction with their bodies comes from comparing their body to what it looked like five, ten or even twenty years ago. We have pretty unrealistic ideas that our body size and shape in our thirties and forties should be able to be what it was like in our twenties, and are disappointed when it isn't. Many women report that they don't want to be stick thin – they 'just want to lose five kilos to be happy'. A study of women in the year after they had given birth found that they wanted to be five kilos lighter than even their pre-pregnancy weight.

As we've said, constantly comparing ourselves is an automatic process: we can't stop our brains from doing it. However, we do have control over what we *do* as a result. If we respond to this comparison with self-critical thoughts, like 'Why have I let myself get like this? I will cut out all carbs tomorrow', not only does this have such a negative impact on our body image, but it also leads us to extreme dieting and exercise measures that aren't sustainable, and shame and depression when we don't stick to those regimes. It's bad for our physical and mental health.

Responding with more self-compassionate thinking, like 'Bodies grow and change all of the time. I've just had a baby, and a stressful year. I will take some time to do some self-care tomorrow', soothes our nervous system and has a more positive effect.

I've always been disappointed with how I look when I looked in the mirror. The only time I remember being really happy was on my wedding day – but the life I was living then wasn't sustainable. It was personal training five times a week and really clean eating and no fun at all. It's just not doable in the long term or feasible when you've got kids.

KELLY, MUM OF TWO, SYDNEY

BELIEVING THAT THIN = GOOD

So now we know that years of cavewomen being prized for their fertility and cavemen for their strength may have shaped early ideals of bodies, but decades of more recent beauty ideals have further shaped our notions of which people are valued in our society. Despite the sizes and shapes of particular beauty ideals over time, one thing is constant: we make a whole range of judgements and assumptions about people based on their appearance.

Along the way, thinness was conflated with health. The past twenty years of 'anti-obesity' messaging has meant that our fear of fat has been heightened, and even praised.

Decades of 'shame and blame' messaging has reinforced that 'fat is bad'. The behaviours associated with thinness, like dieting and exercise, are associated with virtuousness and 'health', even when people diet or exercise in very disordered ways that are very unhealthy. Psychologists and dietitians tell us that younger and younger children are now presenting with this extreme fear of fat.

This core belief that thin is good and fat is bad is termed 'internalisation of the thin ideal' and predicts the development of eating disorders and depression – mostly because we have such a strong idea of how thin we 'should be', but it is physiologically impossible for most of us to achieve this.

The images of women that we see everywhere on television, on social media and in magazines mostly have a Body Mass Index, or BMI (a number calculated by dividing a person's weight divided by their height squared), that would be in the 'underweight' category. The official BMI cut-off for 'overweight' is 25, but a classic early study, published in 1999, found that women generally considered themselves to be 'overweight' at a BMI of around 23. Often, women who have a lower BMI and a roll of fat that emerges when they sit down believe that they are 'overweight'.

It seems ridiculous when you write it down: we all want to achieve, and are actively trying to achieve, a body size and shape that we know can only be achieved by a very small proportion of the population – probably around 5 per cent. Despite knowing that their bodies might never resemble that of a supermodel, women pretty much universally 'just want to lose five kilos', and many think they will be happier and live better lives when they do. And as we'll see below, much conversation revolves around this goal and how to achieve it.

> **We've been really conditioned by the beauty climate in our society to look a certain way, be a certain way, to bounce back after having children. And for most people, that doesn't happen. And so it's about picking apart those ideas that we've been bombarded with since we were very young, and understanding and recognising and growing to love your body for what it is now, and what it's been able to do.**
>
> **LIBBY TRICKETT, OLYMPIC GOLD MEDALLIST SWIMMER AND CHAMPION PODCASTER @LIBBY_TRICKETT**

TALKING ABOUT BODIES

How we feel about our bodies affects how we *talk* about our bodies. And what we say about our own, and other people's, bodies matters.

At a recent networking event Zali attended, she was astounded to move from networking circle to networking circle of women – who had come along to the event, presumably, to make or strengthen business relationships – and have every conversation eventually come back to eating, exercise, bodies and weight. Each time the waitstaff brought around the finger food, there would be an inevitable chorus of 'Oh no, I shouldn't have another one' or a discussion of the diet or exercise plan various women were on. Another woman would join a circle with 'Oh, you look great, have you lost weight?' and a successful businesswoman proceeded to detail her need to lose ten kilos in order to make her ex-husband jealous at a wedding they were both due to attend. All these conversations contribute to our understanding of how women's bodies should look, and how acceptable our bodies are to our particular social groups.

Conversations with other women about our own bodies, or other people's bodies, comments from friends, partners and strangers, teasing and body shaming all contribute to the 'script' that governs how we think we should look. Even being a part of an online conversation or seeing comments about other people's bodies on social media has an impact as we take on the comments and apply them to ourselves.

Many of us can remember particularly hurtful, or even particularly positive, things that were said about our bodies when we were children or adolescents. That throwaway comment or 'harmless' teasing made by someone even thirty or forty years ago can still have an effect today. In one study, researchers found that adult women who had been teased about their bodies as children and adolescents had higher levels of body dissatisfaction up to fifteen years later.

And then there are the things that are said now. For women, much of the conversation between friends and acquaintances centres around our appearance. Stand back and watch some conversations and see how quickly they talk about what the other person is wearing or about their bodies. In many cases, we default to saying negative things about ourselves: a concept called 'fat talk'.

Fat talk among women (and it is more common among women) usually sounds like this:

Woman 1: Ugh, I'm so bloated today.

Woman 2: Well, I think I've put on about five kilos overnight, I've got a muffin top happening, look at this.

Woman 3: You've got a muffin top? No, anyway, I've got a whole muffin bottom as well!

Sound familiar?

These self-deprecating comments come so naturally to us as we simultaneously seek reassurance from the women around us and also try to fit in, by taking part in the shared activity of saying negative things about our bodies. But engaging in this fat talk actually makes us feel worse about the way we look. Researchers have shown that listening to this conversation going on increases body dissatisfaction, but joining in with fat talk has a stronger negative impact.

Then there are the compliments. 'You look great. Have you lost weight?' sounds like a nice thing to say, but this comment single-handedly reinforces the fact that thin is good, and sends the message that you need to stay thin to look good and be accepted.

And finally, in the course of our days and weeks, we also discuss our bodies, and the choices we make in feeding and moving those bodies every day, quite a lot. Our need to eat multiple times a day often brings up a decision-making process and an opportunity to discuss our choices – and our bodies – with others. So often women out at a café will choose what to eat, and then go straight on to talking about their new diet, 'healthy eating plan', or exercise regime.

All of these words influence our ideas about which women's bodies are acceptable to the group. Our drive to fit in and to be accepted is so strong, and our appearance is one of the main ways that we can use to be accepted. All these conversations, which we have been a part of or exposed to throughout our childhood, adolescence and adult years, have a cumulative impact on our ideas about what our bodies 'should' look like. If we think there is a difference between what our bodies currently look like, and what we believe they 'should' look like, we feel dissatisfied, and try to change the way we look.

Listen, grownups. Just because you look different to someone you see on the internet doesn't mean you aren't beautiful!

Nobody is perfect, so you don't need to be either.

Don't believe everything that you see on the internet, because lots of adults get plastic surgery or edit their photos, so therefore, not everything you see on the internet is real.

Don't listen to people who bring you down. Listen to people that bring you up.

Don't waste your life comparing yourself to other people. Life is too short for that. Spend your life doing stuff you love. Like hanging out with your friends, eating yummy food, and playing outside.

LILY, AGE 10

WHAT DOES THIS MEAN FOR US?

We asked the Body Image Movement community to respond to the question 'What did hating your body cost you?' and boy, did we get answers! More than 600 people left comments, and we were blown away by what they said.

We've included this list here because, as we scrolled through these hundreds of comments, it really made us think.

What did hating your body cost you?

Forty-five years of not wearing what I wanted to wear.

It cost me fifteen years of my life spent dieting and treating my body sooo awfully.

It cost me my sense of self. I made bad choices, had toxic relationships and wasn't a great friend because I was so wrapped up in worrying about how I look.

Hating my body had me sidelined for a lot of special memories. Instead of being in the pool with my daughter, enjoying her laughter, I was covering up, afraid of what strangers would think about my body.

Hating my body cost me my peace of mind and the confidence to join in on things that I didn't feel I deserved to do because I was 'too fat.'

Joyful photos with family and friends – avoided them at all costs.

Thousands of dollars trying to hide and fix my body.

Feeling not adequate enough in society to the point I didn't work for nearly twenty years.

Missing out on swimming and cooling off on hot days because I wouldn't wear bathers or shorts.

It cost me my freedom, mental health, social life, doing things with my kids, cost me precious time and moments in life.

It's cost me a fulfilling life – because I've spent my whole life trying to hide from others because I'm not good enough.

Powerful, huh?

Hating our bodies costs us. Relationships, self-worth, joy, dreams, life. Was it worth it?

Umm, that's a no!

Action

We've shared our stories with you. Now it's your turn.

We use stories to learn, educate and connect over shared experiences. Writing about your body story or journey can help you to interpret the things that have had an influence throughout your life and can help you change the 'ending.' Writing our stories is often empowering as we take back control over the narrative and see connections between events. Figuring out who we are, and our own lived experience, can then help us in parenting our kids and what to say when those inevitable conversations arise. It's literally called 'narrative therapy.'

Both of us have found writing and sharing our stories to be incredibly powerful. At the end of each chapter we will include some reflective exercises for you to think about. There is no rush to write your journey, but we recommend it. Write it on paper, type it out, share it, don't share it – it's up to you. If you would like some more guidance, from self-help resources or clinicians who use narrative therapy, there are suggestions in the Resources at the end of this book.

☑ Write about it.

Take a moment to close your eyes, and reflect on some of your earliest memories of your body. Where were you? Who were you with? What messages were you getting? Start there, and begin to journal about these moments and messages that you have received about your body or the way you look, and how that made you feel. Don't edit yourself, just let it flow.

Your story matters. It can help to set a timer for fifteen to twenty minutes and commit to writing the whole time.

☑ Have conversations with your parents and partner.

Our relationships with food, and our bodies, are developed over many years, but most begin in childhood. It can be helpful to have a chat with your parents, and also your partner, in order to get a better sense of what your food and body environment, and their food and body environments, were like so that you can move towards figuring out an approach to use with your kids. Here are some questions to get you started:

- What were your experiences around food, eating and weight in your family?
- Did you ever have any experiences where you felt shame about your body?

3

What the world tells us about our bodies

BEAUTY THROUGH THE AGES

In Roman mythology, Venus is the goddess of love, sex, beauty and fertility. If we were described as goddesses of anything we'd be stoked, but what would we be goddesses of? If you asked us right now, we'd be the goddesses of unmatched missing socks, swearing and ferrying kids around to sports practice. To be completely honest, Venus was probably the goddess of all those wonderful things because she did stuff-all else – have you seen the paintings she's in? If we didn't have to work, do endless loads of laundry, keep up appearances in our WhatsApp friend groups, fill in school permission forms, or attend parent–teacher interviews, we could all be like Venus too. Without all that pressure, it would be a walk in the park to love harder, have more sex and grow unsplit-ended hair past our bums. Easy peasy.

Our frustration and anger have nothing to do with Venus, but rather the preposterous standards of beauty imposed on women for hundreds of years. Beauty ideals and the impossible goal of living up to them have not only diminished our power and quietened our voices, but they've also robbed us of our joy, made us waste our time and money trying to meet these standards, and made us feel quite pissed off, to be honest.

So, let's talk beauty through the ages and take a spin back through Western history. Up until the start of the nineteenth century, artists like Rubens or Rembrandt portrayed the ideal woman as voluptuous and round. Venus had a rounded face and a pear-shaped body. This was beautiful at that time.

After round and voluptuous came the 'steel engraving look' – slight women with small, corseted waists, sloped shoulders and wait for it . . . delicate feet. (Hola, fellow size 9 and 10 wearers, we'd suck in this era.)

By the end of the nineteenth century the 'Gibson girl' emerged, combining features from both of these eras: she was depicted as tall, athletic and thinner than her predecessor, but still curvy with wide hips and large breasts.

And just when we thought the ideals couldn't get harder, the best plot twist was yet to come. Out of nowhere, the 1920s proclaimed a time where women who looked 'boyish' emerged as the ideal beauty. This was about having a straight-up-and-down figure with small boobs and a downplayed waist.

A very short decade later, flappers were out, and Marilyn Monroe was in. The golden age of Hollywood (circa 1930s to 1950s) was all about having an hourglass figure with a slim waist, curves and large breasts – just like a Barbie doll, also invented in this time.

(Are you reading this shaking your head at the ridiculousness of it all? Hold on, there's more!)

The pendulum swung right back in the other direction for the 1960s, because thin was in. Think Twiggy and tiny shift dresses to show off a slender body with long slim legs.

Now for some eras most of us have lived through and remember, such as (in our opinion) the best era in history – the 1980s! Remember the supermodels? They were athletic, tall and toned. They were our equivalent of Venus the goddess. Who can forget the classic quote from Linda Evangelista when she said, 'I don't get out of bed for less than $10,000'? At the time we thought, 'Wow, what a bitch', now we think, 'You go, girl, know your worth!'

Heroin chic was next. We have a particular revulsion for this era. Taryn's brother Jason was a heroin addict and homeless for a time, and Taryn can confirm there's nothing sexy about being homeless or being on heroin. Beauty was defined as being extremely thin and waifish, and you got extra points if you had translucent skin (a beauty goal that automatically left out many ethnicities) and looked frail and neglected. We all cut the waistbands off our jeans so they were so low you could have seen our pubic hair, if we hadn't just waxed it all off.

Notice a recurring theme? They are all white. Beauty standards have been embarrassingly Eurocentric in the past. There have been times in the not-so-distant past where non-white contestants couldn't enter (or win) a beauty pageant, and when magazines in Western countries only depicted one very pale image of beauty. While individual countries used to have their own ideas about what was seen as beautiful, our increased globalisation and connectivity means that now, Eurocentric ideals are also pushed out to other cultures, as seen in the infiltration of damaging skin-lightening creams in South Asian countries, and double eyelid surgery in East Asian countries. While we still have a way to go, thankfully we have a lot more diversity depicted in the media now.

And right now, the postmodern 'beauty' is quite the blend of impossible beauty standards. She has large breasts and a big bum, but a flat stomach. She is thin but not too thin, and has a thigh gap. She has plump lips but not too plump, no lines on her face but does not look like she has had too much work done. She is tanned and has exceptionally manicured, bushy eyebrows. Just when we thought they couldn't put any more pressure on us, they went for the eyebrows. Now, that's a lot of stupid criteria to live up to, isn't it?

Living up to this unrealistic standard takes a lot of time. And money. The sorts of people who meet these standards do it for their jobs. They are models, celebrities or influencers who have the time and support staff to enable them to have nutritionally balanced meals, work out every day, spend time at the salon getting hair, nails, facials, waxing, and everything else on the spa menu done. In striving for these 'standards' you have to give up time with friends and family, give up celebrations and spontaneity, and have everything all planned out.

To look like these 'ideals' you might have spent lots of money on juice cleanses, shakes and miracle products and gym member-ships, or online training programs that you forget about after a few weeks. In striving for these 'ideals' you might have had to slow down or pause your career progress in order to make time and save energy for doing-the-things-you-would-need-to-do-to-meet-these-unrealistic-standards.

So why is it important to understand the history of beauty through the ages and how can it help our kids? Well, for us parents, it's comforting to know that while we have been navigating life, there have been some sinister and powerful forces at play influencing our past decisions about how we feel about our bodies.

The opportunity here is to get on the front foot with our kids, to educate them so they see the silliness of anyone telling them that beauty is a particular shape or size. More importantly, we will arm you with all the information required to gently talk to them about this.

We'll cover more of this in Part Two, but for now, the big question is, who's the jerk that did this?

WHO CREATED THE BEAUTY IDEALS?

Mostly men.

(Sorry, men!)

To unpack this, we need to think about two eras: Before Advertising and After Advertising.

Before advertising, the standards were determined *indirectly* by men. If we start with the cavewomen and then fast forward to the nineteenth-century paintings, during this time women were largely competing for men and their resources, trying to look as fertile as possible. Women might have decided whether to wear massive wigs (hello, Marie Antoinette!), or corsets, or powder their noses with pure lead, in order to be more attractive so that they could marry well.

Advertising and the media landscape that we now know kicked

off around the 1950s – and it was then, and for the next seventy years, that men dominated the advertising field, and were largely telling women how they should feel, what they should do, and what they should look like while doing it. Advertising essentially led to the creation of insecurities around the way we look so brands could provide handy solutions to help us fix our 'faults'.

In their book *Brandsplaining: Why marketing is still sexist, and what to do about it*, Jane Cunningham and Philippa Roberts explained that the early marketing practices of promoting ever-increasing 'ideals' that women needed to achieve, established in the 1950s and 1960s, became accepted practice:

Perfection (and the endless effort to achieve it) should be both the pursuit and the aspiration: complexions should be flawless, homes should be ideal, surfaces should be shining, dishes should be sparkling, the look and the figure should always be perfect, and particularly perfect looking.

It's no wonder the housewives got hooked on the 'mother's little helper' that turned out to be Valium.

But how much has actually changed since then? Media and advertising in the late 1990s and early 2000s was the worst: hyper-focused on thinness, digitally retouched to create completely unrealistic images, with women's hyper-sexualised bodies every-where. Even in the 2000s, men were still dominating the marketing sphere, engaging in practices like presenting everything from the perspective of the 'male gaze', modelling objectification and largely ignoring the voices and opinions of women in generating advertising campaigns. Case in point, Victoria's Secret and Lynx ads.

If you watch ads today, count the number in which the 'authority' voiceover is a man, while the woman is 'helpless' or has a problem that needs to be 'fixed' (dark circles and fine lines?). Count on one hand the advertising that features women that are the actual average of a size 14 to 16, instead of the size 8 to 10 that dominates our screens.

You might not think that advertising works on you, but over time, advertising has become a huge part of our cultural conversation that tells us how we should look, act and live our lives.

Let's look at some prime examples, shall we?

Here are some ads targeted at women over the decades (and what they really mean):

1890s (pictured on opposite page)

A woman has a metal device on her forehead, with a series of beads or rollers under the chin for a 'massage'. It looks like something you would have strapped on before being electrocuted.

What they said: 'Curves of youth will be yours if you will pull the cords.'

What they meant: Strap this contraption on your head immediately to make even the most innocuous parts of yourself smaller, tighter, and more appealing to others.

1950s

A perfectly manicured housewife sits on the couch knitting, while a man ogles her stockings.

What they said: 'Married? No reason to neglect SA. (Stocking Appeal)'

What they meant: Don't let yourselves go, ladies . . . or your husband will leave you.

1960s

A thin model holds a cigarette. Her lips are pursed in a 'sexy' shape as she blows the cigarette smoke out.

What they said: 'We made Virginia Slims especially for women; because women are dainty and beautiful and sweet and generally different from men.'

What they meant: Have your slimmer cigarette and don't think too much – just sit there, darling. Also, don't eat.

1984

Jazzy music plays on TV as a range of slim midriffs are shown on screen one at a time. Out of nowhere, a hand appears and pinches their bellies.

What they said: 'Have you tried the Special K pinch? If you can pinch more than an inch, try the high protein Special K breakfast.'

What they meant: Under no circumstances are you allowed to have a normal stomach that stores body fat.

(This is one of the most damaging diet ads of all time. There is now a generation of women who believe that anything on their stomach they can 'pinch' is wrong. It isn't.)

2015

A very thin woman in black and white wears a bright yellow bikini against a bright yellow background. She has a tiny waist and you can see her ribs. The ad is for Protein Powder: The Weight Loss Collection.

What they said: 'Are you beach body ready?'

What they meant: Heaven forbid you should go to the beach if you don't look like this woman. (After its release, this ad was banned in the United Kingdom.)

Of course, there have been trends in the male body shape over time too, from larger to smaller, to less muscular to more and more muscular. In the 2000s, the beauty industry realised that they could expand their market into the other half of the population and invented a whole range of products for grooming and 'manscaping'. But there has always been an underlying accept-ance that men had an out: if they didn't adhere to the 'ideals', they could still win with financial success and status instead. There has also been an acceptance of a range of body shapes and sizes for men that are deemed ideal and acceptable at the same time, whereas for women, there has always been a narrow and acceptable goal.

The diet and weight loss industry, and entertainment and advertising industries, have all done very well profiting from our insecurities, most of which they themselves created. These are billion-dollar industries and companies. Even the supplements industry and activewear industry, which look miniscule next to the media giants, are worth US$140 billion and US$356 billion respectively. These industries have, over and over, used the tried and true marketing blueprint of:

1. Projecting an unrealistic standard that most people can't achieve;
2. Making people feel bad about not being able to look like the standard; and
3. Getting them to hand over lots of cash for something that won't actually create sustainable change. Then,
4. Ensuring that those solutions fail so you feel so depressed, but also as if you are the only one who couldn't do it, so you hand over even more cash to numb the shame.

And repeat.

Jerks.

When I was in my twenties and thirties, I was so tiny. But when I was that weight, I always wanted to be like the Victoria's Secret models – I wanted the boobs and the hips and the curves, and I wanted to be like them. I still was unhappy with who I was, even in my very thin body. When I had my son, who is eight now, my body drastically changed. Suddenly I was heavier, my boobs grew, and my shape completely changed to be more like these curvy models, but I was still super unhappy with my body. I spent four years of my life trying to get back to my pre-pregnancy weight and shape, but that was never going to happen. It's just so unrealistic to 'go back'. I don't think it's about the weight. And I don't think it's about the fact that your body changes shape. It's something else. It's society telling us that it's not okay to be who we are. We need to be constantly finding and then fixing the things that are 'wrong' with our bodies. Those things are constant, and they keep changing over time. We are trained to always be unhappy about who we are, and how we look.

RACHEL, 41, MUM OF ONE, GOLD COAST

AND THEN WE ARE OLD

You are never the same person that you were yesterday, because it's today.

TARYN

What's another thing all those beauty standards have in common? Youth.

As we get older, all of the usual messaging and advertising around women's worth being their body and their weight still applies. However, there's a new layer, a new message: Women should be youthful. Unlike men, whose power only grows as they age – becoming more believable and more 'distinguished'.

As women's bodies move past their reproductive years, there are multiple physiological, hormonal and physical changes that take place leading to an increase in body fat, and a decrease in muscle mass, particularly as we head towards menopause. During menopause, the decrease in oestrogen levels means that more fat is stored on the tummy. Research has found that women in midlife (an average age of fifty) overestimate what their body size looks like in pictures if they are more dissatisfied with their bodies. Women who are dissatisfied with their bodies in midlife are also more likely to experience anxiety and depression.

Aging also leads to other changes in our appearance such as changes to skin, hair and the way our bodies function in physical and sexual activity. Given that all of our cultural norms of attractiveness centre around young people in their twenties, and the majority of the signs of aging are viewed negatively, we spend a lot of time, energy and money trying to maintain a youthful appearance.

Many women talk about 'feeling invisible' in their thirties and forties.

There's this age – from our mid-thirties to mid-sixties – where we're almost a bit invisible and pushed aside. We've still got that 'ideal' in our head of someone who is in her twenties, and we keep trying to reach that, still have that image of 'perfection' in our heads, until we are around sixty-five, when it's acceptable for us to age. In our sixties it's nice that we've got that soft skin on the back of our hands, and our age spots and wrinkles start telling a story. We're grandparents usually, so it's okay then to be old, but until that point, we keep trying to look youthful and spend so much of our time doing it.

There are forty years – half of our lives really – and probably the best part of our lives where our kids are young, and we should be enjoying things, but we're worrying about how much ice cream we're eating, and whether we should get our hair dyed, or pluck the hairs coming out of our chin.

NICOLA, 42, MUM OF TWO, UK

Oh, the standards. So many standards. And the work slowly increases. In our twenties, it was enough to have shaved our legs, caked on the foundation and sprayed ourselves with sickly perfume. Now we need to wax and curate the hair on multiple parts of our bodies, adding 'chin' and 'lip' to the usual 'eyebrow, bikini and leg' combo. Hair 'should' be dyed, teeth 'should' be white, anti-aging creams and treatments 'should' be applied, all while striving for a thin appearance, despite our bodies' best efforts to make us comfortable.

I have a very public job, and in the media, I get treated in a completely different way if I've gained weight, haven't dyed my hair, haven't done my eyebrows, haven't bleached my teeth, don't wear shapewear – all this stuff to do with appearance. I get far more professional opportunities to get out there and say what needs to be said to make society a better place if I look a certain way. My value in this industry is largely about how I look, and I can't change that system, so despite my extreme misgivings, I do all of those things so I can have the opportunity to speak.

With the messaging you're being given, it's not just an internal thing that you can decide for yourself within yourself. A lot of the messaging is coming from outside. For example, if you're a woman and you are going a little grey and don't dye your hair, people say, 'Ooh, she's let herself go', or other similar sentiments. You're constantly policed and given that message that you need to still somehow adhere to these standards; otherwise, your value is dropping.

GINA, JOURNALIST, MOTHER OF TWO, CANBERRA

Over and over, women told us their body stories. Journeys through size, shape and time. Tales of being smaller, bigger, weight loss and weight gain. Tales of never feeling good enough. As times have changed, there are now a broader range of 'idealised' body shapes – not just one type of body shape, like the supermodels of the 1990s. But one thing is consistent – no matter what they look like, women feel they should always be striving to look different.

Knowledge is power. By looking back over history we can see how messed up and stupid these 'ideals' were. And in the future when presented with an option to choose to buy into the latest fad or 'what's hot', we hopefully opt out and don't get on the misery treadmill of trying to be something we're not and instead just embrace who we are and the bodies we've got.

Action

☑ **Take out your pen and journal in a quiet moment.**

Reflect on how advertising, magazine, film and TV influenced your thoughts about your body. What do you know now that can help you fight back against some of those powerful messages?

☑ **The next time you see an ad, article or Instagram reel that makes you feel bad about your body, stop for a moment, and think about these questions:**

- What am I being sold here?
- Is this actually true? and
- What can I do about this?

Blocking and reporting ads on social media, providing feedback to companies, and generally getting a bit angry about the toxic messaging we receive on a daily basis can help to change 'the system' and 'the industry'. And a bonus: it can make us feel better too.

4

Unlearning what we thought we knew about weight

THERE ARE FOUR MAIN MYTHS that we see perpetuated throughout everyday conversations, advertising, and diet culture:

1. Accepting your body means you are 'promoting obesity'.
2. You need to hate your body to beat it into submission (and be healthy).
3. You can control your weight and shape.
4. You should stay the same size and shape throughout your life.

We're going to tackle each of these head on so that you can be more aware of these myths when they come up, and start to work towards challenging them.

FACT: ACCEPTING YOUR BODY DOESN'T MEAN YOU ARE 'PROMOTING OBESITY'

Every time we talk about body image, someone asks: 'But if we all loved and accepted our bodies, whatever they look like, wouldn't that promote obesity?' The answer is no.

For the past fifteen to twenty years, there's been a war going on that you mightn't have even known about: a 'war on obesity'. Billions of dollars have been poured into research, and every news report about weight has featured anonymous torsos of larger bodies – usually sitting or eating – as they give the same old line of 'Obesity is associated with X, Y and Z'. For years we've been told that being at a high BMI leads to heart disease, diabetes and early death. We'd be writing a whole other book if we were to to go through and explain why BMI is really a very bad indicator of weight status, let alone health status (see p. 57 for our discussion of BMI). But after aaaallll of these programs to try to 'prevent obesity', after all of these horrific ad campaigns, and all of this money spent, what has happened? Not a lot.

There has been no change in weight status at the population level. Why? These programs had the best scientists, were the most well-funded, and had all of the connectedness across systems. But they didn't work, because they essentially made people feel bad about their weight in order to try to motivate health behaviour. It turns out that if you want people to be healthy, what you need to do is facilitate and talk about health behaviours. Take away the barriers, create more infrastructure, create safe and welcoming environments. Focus on health. Not weight.

For a long time, there has been a misconception that we needed to make people feel bad about their bodies in order to motivate them to maintain a healthy body weight. However, the science is now telling us something different. Two decades of quality research have shown that men and women who have positive body image – those who accept their bodies and focus on appreciating what their bodies can do – are *more* likely to engage in positive health behaviours, including physical activity, eating fruit and vegetables, getting cancer screenings, and maintaining a steady weight. Better body image leads to improved health behaviours.

Feeling ashamed about your body is known to lead to weight *gain* over time, not weight loss. This makes sense to many of us who have experience of body shame, but for those who don't, weight stigma researcher Dr Janet Tomiyama describes the vicious cycle. Body shame causes us stress, which leads to a cascade of behavioural, emotional and physiological responses. At the chemical level, when people feel discriminated against or feel shame, cortisol (the stress hormone) is released, which creates a physiological and psychological drive to engage in stress responses such as comfort eating to alleviate these stressful feelings. Over time, this leads to chronic stress, more weight gain, and, usually, repeated failed attempts at weight loss, which leads to greater chances of being stigmatised and feeling body shame, and the whole cycle starts again. Of course, there are a whole range of other physiological, hormonal and psychological reasons why our bodies decide how much we weigh, how much fat we store, and where, but explaining this cycle does make some people sit up and listen. Shame and 'shoulds' lead to stress.

In fact, research is now suggesting that the people who report being judged or criticised because of their weight are the ones who experience the most deterioration in their health, are more than twice as likely to experience mental health concerns like anxiety and depression, and have a 60 per cent increased chance of mortality, regardless of what their weight is. It's not the high weight that causes health problems. It's the fact that some people have a problem with higher weight that causes health problems.

Research has shown that it's often not even your actual BMI or weight status that determines whether you feel stigmatised, it's your perceived weight status. People who *think* they are in the 'overweight' or 'obese' category are more likely to feel discriminated against. This has been proven over and over again in large studies over the past ten years. Participants who were not in that high weight category at baseline and who reported experiencing weight discrimination were 2.5 times more likely to move up a weight category and be considered 'obese' at a four-year follow-up. In a study with children and adolescents, girls who were told they were 'too fat' at age ten by their parents, siblings, friends, peers or teachers were 1.66 times more likely to be classed as being in one of the higher weight categories at age nineteen, compared to those who were not labelled or told they were 'too fat'. In fact, in studies following individuals from the age of fifteen to around twenty-seven years of age, adolescents who don't realise that their BMI is in the 'overweight' category are *less* likely to gain weight.

There is just so much evidence that shows that telling people they are overweight and making them feel bad about it is not helpful and leads to weight gain, not weight loss. Diet culture is what is really 'promoting obesity'.

Making people feel better about their bodies will not glamorise or 'encourage obesity'. Making people feel good about their bodies helps them to engage in healthy behaviours. We have the power to change our own attitudes and behaviours in this area. Hopefully you now know that you don't need to feel bad about yourself or your kids' weight in order to help them to be healthy. Start there, and eventually, we can change the world.

Body Mass Index (BMI)

There is so much that is wrong with using the BMI. So, so much. But it's used in pretty much every research study, so we have to keep using it until someone comes up with something else.

BMI is calculated using a relatively simple formula: your weight divided by your height squared. It's probably taken off because it is quick and easy to calculate. The guy who came up with this was the same guy who conducted the starvation experiments described on p. 62 in this chapter. Insurance companies in the United States started to take on this measurement and the associated categories of 'under-weight', 'average weight', 'overweight' and 'obese'. It really took off because of its simplicity. But it is too simple. The association between BMI and other more complex measures of body fat was only conducted among white men, and we now know that this measure has very poor application in children, women, athletes, and anyone of any ethnicity other than white - that's a lot of people! BMI calculations consistently incorrectly categorise people, thus 'labelling' them as 'over' weight or 'too fat' and contributing to feelings of weight discrimination.

FACT: YOU DON'T NEED TO HATE YOUR BODY. APPRECIATING YOUR BODY HELPS YOU LOOK AFTER IT

Decades of 'anti-obesity' messaging have left us believing that we need to hate our bodies into submission. Health promotion campaigns have mostly mirrored the diet and fitness industry in their approach, which is really to try to shame and blame people into engaging in health behaviours – to point out (usually pretty bluntly) that their bodies are too big, that they are clearly not doing the right thing/doing enough exercise/eating the right foods, giving them some information on how to do this, and sending them on their way. But we know now that knowledge doesn't equal behaviour, and that this shame perpetuates weight gain. So what is the alternate approach?

There is now good evidence that people who have higher levels of body appreciation are more likely to eat fruit and vegetables, engage in physical activity, wear sunscreen, and engage in cancer screening. It turns out that feeling good about our bodies makes us more likely to look after them, in more sustainable ways.

The facts are simple: the more you beat yourself and other people up for your weight and shape, for 'doing the wrong thing' or 'having no willpower', the worse things get. Being kind to yourself and appreciating our bodies can help us feel safe and avoids this negative downward spiral. It focuses on what is important: being happy and healthy.

It's not to say that being dissatisfied with our bodies or appearance can't motivate us to do things, but it mostly drives us to spend more money on short-term solutions that don't work. Lifelong meaningful and positive change doesn't come from quick-fix solutions, it comes from appreciating all the incredible things our bodies can do – from a functional perspective – just as much, or more so, than how it looks.

Appreciating our bodies means that we are driven by intrinsic motivation to move our bodies because it feels good to do it. And appreciating our bodies means that we trust our bodies to guide us towards what we should eat, how much, and when. Never forget, no-one knows your body like you. If you needed permission to trust yourself, here it is (you have to imagine this part): because you know what's best for you.

FACT: YOUR WEIGHT AND SHAPE AREN'T ACTUALLY UP TO YOU. (WELL, NOT AS MUCH AS YOU THINK.)

We actually have less control over our weight and shape than we think. Decades of diet culture, fed to us at every opportunity through the media, advertising, and now social media, have tried to tell us that we are in charge. That if we just do this thing, buy this product, try this new program, then we could have the body that we want. The diet and fitness industry is not based on science, it's based on sales. And selling thinness is soooooo easy.

Now, everybody, sit down for what we are about to tell you. There are more than one hundred influences on body weight and shape, and most of them are beyond your control.

For the longest time, we've been sold the lie that our weight is *not* determined by genetics, hormones and metabolism – that our weight is based on diet shakes, gym memberships, or expensive 'health coach' programs. But fancy genetic research has now shown that your genes influence between 50 to 90 per cent of your body weight. When studies are done comparing identical twins (who have very similar genetic makeup) and fraternal twins (non-identical twins who live in the same family environment), scientists find that the identical twins are significantly more likely to have similar body weight than the fraternal twins. This shows that body weight is a bit more 'nature' than 'nurture'.

The body is not 'infinitely malleable', as much as we'd like to think it is. It is not Play-Doh or plasticine. Your body was designed for a purpose – survival and reproduction – and that's about it. Just as your body regulates your temperature, it regulates your weight.

Our bodies were designed for our stint as hunter–gatherers, to make sure that we could get through the periods in between woolly-mammoth meals by storing fat very effectively, and then defending those fat stores to ensure that we didn't starve when meals were scarce. If you stop and think about it, we humans are very clever!

There is a theory about how our bodies regulate their weight, called 'set point theory'. The idea is that we all have a weight that our body believes is 'just right' for us. If we start to dip below that level, our body will employ a range of strategies to 'defend' our fat stores, and resist weight loss. Just like our body temperature – if we get too hot, our body starts sweating to try to get rid of heat, and if we get too cold, it makes us shiver so we put some more clothes on. The problem is that the 'ideal' body weight according to our bodies doesn't align with the societal 'ideals' of attractiveness, which are actually not physiologically possible for most of us. We think that if a roll in our belly appears when we sit down we are somehow 'over' weight – but our bodies disagree. They are all like, 'I put that there for a reason and you need that'. (Okay, we're going overboard, but you get the picture.)

Therefore, when we start to restrict our food, we can sustain weight loss for a relatively short period of time – maybe a few weeks to a month – but then our body starts to fight back. Suddenly we are overwhelmed with hunger and cravings, and 'unable to resist' certain foods. It's not a lack of willpower, it's actually the body *reasserting* its power. Your body sets off a range of physiological mechanisms designed to save your fat stores just in case the hunters can't bring back a woolly mammoth for your dinner. It's no wonder a six-year follow-up of fourteen *Biggest Loser* contestants in the United States found that they had regained a substantial amount of weight – most of the participants ended up regaining 30 kg or so after the cameras stopped rolling. On top of that, their metabolisms were 2 to 5 per cent slower than when they had started on the show.

They did *what* study?

The same guy that invented the BMI conducted a wild experiment in the 1940s. You can't do this sort of study anymore (hello, ethics) but back then, he moved thirty-six healthy men into the University of Minnesota football stadium for six months. The aim of the study was to observe the potential effects of starvation in war, but we learned a lot more from this.

The men ate a normal diet for three months, and then a restricted low-calorie diet for three months. After the restriction phase, the men had lost all interest in sex, their heart rate and temperature was lowered, and they had less strength and stamina. The men became obsessed with food – dreaming about food, reading about food, looking up recipes – and they became irritable and depressed. It was noted that once the restrictive eating period ended, many engaged in binge eating. (Sound familiar for any of you expert dieters?)

What started out as a study to observe the effects of starvation in war actually became a much-talked about study that demonstrated the psychological impact of restriction, and explains why we don't have the 'willpower' to follow through with our new year's resolutions. It's not that we aren't strong enough – it's that our bodies and brains are hardwired to regulate our weight, so we actually have less control over our weight than we think.

Just as your body defends your fat stores when you start to lose body weight or restrict food, it also tries to dispose of excess energy at the times when we eat more than usual. Decades of seeing charts saying 'Run 5 km if you've eaten a chocolate bar' have made us think that we need to 'compensate' for eating high-energy foods. But our body does it for us.

If we eat high-energy foods, our body spends quite a lot of energy – around 10 per cent of the calories in that food – just digesting and converting what you've eaten into things our bodies can use. Our metabolism increases to deal with these times of higher intake. In one study back in the 1980s, scientists asked a group of participants who had never been at a higher weight to gain 10 per cent of their body weight, and another group of people in larger bodies to lose 10 per cent. Those who gained the weight had an average *increase* in their metabolic rate of 16 per cent, meaning that they metabolised food more quickly. Those who lost weight had a *decrease* in their metabolic rate of 15 per cent – so they metabolised food more slowly. Their bodies were compensating for the change in body weight without them even knowing it, or controlling it.

Relinquish control and trust the process

Maybe it's time to accept that we don't have as much control as we think. Maybe it's time to see through the messaging that sells thinness as health, and profits off our body's psychology and physiology. Maybe it's time that we let our bodies do their thing, trust them and listen to them. Maybe it's not about willpower, it's about mindset.

Shifting our mindset to one of appreciating and accepting our bodies, and focusing on nourishing them and giving them what they need means that our bodies won't fight us. We can engage in healthy behaviours like eating a wide variety of food and lots of fruit and vegetables, we can move our bodies because we want to look after them. We can work with our bodies to do what is best for them, not control everything in an effort to reach an unrealistic goal. This approach feels so much more gentle, easy and calm, takes a whole lot less mental energy and costs a whole lot less money than the alternative.

We never try to change our height. We accept that our genes determine how tall we are, and although we might not like it, we don't spend endless amounts of time on food or exercise regimes to change our height. Some people are dissatisfied with their height. Men and women (but mostly men in this case) will often say that their ideal height is taller than their actual height. But it seems ridiculous for us to think about spending any time or energy on trying to change our height. Imagine how the world would be different if we accepted our weight in the same way.

Diets don't work. Researchers and clinicians have been saying that for a while now. The research has been around for about twenty-five years. Unfortunately, it's just meant that diets have gone undercover and are now in disguise. Rather than calling themselves 'diets' like in the 1990s and 2000s, the 2010s and 2020s version is 'wellness', 'clean eating', 'paleo', or is based around 'whole foods'. It's green smoothies and 'avoiding harmful chemicals and toxins', as well as avoiding our new biggest enemy: sugar. Low fat had a moment, but the last twenty years has been all about low carbs. Our poor cake, bread, potato and pasta friends have been shoved to the side, despite being the main source of fuel that is actually needed for, you know, little things like brain function.

And then there's the other perspective. Anupa Roper is one of those women who has always been naturally slim. Skinny, even. Could never put on any weight. And yet Anupa has become a positive body image advocate and works with young kids around feeling good about their bodies because she never felt good about hers. Now a mum of two kids aged ten and twelve years, Anupa reflects on her body image journey from her home in Leicestershire in the United Kingdom.

It's only in my later years, probably my late thirties, early forties, that I realised how much has been affected by the way I felt about the way that I looked. I've always been small and slim, and at school, I started to realise that I was a lot slimmer than everybody else. Then my PE teacher gave me the name 'Sparrow Legs'. He used it as a term of endearment, but it did make me realise that actually my legs were really skinny compared to everybody else's. And it made me think that must be really obvious, because otherwise, why would I get given that name?

I come from an Indian background, but I grew up in a very Westernised family. My school was predominantly white and so I did feel different. If you're in a larger body, you might feel different than if you're in a smaller body. And if you've got a different kind of skin, it's just another aspect that can make you feel different to others. As a teenager, what I saw in magazines was always white-skinned, blue-eyed, blonde-haired. For me that 'ideal' was like a million miles away. I knew I couldn't possibly look like that, but it also made me wonder: is my skin even beautiful? Because it's not portrayed out there.

Throughout my schooling, I worried about being popular, and being good enough, and whether I looked pretty to the boys and all of that appeal stuff. But not being confident in the way I looked affected so many things. I think I subconsciously made friends with boys in college because I didn't want to be involved in that world of girls comparing and having to be the prettiest, having to be interested in fashion and makeup. When it came to career, thinking about what I might like to do for a job, again, subconsciously, I probably avoided going down the corporate route, because I thought that I looked small and slight and so how could I seem powerful? I couldn't be a lawyer or a director or manager when I'm in such a small body.

As a slim person, I got quite a lot of comments. People would come up to me and say 'Oh, you're so tiny', 'You're so thin', and my extended family would make comments at every wedding or family function: 'How come you're still so skinny?' It would make me feel so nervous and uncomfortable to have people noticing and judging my body like that. I would usually just giggle and wait for them to change the subject. They would put their fingers around my wrist to demonstrate that I was thin. People would ask 'How do you do it?' and say, 'Oh, you mustn't eat anything'. But in fact, I have a really fast metabolism so I'm eating all the time. I actually consciously avoided going to weddings and parties because I didn't want to hear about my size or be told how skinny I am. I don't think people would talk so openly about the size of a person in a larger body, so why were they doing it to me?

The funny thing is that the people in my extended family who commented on my weight never asked how I was, or about my work. It was all about the way I looked, and it was something that I wasn't trying to achieve.

Even in a smaller body, I still think, Oh, I shouldn't have that ice cream. And if I have that ice cream, then tomorrow, I've got to eat fruit. I still get that messaging. Even in a smaller body, I'm not thinking I can just eat whatever I like.

Now that I've started doing this work and started talking about my experiences on social media, I've had quite a few people contact me and say that they used to be called Sparrow Legs at school – that they also got teased about their skinny legs. It's made me want to try to change things for my own kids, and the next generation of kids, so that they aren't held back by their lack of confidence in their bodies either.

ANUPA ROPER, MUM OF TWO, UK
@MISS_SPARROWLEGS

You see? Even in a body that many women would 'love to have', Anupa has still had a lifetime of insecurities, and wasted so much time and precious energy worrying about the way she looks. We can't keep doing this. We need to spend our precious energy doing something else.

Darling Girl, don't waste a single moment of your life being at war with your body . . . just embrace it.

TARYN, OF COURSE!

FACT: YOUR BODY CAN AND SHOULD CHANGE OVER TIME

Much of the messaging we are exposed to tells us that we should be able to maintain the same size and shape throughout our lives – that it is just as possible to be the same size in your forties and fifties as it was in your twenties. I've heard grown up, intelligent women in their fifties lament 'Oh, I just want to look like I did pre-kids' or post a social media 'memory' of themselves from thinner times and comment on how they wish they still looked like that.

As we age, there are so many changes to the way our bodies work – physiological changes to the way we store fat, metabolise things, and build bone and muscle – that affect the way our bodies work, not just what they look like. We can't go back in time. Our bodies can't 'bounce back' after kids. Our bodies are different. Very different. Physically, physiologically, hormonally different.

Laura Mazza started blogging about mental health and body positivity after her second child was born. She is the kind of tell-it-like-it-is mum you want to have on your feed because she's actually real: there's no cookie-cutter perfect white-linen-wearing-with-a-white-couch mama here. Laura says that writing is her therapy, and perhaps her writing can be therapy for others as well. Her first post, all about accepting her post-baby body, went viral. The post included a 'Before' and 'After' photo – before and after motherhood, that is. On the 'Before' side is Laura in a smaller body, pre-kids, looking like an under-wear model. On the 'After' side is a Laura who is happier in her body after having two kids.

Laura explains the 'Before' photo:

I was just eating meat. That's it. On the second or third day, you were 'allowed' certain vegetables but the rest of it was meat. It was so unhealthy. I would go out to dinner and spend the whole time fixated on getting my very specific order right and worrying about food. During pregnancy, I started to eat normally again, I started to eat more healthily, and my body reflected that. And then after I had my first child and my hips got wider, my stomach looked different, I looked different. I felt like I had to tell people, 'I'm still the same person. I'm the same personality, I just look different.' And sure, I can wish to have that skinny body like I did. But I don't want to go through what I went through to look like that. I feel like the pressure that we have on us is to look like that. The pregnant body is celebrated. But as soon as that kid comes out of you, it's not celebrated anymore. And you're not allowed to show any aftermath effects of having a baby, which is just ridiculous.

For mums, it's hard because our bodies change physically. But there's also so many more aspects to it. I gained a lot of weight being on antidepressants, and I had to go on antidepressants because I had postnatal depression. And then with a baby, there's no time for self-care and stuff like that. People have this expectation of you to not view yourself as sexy anymore when you become a mum. And then if you gain weight, it's like you definitely shouldn't consider yourself attractive because you're not 'looking after yourself.' But the best some of us can do is eat the toast scraps off the kids' plates and grab whatever we can to eat whenever we can. After having my third, I lost a lot of blood and my body changed completely. I've never had the same energy levels after that.

When I gained all this weight, it was like I was disrespected. Like I wasn't the same person anymore. I had three kids, I went through hell, I was exhausted. My body physically changed. I've got stretch marks, my belly button sits much lower. But inside, I'm the same person. So why do I have to be treated so differently – why can't I be respected? And then the same goes for someone losing weight. They're treated like they're not the same person too. The singer Adele – she is exactly the same person inside, and is also a mum. Everyone has something to say about your body, and society doesn't let you have body autonomy. You can't be happy with it if you're fat, and you can't be happy with it if you're skinny. Because you should always be something, you know.

So because I wasn't respected, I didn't celebrate my body either. I didn't buy the sexy clothes. I bought stuff that would hide my body. I thought I would get a new wardrobe when I lost weight. I was worried about how I looked. I didn't want to show my husband my stomach and stuff like that, it was just ridiculous.

And then one day after having my second kid I was getting out of the shower, and in my head, the voice said 'Ugh – don't look at yourself.' And I thought, 'Why? You look like this because you've had two children.' That's a pretty big deal. People would kill to have two children. I've had a miscarriage, I know what that heartbreak feels like. So I wrote about accepting and loving your body after having kids. I wrote it because I wanted to share it with other women so they know they're not alone, and it's okay to be okay with the wonder that is your body right now.

The photo blew up. The story blew up, and it was so validating. All this time I spent being ashamed. It was so unnecessary when I just had to talk myself out of those bullshit thoughts. I learned that not everybody was looking at me with that expectation to return to the 'Before' image. That was actually all in my head.

Five years later, as my relationship was ending, I had a conversation with a friend (an ex-friend now!) who said, 'You can't leave him. Who would want a chubby mum with three kids?' and I really believed that. Anyway, the relationship ended and I thought, fuck it. This is who I am. This is what I look like, if they don't like it . . . Well, actually I'm surprised by how many men like it.

I assumed I had to apologise for my body, which housed three kids and didn't look like it did in my early twenties. I thought that no man would want a woman who has more weight on her, who has stretch marks, cellulite, who has kids. But boy, was I wrong. As a single woman with cellulite, stretch marks, a stomach that has stretched and deflated three times, I've been told that I'm sexy more times than I can count. Every bit of me – and I now believe it too.

LAURA MAZZA, MUM OF THREE, MELBOURNE
@ITSLAURAMAZZA

It's so universal, isn't it? That moment of looking in the mirror and not recognising what you see. The overwhelming feelings of failure, and the thinking that losing weight will change all of that. This is so similar to all of the stories of so many women that we speak to. We hope that reading this story makes you feel less alone, less broken, and less like this was somehow all your fault. The other side of the story is also something we hear often – women who realise that they can stop hating on their bodies are so surprised by how easy it can become. Women talk about how light they feel without wearing the weight of others' expectations about their bodies. And women talk about how that shift in mindset and 'middle-fingers-up at beauty ideals' attitude is what gives them the confidence they were seeking by shrinking or changing their bodies. So will you try it?

We've already discussed the complete physical, physiological and psychological changes that occur during pregnancy and post-partum. Similar hormonal and environmental changes occur for those who come to motherhood and parenthood in other ways as well. You might have accepted the fact that your feet were a totally different size and shape, and that your shoulders and hips were wider forever, but most women blame themselves for 'failing to lose the baby weight' or 'letting themselves go' in parenthood. That weight is physiologically designed to stay there, safely stored away on your stomach, thighs and butt, just in case there is a complete lack of woolly mammoths to eat for a while, and you need to give your children all of the nuts and berries you can find, surviving off your fat stores and prioritising their growth. Our bodies haven't moved on from the Stone Age.

Taryn

DIET: The first three letters of this word spell 'DIE' – surely it's a sign . . .

When I did my bodybuilding training, I was going to the gym and eating all of the things that were meant to be 'healthy' but I was so broken inside. I was prepared to do just about anything to achieve my 'bikini body', but focusing so much on my appearance meant that I neglected other areas of my health and life. I became very one-dimensional.

Putting all my health goals into one basket completely changed my health metrics from how I felt and moved in my body to how tight my bum was, how toned my arms were and how flat my stomach was. (Sidenote: on stage at the fitness model competition, I still had to glue my excess tummy skin down into my very small briefs. And yes, you read right – glue!)

It was on stage, under the bright lights, with the judges making notes about my body that I had a big revelation – everything I had put my body through for the past few months was just not worth it. Having a 'hot' body actually didn't make me happier, it made me grumpier (bye-bye, chocolate!), it excluded me from feasts with friends ('I'll have chicken and broccoli, thanks') and made me less fun ('No margaritas for me, just a water, thanks'). (Okay, okay, drinking doesn't make you happier but, on occasion, it sure makes things funnier.)

When I stopped punishing my body and started valuing health not just as encompassing physical goals but also emotional, mental and spiritual, I became a much nicer, more grounded and happier person. Instead of going for a run to burn calories, I'd go for a run because moving my body in such a dynamic way with the tunes blasting made me feel really good.

I'd hike up mountains and, instead of checking my watch to see my stats, I'd look at the view. Rather than being a slave to the gym and an inflexible schedule, every day I'd make a choice about how I wanted to move my body. During hectic times I'd still enjoy lifting weights (I think there is something about grunting with heavy weights that expels demons from your body!) but on occasions of overwhelm or stress, I'd choose gentle and nurturing ways to move my body – either swimming or yoga. The rules were gone, and intuitive moving was in.

Removing the metrics of calories burned, time spent at the gym, kilometres run and kilograms lifted allowed space for me to focus on how my body felt. When I was connected to how my body was feeling, it gave me an overwhelming sense of appreciation for all the ways in which it could move and all the things it could do. Dance, swim, run, hike, sway, lift, sashay even! What a glorious feeling it is to move your body without the burden of 'Am I doing enough to lose weight and look good?'

I found the same freedom in developing a positive relationship with food. Instead of using dysfunctional and restricted eating to look a particular way, I'd choose to eat foods that fuelled my body and gave me lots of energy. I learned about intuitive eating and health at every size.

Finally, I could have my cake and eat it too! No more guilt, calorie counting or punishment.

Just pure joy, like chocolate, or an extra hour back in your day.

News flash: You can just get new pants

So many women identify with their clothing size. They associate with those numbers so hard, and they are so definite about it. We feel shame when we have to buy something labelled with higher numbers, elation when the numbers are lower. But it doesn't have to be that way . . .

Sara Ibrahim @simastylistlondon is a sustainable fashion stylist. She spends most of her time with her clients removing the layers of all of the negative thoughts and feelings that they have about their bodies, and what they 'should' wear. It's a huge, emotional excavation.

'Hating our bodies is so democratic. It doesn't matter if you are rich, poor, from England, from Europe, posh, not posh, what industry you work in, whatever colour your skin is. The one thing that women say to me is "Oh, I don't like this", "Oh, this used to be smaller", and "Sara, can you just make me look tall and thin?"'

Sara then teaches them to know their bodies, align their wardrobe with their priorities in life, and forget about the numbers.

'I meet completely different people in our second session,'

Sara says. 'I don't even recognise them. They just have so much confidence – they carry themselves differently and they actually look like a different person.

'I want to start a revolution. A quiet, silent revolution. Where women acknowledge themselves from the inside, they know how beautiful they are, and how to wear clothes that make them feel beautiful on the outside too.'

We want to empower women in different ways. To buy new pants if the ones you have don't fit. To wear the things you love, that make you feel good. Because life is short.

Repeat after me: My body will take on many shapes in my lifetime. It is my character that matters most!

People change. Bodies change. It's the whole point to life. The key to getting through all of this is in accepting your body, your appearance, and the fact that they will change over time. This will help you to be happier, healthier and way more fun to be around!

Action

☑ **Write a letter to your younger self.**

Actually sit down with a paper and pen, set a timer for ten or fifteen minutes, and start writing. What would you tell yourself, now that you know the things you know?

☑ **Can you come up with a word or phrase that captures this? One that you can write down everywhere, remember and say to yourself often?**

5

Be kind to yourself

SURE, IT MAY BE A convenient hashtag, but you don't need to #loveyourbody. For people who have been hating their bodies for years, that can be a pretty unrealistic target. #Appreciateyourbody doesn't quite have the same ring to it, but it's more like what we are after. You can like some parts of your body, but research now shows that physical and mental benefits come from the level of *appreciation* of your body. That appreciation can be about the way your body looks, but it can also be about what it can do.

> **Loving your body isn't believing your body looks good; it is knowing your body is good, regardless of how it looks. It isn't thinking you are beautiful; it is knowing you are more than beautiful. It is understanding that your body is an instrument for your use, not an ornament to be admired.**
>
> **DR LINDSAY KITE AND DR LEXIE KITE**
> **CO-AUTHORS OF *MORE THAN A BODY: YOUR BODY***
> ***IS AN INSTRUMENT, NOT AN ORNAMENT***

Sometimes, in recognising that we need to appreciate our bodies more, we can get a little obsessive about it and start 'policing' our thoughts, trying to block or remove any negative ones from coming anywhere near our brain. Newer acceptance-based approaches allow us to have negative thoughts and feelings about our bodies from time to time, and allow ourselves to experience these thoughts and feelings without acting on them, trying to avoid or change our thoughts and feelings. In other words – feel the feelings!

BODY IMAGE FLEXIBILITY

The key to appreciation is to stop those thoughts and feelings from making you feel shame and causing you to avoid the things that you want to do, and instead move towards more mindfully accepting and appreciating our bodies. For example, you might wish that your body looked different in a swimsuit. But as long as you can sit with those negative thoughts and feelings long enough to wear the swimsuit anyway and have fun at the beach, then you can start to have some more positive experiences of your body. It's about reframing some of your brain's self-critical thoughts. Body appreciation at the pool or beach could look like this:

1. **Stop comparing.** Instead of 'Everyone else has a better body than me', you could think 'Bodies come in all shapes and sizes'.
2. **Appreciate functionality.** 'Ugh, my arms are wobbly', could become 'My arms are strong enough to play with my kids in the water'.

3. **Do what feels good.** Instead of 'I don't want anyone to see my body so I will sit here and hide it', think 'I will just walk faster into the water as I will feel less vulnerable there'.

Dr Jennifer Webb explains: 'Body image flexibility is about understanding how we relate to ourselves and our bodies. So, for example, if I think, "I hate my body, I'm fat", body image flexibility is trying to honour that those are authentic thoughts, and being more conscious of how having those thoughts affects doing things that matter to us. Does having the thought that "I'm fat", or "I hate my body" prevent you from engaging in activities that are meaningful to you? Once we have an awareness of that, we can develop skills like mindfulness, self-compassion, and other kinds of acceptance skills to sort of hold those thoughts and associated feelings – and still do the things that we want to do.'

Dr Webb gives us a brilliant example. Just imagine that you've had a shower and as you step out onto the bathmat, you catch a glimpse of yourself in the mirror. You could go down a spiral of self-critical thinking, where you compare your body to what it looked like in previous parts of your life, or you could be upset with things like skin conditions, cellulite or sagginess. Body image flexibility encourages you to be curious about the thoughts and feelings that you might have in that moment – not to avoid them, but to connect in an authentic way.

- Think: How do I want to spend the time that I have today, right now? Do I want to stay caught up in these thoughts about not liking my body? Or do I want to connect with my body as the vehicle that will help me engage with my family, my work and the world today?

- Try: Putting on moisturising lotion or something that takes you away from the experience of judging the body and to nourishing the body instead. As you move over the different parts, notice what that part of your body does for you, and why that is important to you. Focus on giving love to those parts of your body.
- Think: Can I still recognise that even though there are aspects of my appearance that I'm not really on board with right now, I'm just going to get dressed in something I am comfortable in, that makes me feel good, and I will do the things that matter to me today anyway?
- Experiment with creating some distance from the thoughts: For example, instead of saying 'I feel fat', perhaps give yourself a little distance or perspective by saying 'I am having the thought that I feel fat'.
- Reconnect with your values: Would you want that thought to be written on your tombstone? 'Here lies Donna – really should've lost a few kilos . . .' No, you want people to remember you because of who you are, what you do and what you mean to them, not based on the number written on the tag of your pants. Although it may sound morbid, there is nothing like remembering we still have this moment today while we are still living to jumpstart moving in the direction of our values.

This is similar to ideas you may have come across in meditation or mindfulness sessions. Just notice your thoughts: don't listen to them, believe them or shoo them away. Your thoughts are not facts. Hold your thoughts, make space for them. You can experience those negative thoughts and feelings about the body without ruminating on them and without acting on them. Let them be, let them pass. Be curious about new thoughts that we can bring in, like being appreciative of our body functionality, or liking the way other parts of our bodies look instead of just focusing on the bits we don't like. Taking this approach, and combining it with self-compassion, moving your body, and eating more intuitively will lead to a much more authentic version of body positivity than you can show on Instagram with a hashtag #BOPO.

The aim for you as a parent is to improve your relationship with, and appreciate, your body, because this will be good for you, but also for your kids. There isn't really a 'goal body image' or a number we are trying to reach, it's more of a feeling.

So, we've convinced you that you should appreciate that body of yours, but *how* exactly do you achieve that? We can give you all of the information we want, but it's not likely to change your attitudes or behaviours without action. You need to know all of this in order to rewire your existing understanding of the way that bodies, weight and wellbeing work together. This knowledge will help to prepare you for action and keep you going, but you will have to do the work.

SELF-COMPASSION

It's one thing for others to say mean things to us, but what about when we are the mean girls to ourselves?

Think of your bestie. Now imagine saying to her:

You are fat.

You are ugly.

Gosh, your husband wouldn't want to have sex with you, you're the size of a whale.

Wow, you've really let yourself go.

That cellulite on your legs is so gross.

Your tummy is a mess, look at the way it jiggles.

You are looking old and run down.

You shouldn't wear a sleeveless dress, your tuckshop arms are hideous.

You just wouldn't say it, would you? We would never say such mean and cruel words to our best friends, so why do we think it's okay to say those things to ourselves? Sometimes we are our own worst critics, but it doesn't have to be this way. We can learn to quieten down the inner critic and be more neutral, and then graduate to being more forgiving and eventually get to nirvana – a state in which you walk through life with a kind voice in your head that champions your every move!

It wasn't that long ago we would hear the word self-love and just want to eyeroll. That's because we've spent more years of our life hating our bodies and being more closely acquainted with the inner critic than the inner champion.

But now that we're a decade into the world of self-love living, not in a million years would we go back. Walking through life with a friendly positive voice chanting away in your head, saying 'You can' and 'You've got this' is like having a superpower. Self-compassion and kindness to yourself will give you a spring in your step and an undeniable edge, in everything you do.

It's alarming the amount of people – women in particular – who are nothing short of cruel to themselves. The things women say about their own bodies brings us to tears. How can our bodies that have done so much for us be the subject of our own vitriol and nastiness? And are we really that surprised that our kids adopt some of our body dissatisfaction when we are so cruel to ourselves?

We must take action. You're in the right place.

WHAT IS SELF-COMPASSION?

Essentially, self-compassion is treating yourself with the same kindness that you would a good friend. It involves speaking to yourself, and treating yourself, with kindness rather than criticism. Self-compassion is basically the antidote to perfectionism and shame, and those two things are behind so many of the problems that we experience.

Dr Kristin Neff in the United States has led the way with the study of self-compassion. She outlines the three main components of self-compassion as follows:

- Self-kindness (as opposed to self-judgement): Being understanding and kind to yourself when you are experiencing challenges and suffering.
- Sense of common humanity (as opposed to isolation): Recognising that you are not alone in experiencing these challenges.
- Mindfulness (as opposed to over-identification): Being aware of and feeling negative thoughts and feelings, rather than avoiding them or becoming too attached to them.

It's important that we are kind to ourselves, particularly in parenthood, but very few of us are wired for self-compassion. And you can't just click your fingers and make it happen. How many times have you looked at a post on social media that tells you to be kind to yourself and thought, 'Yep, I definitely need to do that' and then operate exactly as you always have done, beating yourself up about everything? With practice, we can turn down the self-criticism and turn up the self-compassion towards ourselves and our work, our parenting and our bodies. Learning how to be compassionate to ourselves first will help us to be more compassionate with our kids, and also model and teach a compassionate approach to them.

THE SCIENCE BIT: WHY SELF-COMPASSION WORKS

When the world (and Dr Brené Brown) started to talk about shame, we searched for programs that could help. While guilt is the thought or feeling that you've done something bad, shame is the thought or feeling that *you* are bad – a bad person, a bad mother, and so on. It's a lot deeper. We couldn't find any specific interventions to overcome shame, but what we did find was self-compassion.

There is now a huge number of scientific journal articles and even more studies that have been done around self-compassion, mostly in the past ten years. Studies that bring together all of the studies (called 'meta-analyses') have confirmed that self-compassion leads to improved wellbeing. Adolescents and adults with higher levels of self-compassion have lower symptoms of depression, anxiety and other mental health issues, as well as improved happiness, better physical health and immunity, and being more likely to engage in physical activity and sleep better.

When researchers evaluate self-compassion intervention programs, they find that participants report being happier, eating better, feeling better about their bodies, and losing weight. Anxiety, depression and eating disorders are reduced. In the last chapter we introduced the research that shows that shame about our bodies and weight leads us to eat more, and the stigma associated with being in a bigger body leads to the negative physical outcomes that most people assume are the result of being at a higher weight. Self-compassion may be the solution to reverse this.

Interestingly, none of these self-compassion intervention programs focused on bodies, weight or body image to have that effect, indicating that improving self-compassion in general can have a broader impact. Many self-compassion programs are relatively easy to access and practise on your own, and don't require a therapist. This makes self-compassion a very effective intervention that can lead to improvements in mental health for pretty much everyone.

Increasing our levels of self-compassion can improve body image, mental health, happiness and overall wellbeing. This may be because people make a mindset shift towards self-compassion rather than self-criticism, and therefore experience lower levels of shame in all aspects of their lives.

SELF-COMPASSION IS THE OPPOSITE OF PERFECTIONISM

Perfectionism is often thought of as being a relatively positive trait (hands up if you've ever gloated about it as your 'weakness' in a job interview). Perfectionism has also been recognised as a personality trait common to people who experience eating disorders – it's a way of thinking that facilitates the development of ridiculously high standards, and the never-ending striving to achieve them that can have such serious health impacts.

Being a perfectionist can have other implications for our mental health in multiple different settings: at work, education and parenting, leading to depression, anxiety, stress and burnout. We get into cycles of 'never-enoughness', thinking that if we work harder, we will do better (and be more worthy of love and attention), but in working harder, we exhaust ourselves, feel like failures, and feel shame. We fall in a heap, but usually get back up again and repeat the cycle again.

There are very few paths out of this way of thinking, but self-compassion is one of them.

That's not to say that it's always easy. Some people find it difficult to shift their thinking towards being kind to themselves. This will depend on experiences that you might have had. If you have experienced significant trauma, it would be a good idea to practise this with someone who specialises in compassion-focused therapy (CFT) or someone to guide you rather than attempting it on your own. The people who find self-compassion to be hard are often the exact people who need it the most.

So this is all a very long way of saying that it's a good idea to practise self-compassion. And by doing this yourself, you will be able to model and teach it to your kids, which could help improve their physical and mental health.

SELF-COMPASSION IMPROVES YOUR PARENTING

Being less critical on yourself is good for *you*, but practising self-compassion can also make you a better parent, in direct and indirect ways. When parents are kinder to themselves, they have less depression, anxiety and stress, all of which has an impact on children.

Here's how that could play out in an everyday scenario: When your child is being loud/rude/rambunctious in a shopping centre or the supermarket and you have tried all of your usual tricks but nothing is working, you might start to have critical thoughts of 'I'm such a bad mother' – which, when you are experiencing anxiety or depression, can quickly spiral into helplessness and hopelessness, and even more unhelpful thoughts. This can lead you to snap at your kid, and they might finally be quiet, but then you feel all sorts of shame that you yelled, and you sense the judgement of the people around you and hate that you had to do that to your child.

Being more compassionate in that situation might look like responding to your 'I'm a bad mother' thought with thinking about some of the context for the behaviour (e.g., 'Actually, the kids are all hyped up from that birthday party and the cake/ice cream'). You might stop and take a breath, realise that it's unhelpful to be judging yourself at that moment. Notice that no-one around you actually cares about how noisy your kids are, and that one lady who looked at you weirdly was trying to tell you, 'It's okay, you've got this.' The kids eventually move on to another, more shop-appropriate game, and you have skated through a potential shame-storm unharmed. Well done, mama.

Taryn

Do you remember the days when the local maternal and child healthcare nurse would come to your home to check up on you and your newborn? When Mikaela was a newborn, the nurse measured and weighed her and then sat down to chat with me. At the time, my older child Cruz was fifteen months old, and he joined me on my lap as my peaceful peachy Miki slept in her portable carrier on the bench. As Miki was my third child, I felt pretty comfortable and confident with how she was developing so I used the opportunity to raise a concern I had about Cruz with the nurse. I said, 'Cruz is doing well, but I'm worried about his speech, he's not saying many words.'

At that exact moment, Cruz knocked over a cup of milk and said 'Shit.'

I looked at the nurse and nervously said, laughing, 'I guess he doesn't have any problems after all!'

Children learn so much from how we are being and what we are doing rather than what we are saying. Those little sponges absorb everything! Of course you want your little sponges to be soaking up the goodness – so if you are waiting for a sign to start working on your own self-compassion and body image, this is it!

PRACTISING SELF-COMPASSION

Becoming more self-compassionate is not a linear process. Practising self-compassion becomes more and more automatic over time. Every time you practise, you are training your brain to respond in a kinder way to the things that come up in life, rather than being critical. There is no end destination where you reach the magical zone of everything-being-okay. You just keep going.

Keep reminding yourself, and one day you will look back at a situation and go, 'Huh, that used to trigger such a downward spiral, and now it doesn't.'

Self-compassion is something that you can practise, a way to respond when you are stressed or suffering, and an overall approach to your relationship with yourself. By recognising and moving through the three steps at a challenging time, by listening to self-compassion meditations, and by engaging in self-compassionate writing activities, you can slowly rewire your brain to respond more automatically with kindness instead of criticism.

Start by recognising that this is a hard or challenging moment. Dr Neff says, 'This is a moment of suffering.' You might use 'Arrrgh, this is hard.'

1. **Feel the feeling:** Stop and notice how the situation makes you feel and name that feeling. 'I'm feeling frustrated because I've asked my kid to put on their shoes seventeen times, and he's still not wearing any. This makes me feel ineffective, and like a terrible parent.'

2. **Recognise the reality:** Recognise that this is actually really common. Who else might feel this way? 'I'm sure I'm not the only one battling against kids who won't do what I ask. Most parents I've talked to say they have "one of those mornings" quite often.'

3. **Choose kindness:** What would a friend say to you in response to your thought/statement? 'I'm under a lot of stress at the moment, it's normal to feel a little frustrated in this situation. I'm doing a great job of keeping things together really.'

Using this three-step process can help you from spiralling into a beating-yourself-up moment. Once you practise this and turn up that compassionate voice in your head more often, you turn down the critical one. Over time, the compassionate voice will come more easily and naturally, and the critical one will be muted and muffled.

Other ways to practise self-compassion include using these three steps in writing or meditation. It can be helpful to practise when you are not in such a heated moment.

If I'm putting on a pair of jeans that fitted me last month, and they don't fit me anymore, and the critical voice pops up, instead of going down that path, I need to ask myself: What do I need in that moment?

I need to be really gentle with myself.

I need to take off those damn jeans.

And I need to do something in that moment that helps me be kind to myself and my body. That might be saying nice things to yourself, but we have to do more than talk. We actually need to do something with our bodies and to our bodies that helps us to heal. Respectful actions and loving actions. Moving, and nourishing our bodies in mindful ways. So that even if we don't 'love ourselves' 24/7, we are practising the actions which show love, respect and care for ourselves, even when we might not feel it yet.

FIONA SUTHERLAND

@THEMINDFULDIETITIAN

Action

Self-compassion writing tasks

Evidence suggests that writing and journalling are really helpful in managing our stress and anxiety, by helping us to express our feelings and take a different perspective. You can type on your computer or your phone, but there is something special about the physical act of handwriting and letting those thoughts and emotions flow out of you. Here are some writing prompts to help you engage in this activity.

Find some time and space that you can devote to this and grab your journal and a lovely pen. Try one of the following prompts:

☑ **Imagine you are having a bad body image moment.**
You might be worried about a big event that is coming up, or you've seen yourself in a photo and started being critical to yourself. Use the three-step response framework above to write a response to yourself to explore your feelings and practise speaking to yourself with kindness. Set a timer and write for ten minutes.

☑ **Write yourself a letter from an imaginary kind friend, the sort of friend who wants the best for you, would never judge you, and is endlessly kind and supportive.**
The letter may be in response to a challenging parenting or body image moment, or more general, depending on what you need. Set a timer and write for ten minutes.

Self-compassion meditation

The exact meditations and exercises used in many of the studies mentioned above are freely available. We've adapted one below for your parenting. There are more available in the resources section at the end of this book.

Just sit back in your chair, take a deep breath, and close your eyes for a moment (as long as you're not driving!). That's it. Now, take another nice big, slow breath.

Picture a tough situation that you have had with your kids lately. Anything that comes to mind is fine. Replay what was happening in that moment.

First, think about how you were feeling in that moment. What emotions came up for you? Anger? Fear? Confusion? Frustration? Sadness? Grief?

Allow yourself to feel those feelings. Acknowledge how you were feeling.

Yes, parenting is hard.

But let's take a moment to consider everything that is going on for your child in that moment. Take a deep breath and imagine the physical, emotional and cognitive challenges and changes that their body is going through. Imagine the influences on your child's thoughts, feelings and actions. I want you to visualise your young person now, and send them some compassion. Being a kid can be really hard.

Let's send them some compassion now. Repeat silently after me, in your mind, to your child:

May you be strong.
May you be patient.
May you be kind to yourself.

Parenting is hard, and it can be hard to treat your kids with kindness when they are angry with, or dismissive of, you. But you are not alone in feeling this.

Next, visualise taking a step back, or zooming out from your child and your own experience, to picture all of the parents of your child's friend group. Do you think that they struggle with parenting too? And now all of the parents of the kids at your child's school – are they struggling with this too? And zoom out again, to visualise all of the parents in your town or city, your state or territory, your country, and around the world. All of these parents are feeling similar feelings, and experiencing similar struggles. You are not alone. All parents feel this way from time to time.

We are going to send all of these parents some collective compassion:

May you be strong.
May you be patient.
May you be kind to yourselves.

And now, come back to you. The parent who has always been there for your child, who gives up so much of their life for them. You have given this child love and have been a guide and teacher. There was no manual, but you figured out their unique needs and met them as best you could. No-one can love and support this young person like you can. Although it is hard, and you feel exhausted sometimes, you are doing the best that you can, and you will be able to keep going.

Now give yourself this kindness:

May I be strong.
May I be patient.
May I be kind to myself.

While you are in this moment of stillness and kindness towards yourself and others, what comes to mind, what do you need to remember?

As you slowly come back to the room you are in, and to the present moment, take some time to reflect and write down the words that came to you, or what you need to remember to go forward with.

(ADAPTED FROM GUIDED SELF-COMPASSION MEDITATIONS BY DR KRISTIN NEFF)

6

Appreciating your body: Action!

IN CHAPTER 5, WE LOOKED at moving towards being kinder to ourselves. Now it's time for action. There are so many things we can do to create change here. To change our own mindset, to approach movement and nourish our bodies from this more compassionate place, and to change the media and social environments we are in throughout our lives.

Don't skip this chapter. All of these changes we outline here are things you want your kids to know. All of these changes will inform your conversations with your kids. All of these changes will help you to role model more positive attitudes towards bodies, food and physical activity.

APPRECIATING WHAT YOUR BODY CAN DO

People who appreciate what their body can do rather than focusing on what it looks like generally have a more positive body image. Dr Jessica Alleva from Maastricht University in the Netherlands has developed a program that promotes appreciation of body functionality through journalling – writing about what your body can do, and why that is important to you. These prompts encourage you to go beyond seeing your body as an object to be admired, and instead see your body as a vehicle that lets you experience the world and interact with others – and realise that it doesn't really matter what that vehicle looks like.

Reframing the conversation that you have about your body to be one of gratitude for the things that it can do rather than what it looks like can improve overall body image and wellbeing. This approach can work as it reduces objectification – the extent to which we see ourselves as objects to be admired. Appreciating functionality encourages you to recognise that your body does more for you than you realise, but most of all, that your body is the thing that helps you do all of the things that are really important to you – like cuddling your child, helping people, making a difference in the world. Your body *allows* you to do these things that we value. There are no established 'ideals' of good body functionality, so it's harder to compare. Get started by taking a moment to think about all of the things that your body does for you in terms of experiencing your senses, enabling you to interact with others, to move and be creative. Then access the full list of Resources at the end of the book.

All the things your body can do . . .

It would be easy to think, *Yeah, yeah, I know I know, my body does a lot.* What about actually going back over your list and looking a little deeper, really considering all of the beautiful things your body does each day, without you even thinking about it. Think about the purpose of your body rather than just its functionality.

What some people might write for this list

Eyes that can see.

Ears that can hear.

A nose that can smell.

Arms that can carry.

Legs that can run.

Feet that keep me balanced.

Vocal cords that help me sing.

Tastebuds that allow me to taste.

Hands that can hold things.

A heart that beats and keeps me alive.

A body that regulates my temperature.

A stomach that digests my food for me.

What your list could look like

Eyes that can see my child take their first steps. Eyes that can see my child smile.

Ears that can hear my child fart followed by the beautiful sounds of uncontrollable laughter.

A nose that can smell my newborn, or my teenager wearing too much Lynx.

Arms that I can wrap around my kids. Arms that carry a sleeping child.

Legs to help me chase seagulls at the beach with my toddler.

Feet that keep me balanced when bouncing on the trampoline.

~~Pelvic floor that can~~ . . . Actually, never mind.

Vocal cords that can sing sweet lullabies and yell 'Dinner's ready.'

Tastebuds that scream in unison with my child's when we lick the bowl when baking a cake.

Hands that can throw a ball for my child to catch. Hands that I can hold theirs in.

A heart that's so full of love for my child it could burst.

Our bodies are magical. We just have to see them through the same lens of love that we see our kids with.

Our bodies allow us to experience life. To be there for people, and to do the things that matter. This is important to us. Much more important than whether or not we have wrinkles and stretch marks and cellulite. Much more.

EMBODIED MOVEMENT

Ever had that moment where you've been dancing or walking or doing yoga and you just feel so *good* afterwards? It is a fact that moving your body can make you feel better about the way it looks. Even just a short spin riding a stationary bike for twenty minutes – one of the most boring types of movement, in our opinion – can improve body image. This is not due to that activity changing your weight and shape, it is because you feel a sense of functionality, achievement, and being in and at one with your body (embodiment). Exercise boosts mental health and reduces depression and anxiety. In fact, the psychological and physiological benefits of exercise are so strong that some researchers have stated that exercise should be classified as a drug. Women who focus on the benefits of exercise for the functionality and health benefits (i.e., fitness, strength, confidence) rather than on appearance are more likely to stick with their physical activity engagement for longer – long enough to gain all of these benefits.

The trouble is, although there are so many great physical and mental health benefits of physical activity – and we all know this – it's just so hard for us to do it! Fitting in physical activity these days usually comes with an alarm that wakes us up way too early, or a sense of guilt when we get to the end of the day and say 'Maybe tomorrow!' Moving our bodies is actually really hard. There are the usual barriers of time, cost, access, someone to mind the kids, having the energy to move when you haven't slept properly in years, having the right gear, being injured etc . . . But many people also avoid physical activity because they are afraid of judgement and what other people will think of them, from joining team sports, participating in group exercise, to being active in public. We tend to have this idea in our head of what 'fitness' looks like, who does it, where, and what you wear while doing it. I bet you imagined an ad for a gym in that last sentence! Here's the thing: we've grown up thinking that exercise has to be a) hard, b) boring, and c) timed/recorded/noted on a machine or watch or fancy chart. But actually, all movement counts, even picking-up-a-thousand-kid-toys (ugh). Moving on from cleaning up, all of those juicy brain benefits are much more prominent when you are actually having fun. So try some new things, in whatever clothes and settings you feel comfortable in, high five yourself (or a friend) every time you notice your muscles moving or your heart beating a little faster. The more you do it, the more you will feel like doing it – even if parts of you do wobble more than the person on the ad for the gym!

Championing movement

One of the conversations we looked forward to the most in writing this book was with Libby Trickett. Libby writes beautifully about mental health and body image after having babies (she has three girls, aged six, three and two) in her book *Under the Surface* and talks about it on her podcast *All That Glitters*. Libby has an amazing perspective on all things related to moving our bodies. When we chatted to her, she said:

One of the things I'm really grateful for when I was swimming is that I learned that my body is capable of pretty fucking cool things.

So I am able to push to a level of pain tolerance which kind of lights me up and makes me quite excited, which, I know, is kind of weird and bizarre. But I think most athletes would have that to some extent, because we have to push our bodies every single day, multiple times a day, to achieve something that you get an opportunity once every four years to do. So even though when I was competing, I did battle the feelings of 'being enough' and trying to prove my worth and prove my value, I did innately trust that my body was capable of really cool things.

My body is now twenty kilos heavier than when I competed for Australia, and it has run two half marathons, three triathlons, it's birthed three children, and breastfed three children. It's incredible what it's been able to do. Sure, my boobs look like lemons in socks, and my tummy is soft, and my youngest loves to play with my belly, and I got terrible chub rub running those half marathons. But I get to experience this world in all its glory. We're conditioned to feel crappy about our body, and our lives, and our looks, and not achieving enough in this world. But if you surround yourself with positive content, follow positive people, and start to be aware of your own narrative that you say to yourself, I think you can get to a point of not just accepting your body, but actually loving it most of the time.

Since having my girls, I've been walking, and running, and I love doing weights because that makes me feel physically strong. I've recently started *swimming again – it's just a joy for me – but I totally suck at it! I have to consciously block out when they say my times, and I'm trying to do a lot more back-stroke because I didn't compete in that before, so I don't have any connection to what time is good for me or not. But the reality is, I will never be at that level; I was training thirty-five hours a week, day in and day out for fifty weeks a year. There's no way that I can ever get back to that level again, and that's okay. So I'm really slow, but I just think to myself, you've still got a great workout, you still get a great connection with people who share the same joy in the water as you do. And yes, it's hard to get up and do it at five o'clock in the morning, it's a massive commitment, but I'm making that for myself because I know that I'm a better human when I'm exercising, and I'm also making that commitment for my family because I'm a better human around them as well.*

I feel good in my body, I feel good in my mind, and I feel a connection with a community.

I think the biggest thing that I've learned is that it takes time, and it takes patience, and it takes aware-ness of those voices and those thoughts that we all have. But after all this, I've been able to recognise that my body is amazing. It's incredible.

And that's the gold medal that you get at the end of a swim, a ride, a yoga session, gym class, dancing with your kids in the loungeroom. It feels good!

Participating in embodying *activities* – those that empower women to be aware of, attentive to, and experience competence in their movement – is important in developing body appreciation and mental health. This means things like yoga, stretching, and some forms of dance – anything where the focus is on being in your body, and on moving because it feels good, not for what it looks like – are good for you.

Studies of people who practise yoga regularly find that they are more likely to appreciate their bodies, and studies of people who engage in a series of yoga classes have shown that body image improves. Similar changes are seen in studies where women are introduced to expressive dance programs. Yoga and dance both encourage embodiment – to really be in the body, and let go of the cognitive control of our bodies and ourselves. These styles of movement also encourage us to appreciate the functionality of our bodies, and to heal.

If your current physical activity options aren't like this, think about what you might enjoy more. Ditch the guilt and the 'shoulds' and just move in a way that feels good to you. Get started by putting on some music and moving the way your mood desires. Go for a walk among nature. This movement is invaluable for your body image and wellbeing. Dr Megan Lee, body image and intuitive eating researcher, says:

Stop exercising to punish yourself for what you ate the night before. Stop going to the gym and forcing yourself to do things that you hate. Go and move your body in ways that make you feel good - you enjoy dancing, go. Go ride a bike with the kids. If you like to go to the gym, go! Don't just do the cardio workouts because you think that that's going to make you burn calories or lose weight. Do some strength training – that's awesome for your body when you get older.

INTUITIVE EATING

So if diets don't work (and if we've known this for a loooong time), what's the alternative? Intuitive eating is a practice first described by Evelyn Tribole and Elyse Resch, who came up with ten principles. This approach is all about listening to your body, to your cues of hunger and satiety, and what you feel like eating. It's a guide to eating if you are not dieting. Most people assume that they would eat only chocolate bars and ice cream if they 'let themselves' listen to their body, but it's just not the case. We've all experienced that time, maybe over Christmas, or a holiday somewhere exotic – where you just ate exactly what you wanted, when you wanted to. For the first little while, it might have been all chocolate and croissants, but then after a few days your body starts to say 'Hey, how about a salad?!'

Ten principles of intuitive eating

1. Reject diet culture and mindset
2. Honour your hunger
3. Make peace with food
4. Challenge the food police
5. Discover satisfaction

6. Feel your fullness

7. Cope with your emotions with kindness

8. Respect your body

9. Engage in joyful movement

10. Honour your health

EVELYN TRIBOLE AND ELYSE RESCH, *INTUITIVE EATING*

Women who engage in intuitive eating have better body image, and actually eat healthier (more fruit and vegetables, a greater variety of foods) than those who are restricting. Research has also found that women who follow intuitive eating principles have better self-esteem, are less likely to engage in disordered, emotional or stress eating, have lower levels of depression and have higher overall psychological wellbeing. *And* women who are eating intuitively maintain a more stable weight (instead of yo-yoing) over time.

Dr Megan Lee has just finished her PhD, where she interviewed people about food and mood. Many of the women described these intuitive eating practices as beneficial for mental health. As someone who follows this approach herself, she is quick to emphasise that there are two areas where people usually struggle with the idea:

The first is in losing control. With this approach, you need to give yourself permission to eat what you want, to remove any food restriction. Most people think that that means that they will eat a thousand bowls of pasta and a twelve-pack of doughnuts. That's not what intuitive eating is about. Intuitive eating is about eating what you want in the moment that you want it, and not having any food restriction, but knowing how that impacts your body.

The process of eating intuitively, of trusting and listening to your body, means that you also become more connected to the feedback that your body gives you after you have eaten of whether you feel energised or sluggish, and then use that education that your body is giving you to inform future choices.

If you're deprived, then what happens is you go and binge on those things that you want, because you've been stopping yourself from eating them. So once you get into a mode of intuitive eating and understanding what your body is telling you, it is good for you. In that moment, then you can be released from the thoughts of 'I should eat this or I should eat that.' You eat what you want, when you want.

The second concept, and this is the one I find the most difficult, is worrying about my body conforming to the thin ideal. I'm not immune from wanting to change my body sometimes. We've been programmed into weight-focused thinking since we were kids – thinking that we have to be small, we have to be thin, we have to look a certain way. The media is constantly giving us images of how we should look even though the people in those images are photoshopped so dramatically now that they don't even look like themselves in real life. And then we're trying to be them. We're trying to be the photoshopped versions of people who don't even look like that. Removing weight-focused thinking is the scary part about intuitive eating that makes it difficult for most people to do, because you have to then throw away all your scales and accept yourself for who you are.

GO ON A MEDIA DIET

Our mindset and our attitudes in our head and heart are really important. But we have to change the things that we see, hear and experience as well. Given the huge influence of media images and social media on our lives, it makes sense to consider if we can reduce our level of exposure to any of these negative influences.

The 1980s and 1990s was a time when big corporations decided what would be in our magazines and the images that we would see. We're not used to being in control. But we're now in control! We now have so much more power over what we are exposed to. We can follow and unfollow with the click of a button. But so many people expose themselves still to these very narrow beauty ideals, following 'fitspiration' (more on this below) and 'Before' and 'After' photos, and accounts that show nothing but thin models all the time. It's just not good for us.

Decades of research indicate that there are negative effects of viewing images of thin or muscular individuals that depict and also influence societal 'ideals'. In one study, researchers invited people to a lab, asked them to complete surveys, then showed half of the group images of models and advertising depicting the thin or muscular ideals for men or women, while the other half saw images of nature or cars (or anything that wasn't human bodies), and then had them complete another questionnaire. When researchers compared the scores from before and after, they consistently found that both the men and women who saw the thin or muscular models walked out of those rooms more depressed and more dissatisfied with their bodies than those who looked at trees for a while.

This same effect is seen in social media. Instagram has the strongest influence on body dissatisfaction, because of the focus on images and its capacity to expose people to a large number of idealised images in a short space of time. One research study found that women were more dissatisfied with their bodies, and more depressed, after viewing Instagram content for just seven minutes. We know the two of us definitely spend more than seven minutes a day on IG . . . eek!

The damaging impact of retouched images has led to calls to label airbrushed and photoshopped images, warning consumers about their effect on their mental health. Despite a few countries mandating some sort of labelling or banning of digital alteration and many experimental studies that used a range of different warning labels, none of the approaches to labelling these images led to consumers feeling better about themselves. None of them worked. Researchers have therefore concluded that adding post-production labels to images is not a potential strategy for alleviating the distress caused by exposure to images of unrealistic bodies. The only option is to depict more realistic bodies.

When researchers, including our colleague Professor Phillippa Diedrichs, conducted the same studies as described above but instead showed models that were more diverse in terms of size, shape, and skin colour, the participants walked out of the room feeling better about themselves. They had a more positive body image, and were less depressed. Minor adjustments in the size of the model – from an Australian women's size 8–10 to an Australian size 14–16 (the average size of women in Australia) – eliminate the negative effect. The same thing happens with men.

Many people think that looking at images of thin models, celebrities and peers will help to motivate them to achieve that body themselves; inspire them into thinness or fitness. We now know that this isn't the way that our brains work. Feeling bad about our bodies won't help us look after them. Case in point: fitspiration.

#FITSPO . . . UMM, NO

You might not have called it fitspiration, but you've probably seen it. You know, the motivational quotes next to images of very slim, very toned, very muscular women (who magically also have boobs), wearing matching activewear. Sometimes featuring a 'glow' of glistening perspiration. And a catchphrase like: 'Remember why you started', 'Sweat now. Glow later', or 'You will never know your limits unless you push yourself to them'.

Fitspiration was originally intended to motivate women to exercise. However, given how our brains are wired, as soon as we see this content, we instantly compare ourselves to the bodies in the image. This drives down our body image and makes us even less likely to exercise. Dr Ivanka Prichard, an expert in fitspiration, has conducted studies that have confirmed that viewing fitspiration images leads to greater body dissatisfaction, and it is actually worse for body image than viewing images of thin women. Probably because the images are generally sexualised, reinforcing the 'bodies as objects' thoughts and feelings, and maybe because we feel guilty about not exercising as well as the negative effects of comparing our bodies. In some studies, participants reported that fitspiration inspired them to exercise, but this did not translate into increases in exercise behaviour.

But Dr Prichard brings us some good news too: 'What does inspire us is seeing more diverse fitness images – women of all shapes and sizes enjoying exercise. Our research shows that women can be more motivated to exercise and feel better about their bodies – just by increasing the diversity of images we are exposed to that focus on joyful movement.' Evaluations of the #thisgirlcan and #jointhemovement campaigns that depict more diverse women engaging in a range of traditional and non-traditional forms of movement, in very 'real' ways, found that these campaigns had a positive short-term impact on body satisfaction and intentions to exercise.

'Before' and 'After' photos have been a longstanding institution in the weight loss world. But now more than ever, they are made really public. People post them – or gyms make them post them – on social media for the world to see. This induces a different type of social comparison, as we compare ourselves to *both* the 'Before' and 'After' of someone else and the amount of weight that they have lost. This has a pretty powerful negative impact on our body image. These images also tend to reinforce the concept that our body weight and shape are really changeable (which they aren't) and that our appearance and weight are the most important things about us (which again, they aren't).

More positive social media content that promotes the cele-bration of all body types and promotes diverse-sized bodies to reject the idea of narrow societal 'ideals' is out there, and it is better for you. So, if you really want to motivate yourself and make yourself feel better? Follow some body positive accounts.

I took a bikini selfie (eyeroll) for Instagram, but I was really disappointed when I saw the photo because I had cellulite all up the back of my legs. I thought, *Oh I'll just photoshop that, throw a filter on it, it will be fine.* But when I saw the edited image, I looked like a Barbie doll, and I had this realisation that people would be comparing themselves to my fake body. It's just not right. So I uploaded the original, unedited image, and it's actually been the one that I've got the most likes ever for: people were saying 'Thank you so much – this is what I have been wanting!'

AMY SHEPPARD, SINGER/SONGWRITER AND POSITIVE BODY IMAGE INFLUENCER @AMYSHEPPARDPIE

Following clothing brands that cater to a wide range of sizes but also celebrate women in these sizes on their social media feeds is also really helpful for normalising the glorious, vast range of different shapes, sizes, colours and flavours that our bodies come in. Try being really intentional about the images that you let yourself see, and reward the brands that do this well by engaging with them around their diverse content. The more we as consumers support these brands, the more they will feature this awesome diversity, and the more we and other women can benefit from it.

You can still use social media. You just need to look at how you use it, engage with body positive accounts and follow brands that use diverse-sized models. Unfollow, unsubscribe and mute any accounts with images of thin models or influencers, fitspiration, 'Before' and 'After' weight loss photos, and anything else that makes you feel bad (like images of clean houses). The ones that make you feel bad can have a huge impact on your Insta experience and your psychological health.

PHYSICAL ENVIRONMENTS, FRIENDS, AND FAMILY

Once you've fixed your social media feed, it's time to move on to real life. Are there any friends, places or people that make you feel bad about your body and yourself? Mute, block and unfollow them too! Okay, so this might be a little harder in real life, but here are some suggestions.

If someone starts saying negative things about *their own body*, you have two choices – shut it down, or divert the conversation. To shut it down, you could try talking about how you have read this book, and research shows that these sorts of conversations are bad for our mental health. If there are kids around, use them as a reason not to talk about your appearance. Diverting the conversation by changing the subject avoids the immediate situation, but it might come up again.

If someone says something negative about *someone else's* body, we would love you to start calling it out. You know quite a lot about this area now that you've read this far into this book.

A simple 'It really isn't helpful for us, or our kids, for us to be talking about people this way – let's talk about something else instead' usually diverts the conversation, and might make them reconsider saying it again.

If someone criticises *your* body, it can be helpful to have a response prepared – such as 'Oh, this? I don't worry too much about what it looks like. I focus on what's on the inside, and you should too.' (This is a tough one. You may feel shame in the moment, making it harder to respond.) Often we are so shocked at what the other person has said, and so busy trying to cover up our outrage, that our brain doesn't have time to come up with an informed-yet-witty response. Practising what you are going to say can help, and there are more suggestions coming in this book.

If someone says something positive about weight loss, you could divert by talking about your outfit, shoes or makeup, or respond with 'No, I'm actually working on accepting and appreciating my body as it is', just to see their response!

One mum reported success here:

My grandmother is constantly telling me I look tired, and finally one day I said, 'If you're not going to help me *be* less tired, then please stop pointing it out', and that seems to have worked!

MONICA, MUM OF TWO, SYDNEY

Taryn

While walking through the school yard, a mum I didn't know came rushing up to me and in an excited voice exclaimed, 'You are so inspirational!' I was confused. Was she referring to the fact that I'd brushed my hair, was out of my ugg boots and had got my three kids to school before the bell?

She went on, 'I've been watching you drop the weight over the past couple of months, you are so inspiring!'

I responded with, 'Hi, I'm Taryn.' I looked down at my three kids, who were as perplexed as me.

When did weight loss become inspiring? Saving the planet, rescuing injured animals, fighting against human trafficking: all inspiring. Weight loss: not so much. **If we really want to make the world a better place, please let's not comment on anyone's weight loss or weight gain again.**

WATCH *EMBRACE*

Another easy thing to do to improve your body image is to get a group of friends together, or just yourself, and watch the film *Embrace*. It was made for mums. Research conducted around the film found that it has been helpful in improving body image for most of the people who see it. You will laugh, you will cry, you will be grateful for watching it.

It's a lot. You're already busy doing a million things. And we've just asked you to do more. But it's worth it! For you, and for your kids. Often when we're reading books like this, we skip the bit where they say: 'Now put this book down and go and do X, Y, Z' – please don't!

Action

Throughout this whole chapter, you've been reading about taking action. Now it's time to actually do it! Block out some time in your diary and move through this checklist:

☑ **Grab a pen and paper, set a timer for ten minutes, and don't stop writing. Here's your prompt: What are the things that you appreciate about how your body allows you to interact with others? Why are these things important to you?**

☑ **Block and unfollow the fitspiration and other social media accounts that make you feel like you should change your body. Replace with some diversity.**

☑ **Prepare witty responses to shut down or divert conversations and comments about your own and other people's bodies.**

☑ **At mealtimes, check in with your body to see what you really need/want and how much. Try eating intuitively for a day, or a week. How did it feel?**

☑ **Try out some new movement that you find fun and that helps you to feel more in tune with your body. What did you learn about what your body can do?**

7

Role modelling body confidence

IMAGINE THIS. YOUR CHILD WALKS in on you trying on a new outfit in the mirror. You are smoothing a new dress over your stomach, checking the back to see your butt. Then your brain starts letting your thoughts out, and you say, 'Hmm, I think I'll take this back, it's a bit tight across my mum tum,' as you grab that roll of flesh below your bellybutton and jiggle it for effect. You're just making conversation and saying what you're thinking, but in that moment, your child learns big lessons that will stay with them throughout their life: about what women should look like, and how they should speak to themselves about their bodies.

The things that you say about yourself and others act as vicarious learning for your kids, who are trying to figure out how the world works, how to fit in, and how to belong. Making comments about your own weight ('Ugh, there's no way I'm getting in the pool today, I'm sooo bloated,') or about others' bodies ('You look great, have you lost weight? Well done, you!') sends subconscious messages to children about how adults should behave. It tells them that appearance is one of the most important things that makes you a good or bad person, that makes you worthy of love and attention, and whether you should or should not engage in certain activities.

We know that you want your kids to feel great about their bodies. And we know you are busy. We definitely don't want to add another thing to your to-do list. That's why we're going for the approach of building your own body image so that you are *automatically* better able to support your kids in developing their own appreciation of their body. Being body confident is one of the best ways to build your kids' body confidence. Show them what you want them to believe about their bodies.

> **'Do what I say, not as I do' doesn't really cut it with kids anymore. They are always watching, always learning, even when you least expect it!**
>
> **TARYN**

THE RESEARCH ON ROLE MODELLING

Parents are a strong influence on children's body image in direct and indirect ways. Direct influences are things like making comments about our children's weight and shape, encouraging them to diet or the food we serve and make available in the home. Indirect influences are things like the attitudes that we have about our own bodies, and the things we might be doing to try to change them; for example, changing what you eat to lose weight or starting a new exercise regime.

Research suggests that mothers are one of the strongest influences on the body image attitudes and behaviours of their children – particularly by role modelling attitudes towards our bodies, and the behaviours that we engage in based on our thoughts and feelings about our bodies. Children learn a lot about the world by watching other people, particularly up to the ages of six or seven. They learn from us, and role modelling takes place even when we are not aware of it, or are not actively trying to teach them something. In fact, they are more likely to pick up on and remember the things that they see that have an emotional component than the 'lessons' we give them intentionally.

Studies have shown that when people verbalise their thought processes and actions and show how they engage in problem solving or managing anxiety, this can provide a 'road map' for observers to develop their own responses. Many research studies have confirmed that the things that mothers say and do in relation to their bodies can impact on the body image of their children. Most of those have focused on the modelling of negative attitudes and dieting and disordered eating behaviours. Fathers do have an influence, but the majority of role modelling is from the mother.

Some reflections on role modelling

My mum was an athlete. She was a netballer and competed in the 400 metre hurdles. I think she had come to terms with a lot of things in the body image space. I've never actually heard her use self-deprecating language, or speak about her body in a negative way, and that's been an incredibly positive influence. Whereas speaking with other friends it's often their mums' own body dissatisfaction, if it hasn't been addressed, that trickles down, and really impacts the way they felt about their own bodies. It's almost like this inherited body image.

JASMINE, 23, MELBOURNE

It took me a while to realise that I grew up in an environment where people didn't talk about bodies. My parents didn't align with traditional gender roles: my mum was a feminist and an economist, Dad was an artist. So there was no talk about dieting or criticising herself or other people about their weight, but we also didn't talk about other aspects of our bodies, like periods and sex. I didn't even tell my mum when I got my period. I tried to hide it, and deny it, and I was left to navigate many body-related experiences with my peers in rather unfortunate ways.

KELLY, 42, BOSTON

I remember Mum putting on makeup. I used to love watching her put on makeup and get dressed up when she went out, but she never talked about her body in front of us. I remember her going to Weight Watchers when I was in my teens, but she never talked about it. I think I want to do that for my kids – not just 'not talk about it' but actually be body positive.

EMMA, 34, SYDNEY

I grew up in the seventies, in that era of dieting, body concerned parents, and now we're this sandwich generation who's desperately trying to deal with their own stuff, and then raise body confident kids.

FAYE, 45, MELBOURNE

Zali conducted some research with colleagues as a part of the Body Confident Mums Project. In 2019, they published research exploring the role modelling of mums, and how that was related to their own body image, and their diet and exercise behaviours. The mums who had a better body image themselves were more likely to agree that they were good role models for their children.

And all of this positive role modelling? It can have a beneficial effect on you too. Researchers have found that when they trained women in their third year at university to deliver a body image program to first year university students, the older women's body image improved to a greater extent than participants who received the program. This was explained by the fact that, to come across as a convincing leader implementing the program, they needed to have that attitude themselves, and therefore made more progress personally in order to fulfil this role.

This can also be applied to the parenting context. We want to develop positive body image for our kids, so we need to start 'acting' like we have this to role model appropriately, which might benefit our own body image over time.

CAN YOU FAKE IT TILL YOU MAKE IT?

Absolutely.

Our research shows that you can try to fake it until you make it, but it's much more effective if you really feel it. This is particularly important if your kids are aged 0–10 years, as you are likely to be the strongest influence that they have on their body image. So, take a deep breath and think about what it is that you want to pass down to your children. What do you want them to believe about their bodies and themselves? How can you support this process by really showing compassion towards yourself and others, and your appreciation of what your body can do?

Ginger Gorman is a social justice journalist. She told us about a time she pitched a story about role modelling body image to her editors, prompted by a 'crisis situation' with her daughters in relation to role modelling and body image.

I'm a person who's never had good body image myself. I was always slightly overweight as a child and have always had that battle that a lot of women have, where you have a really uncomfortable relationship with food. This is complicated by a number of medical issues that make it really hard to lose weight.

So I've always had a difficult relationship with weight. And I was always really conscious that, when I became a mother,

I didn't want my kids to have that same relationship with their bodies. I have two daughters, aged eight and eleven, and I had carried with me this hope that I would not pass on my own body shame and my own feelings of despair about my body to my children.

But then, about six months ago, I had this crisis point. I had put on a bit of weight during the COVID-19 lockdown. My kids were in my bedroom, and I was looking in the mirror and I said something about having a 'mummy tummy'. And then I said it again, later that week. It was almost subconscious – it spilled out without me thinking about it. Reflecting on it now, it was really just me expressing my very much internalised body shame and loathing. But then one of my daughters started repeating it back to me: 'You have a mummy tummy' and telling strangers 'My mum's got a mummy tummy'. Around that time, she also started saying things about the things she didn't like about her own body. So I had sirens going off in my brain. I was thinking, *No, I just will not have a child who feels this way, and has this backpack full of rocks dragging her down*. I felt like I was giving her a road map to this sort of body-shaming hell, and that was being magnified by popular culture. Instead of being a force for good against these horrible societal norms that teach women to feel shame about their bodies, I was actively leading her directly down that pathway. I realised that I was actually passing on my feelings and thoughts about my own body to my kids, and that they were internalising them, on some level. I knew that this had to be a point of change in my parenting.

I pitched an article about 'How to role model positive body image to your kids when you don't feel it yourself' [which was published in *ABC Everyday*] and started contacting experts and doing a lot more reading on the topic.

Some of the advice was to consider questions such as: What actually are the things that are good about my body? And what do I admire about my own body that I could tell my children? My response was: I'm really proud of my body for making these beautiful children, because I love my children so much, and they're such special little humans. So the next time my kids said something about my 'mummy tummy', I said, 'Actually, I'm really proud of my body because it created both of you.'

I remember my little one looking at me wide-eyed as if she was thinking, *Oh, yeah, she's made a baby, that's actually pretty clever.* It was interesting, because after that, I did feel proud of my body. I wasn't just saying it, I actually was proud. I guess it had this effect of almost tricking myself into believing that my body was strong and powerful. Once I started saying the positive things, I started feeling them.

So yes, you can fake it, but it's hard to fake it all the time! That's why we're focusing on you, to help you appreciate your body and treat yourself with kindness so that you can nurture these same feelings and qualities in your children. The more you do the work yourself, the more easily you will naturally pass this positivity on to your kids.

WHAT DOES POSITIVE BODY IMAGE LOOK LIKE?

It's a bit hard to role model something that you don't fully feel yet . . . so here's some more insight into what a positive body image looks and feels like. It's not just about #loveyourbody. It's a bit broader than that. The concept of positive body image is relatively new in the research space. It's only been around for the last ten years or so. Professor Tracy Tylka from Ohio State University defined positive body image as 'an overarching love and respect for the body', and alongside other scholars in the field, has described the components of positive body image as:

1. **Accepting our appearance:** Appreciating and accepting what our body looks like, and all of its unique strengths and abilities, even if you are not completely satisfied with how it looks, or if it looks different to cultural 'ideals'.

2. **Appreciating functionality:** Respecting and being grateful to our bodies for all that they do for us, and what that means for us. For example, the fact that our bodies let us interact with loved ones and do creative things.

3. **Strength-based approach:** Recognising the good things about your body rather than dwelling on imperfections.

4. **Protective filtering:** Having a protective mental filter whereby you can interpret any negative societal messages about bodies, and not let them creep in. For example, recognising that we cannot completely control our weight, and that the majority of images of women portray unrealistic and unachievable standards that most women are unable to live up to.

5. **Body image flexibility:** The ability to accept our insecurities about our body without letting these thoughts and feelings interfere with us engaging in things that are meaningful. For example, going swimming despite feeling self-conscious in your swimming costume.

In short, positive body image is not about liking what you look like or #lovingyourbody, it's about respecting, accepting and appreciating your body, and treating it accordingly. It's not about never having another negative thought about your body, it's about not letting that stop you from doing things.

Women share what works for them to role model positive body image

I think for me, sometimes it's what you don't do. It's about *not* showing them your insecurities. It's about *not* using that negative language. It's about *not* saying 'Oh, well, if I have that ice cream, I will have to go for a run tomorrow.' Making sure that your children don't hear that language, or they don't hear you say 'Oh, I look awful in this,' or 'That photo is terrible, let's delete it.' You can delete it quietly. It's okay to have insecurities and body image issues, but it's best not to share them with your kids constantly. The time that you can share them is when you are having a talk with them about their own concerns, and you can share that you feel that way too sometimes, and it is okay to have body image issues, and there will be days where you don't feel as confident. Because otherwise they will worry on the days where they feel like that. So it's a balance.

ANUPA ROPER, UK

I have a rule that I don't trash myself or my body – whether that is looking at photographs or when I'm getting dressed. If I've got nothing nice to say out loud, I definitely won't say it. That doesn't mean I don't sometimes think those things or feel that way, I am a woman living in a very image-obsessed world, so there is ongoing work to do to keep an accepting and compassionate attitude towards my appearance, but I try my best to avoid discussing my body and also other people's bodies too. We are not objects and we are more and need to be more than how we look.

CLARE, MUM OF TWO, MELBOURNE

I still have it in my head that I'm going to be much happier when I'm skinnier or when I'm a little bit smaller. That's still in my head. But I'm working on it and I'm on a bit of a journey to try to be who I need to be for my kids. My baby needs my body, and she loves my body. So I've really got to love my body.

EMMA, MUM OF TWO, SYDNEY

HOW DO I ROLE MODEL POSITIVE BODY ATTITUDES AND BEHAVIOURS?

The whole idea here is to say some things out loud to contribute to the messaging that your kids receive about bodies and body image. You want to talk through things that you might not naturally be drawn to say out loud, to help create a more positive road map for your kids. Overall, we want kids to celebrate a diversity of bodies, and to appreciate their own body functionality, and not to see appearance as important.

You might like to write out scripts for these conversations, or think of some times that you could bring these things up.

Here's how to role model positive body image.

Words matter

Try not to say negative things about your body in front of your child. This can take some practice, but it is worth it. Every time you catch yourself about to say something negative about your jiggly tummy, try to flip it to a positive about the functionality of your body. You can try the 'Red Riding Hood' approach, as in, when your kid asks something, you respond with, 'All the better to see/hear/smell/eat you with, my dear.' For example:

'Mum, why are your arms so floppy up here?'

'Oh, yes, they are floppy, aren't they? They make my hugs so much nicer.'

Judgement be gone

It's really important not to comment on other people's bodies in a positive *or* negative way. No 'Oh, you look great. Have you lost weight?' or 'Wow, she's really getting big' behind their back. None of that. We generally say these things to voice aloud the automated self-comparisons that are happening in our heads, but they teach our children more about how to judge others and can become the voice inside their heads when they judge themselves. Instead of this, try practising compassion towards others. Take a deep breath and send kindness instead of judgement their way or at least don't say anything out loud. You could think or say non-appearance-based compliments like 'You look so radiant today – your energy is amazing!'

More meaningful compliments

You look happy.

I love your choice of outfit.

You inspire me.

I love the way you think.

You're fun to be around.

You should be so proud of what you've done.

I wish there were more people like you.

Thanks so much for helping me. You're so great at that.

You make me feel so much better.

You look like you're having fun!

You have such great energy and enthusiasm.

I love talking to you.

You're a great listener.

Tummy talk

You can verbalise and model listening to your body. For example, when you are done eating, you can say, 'I think I'm full now, so I'm not going to finish all of this,' or 'I'm still really hungry, I'm going to have a bit more.' Explicitly modelling this helps to teach children the reasons why you are doing what you are doing and shows that you listen to, and trust, your body.

Move, Mama

Talk through why you want to move your body, and what you get out of it before or after you sneak out the door for your walk or class. Before you go you can say: 'I'm feeling a bit blah, I might go for a walk to clear my head' or 'I love seeing my friends at my gym class'. Afterwards you can talk about feeling strong, that your muscles feel tired from all of that hard work, and that you are proud of yourself for what you achieved because you tried hard and persisted.

Ditch the diet, or at least the diet talk

We don't want to oversimplify the relationship between food and weight – that is, that eating cookies can make you gain weight, and eating a salad helps you lose weight. Try to talk about listening to your body, to what, when and how much it wants and needs. While you're at it, you want to avoid demonstrating that you are using food and exercise as punishment. Try to show that your body is worthy of love, movement and nourishment regardless of how you might have treated it in the past.

Increase self-compassion

This is easier if you have done the work yourself first. Try to bring a self-compassionate approach to everyday events to model a kinder reaction, response and conversation with yourself. (Refer back to Chapter 5 for more detail.)

Counteract negative messages

Minimise access to media that promotes beauty 'ideals'. When you see negative body attitudes or thin characters on a show, you can try to model some media literacy – question why they might have used those people in those images (usually because they want to sell aspiration), what might have been done to alter an image (like photoshopping), how genetics have made the model/celeb/influencer look like that and how unrealistic it is for people to try to change themselves to look that way.

Value difference in appearance

Point out all of the different shapes and sizes of people, dogs and flowers in storybooks, and in real life, to celebrate the great things that this diversity brings. Model your acceptance of people with varied and diverse appearance by talking about the things you like about your friends or colleagues who look different, or pointing out diversity and strengths in media or on social media.

Role modelling positive self-talk

Talking about your stomach

Instead of: Well, it's because I had you in there and then I ate too much cake.

Say this: Yes, my tummy is soft and squishy, *and* that makes it much better for cuddling you. [insert cuddles here]

Talking about other people's bodies in a positive way

Instead of: Oh, you look great. Have you lost weight?

Say this: Wow, you look so radiant right now.

Talking about other people's bodies in a negative way

Instead of: Wow, Sandra has really gained some weight during lockdown.

Say this: [Literally anything other than commenting on someone else's weight gain.]

Talking about eating

Instead of: I have to eat a salad because I need to lose weight.

Say this: I love eating all of these veggies to make my body feel good.

Talking about exercise

Instead of: I'm off for a run to try to lose this. [wobbles muffin top]

Say this: I think a run would really clear my head right now – I'm off!

Looking at your reflection in the mirror

Instead of: Ugh, why am I so fat and *old*?

Say this: I love that my [body part] can [function] so that I can [what that means for you]. For example, I love that my legs are so strong so I can chase after you.

> ## This is a critical intervention for most women, and a lot of men too. As parents, we need to spend time analysing the amount of body shame we carry, and working out ways to unpack it so that we can bring up healthier and happier kids. It's a big burden to carry, but think how much lighter our kids' lives will be and how much more productive they will be if they're able to go through the world full of grace, feeling whole and accepted, and loving their body.
>
> **GINGER GORMAN, JOURNALIST**

There's a reason why we've presented you with all of this information. We're trying to arm you with all of the key things you need to know to be able to a) change your own attitudes and behaviour, and b) explain things to your kids (often while also trying to reverse parallel park or cook dinner – why do they only ask hard questions at the most inconvenient times?!).

So now that you know all of this, you can apply it in your life. Catch yourself thinking negative thoughts, reframe them, and treat yourself with more kindness. Unravel the years of diet-culture messaging you've received and start to listen to, and trust, your body. Accept that your body has and is changing, and figure out how to nourish and support it rather than punish and beat it into submission. Realise that you are enough. You are worthy. Just as you are. And you always have been.

And once you do that? You start being the example of enoughness and body confidence that your kids need to see to grow up in this world that keeps telling them that they should be trying to change this, that or the other in louder and louder ways. We break the cycle. It's hard, but it's worth it.

Action

You didn't think you could just read that last paragraph and have those things magically come true for you, did you? You do have to do the work as well!

☑ **Take a moment and close your eyes. Imagine the example you want to set for your kids. What do you need to start or stop doing, and who do you need to be being in order to make this happen? See it. Then write it down.**

☑ **If you are already role modelling all of the good things to your kids, start to think about their other influences – extended family, grandparents, family friends – that communicate messages about bodies, weight and worth to your kids, directly and indirectly. Are there things you need to ask them to do – or not do – in order to align with your vision?**

part two

---

building them up

A no-shame approach

Parenting is hard. Full stop, end of story.

But parenting school-aged kids gets harder, in less-obvious ways. We are no longer required to literally spoon the food into our babies' mouths; they can now prepare their own sandwiches and eat them all on their own (making a mess along the way, of course). However, along with the reduction in neediness and physical labour comes a relinquishing of control. We are used to being able to control what, when and where our children eat, who they play with, and how they spend their time. Once children move towards adolescence, all of that can change, which can be a challenge.

We have a choice. We can be guided by our fears, or we can lead with love. No prizes for choosing which one might be a bit of an easier ride for everyone. It's easy to be afraid of all of the things that can 'go wrong' and all of the bad things that can happen as our children gain independence from us and move out into the world. But when we are afraid of things, we try to control them, and you literally can't control everything in parenting kids through this stage, at this time.

We can't control everything, and nor should we. We can't protect our kids from ever getting upset or having something bad happen to them. Sometimes, things need to go wrong for us to learn from those experiences. Kids need to experience emotions – even the 'bad' ones. We can't stop everything bad from happening. The whole idea is that we support our kids through these challenges, and model how to respond.

In this next part of the book, we will talk through some of the key opportunities to create a more positive body image environment for your kids, and how to manage some of the body image-related situations that come up. Things like being teased about the way they look, managing social media, and encouraging healthy food and movement without becoming obsessed. There are some gems of wisdom here, all shared from the amazing experts, parents and expert-parents we spoke to, all over the world.

Here's the thing, though. There is some very specific advice around some aspects of parenting – there is a lot to know, and there are some guidelines that you could follow and response frameworks you could use. But if all of that gets overwhelming, here's what you need to know: it's actually not possible to manage this perfectly. There is no perfect. Even people with all of the research knowledge, all of the clinical expertise, and people who literally do this for a living struggle with managing these situations and conversations when they come up.

You are already doing an amazing job for investing in this book, and managing to find the time to actually read it, so let's dive in.

Feeling the failure and doing it anyway

Zali

So, having three kids means there are some standards that slip. We definitely brush our teeth often, but I just didn't think that making kids floss every day was an actual thing. Every time I went to the dentist, or took the kids, they talked about flossing, but I kind of thought that most people, like me, smiled and nodded and thought, 'Lady, you have no idea what bedtime looks like at our house if you think I can floss twenty teeth times three kids on top of all of the other things we need to do.'

I was feeling pretty good about managing to get all three kids to the dentist on this particular day – again, it was probably a bit over the six-month mark, but hey, life is hard, and busy.

So the kids are having their teeth checked, and it turned out that one of my daughters needed some silver caps on some cavities. And the dentist made me feel bad about not flossing their teeth all the time.

I was looking at my three kids going nuts in this dental office, thinking, 'Do you really think I can wrangle this? It's hard enough to get them to brush their teeth, let alone floss.' After the lecture, the dentist proceeded to demonstrate how easy it is to floss a child's teeth by lying the kids back in her dentist's chair (which I do not have at home) and flossing one child's set of teeth, saying, 'See, it only takes a few minutes.' Feeling the shame of being a 'bad mum', I spent lots of money on special flossing devices and got into the car vowing that I would brush and floss all three kids' teeth each night, and gave the associated lecture to the kids. But the real finger waggle was directed at myself.

Of course, we were all very motivated to floss that night. But then, two days later, the novelty had worn off for the kids. One of them had already lost their special flossing device. So the next thing I was like – well, maybe we can just do it every

second night, spending the ten minutes trying to convince
them all to let me floss their teeth and the ten minutes of
actual flossing. Fast forward six months later, and not only
do I not floss their teeth every night, I've also changed our
dentist. I just don't want to see that person again. And I don't
want to feel that shame. I don't want her wagging her finger
at me, so we went somewhere else.

We tell this story to illustrate the fact that shame doesn't
motivate positive behaviour change. We would hate for you to feel
shame here. Because we recognise that as body image experts it's
very easy to give this advice – but we recognise that some of the
'easy conversations to have' might not be so easy for you. They
might actually be a challenge to incorporate into your parenting
life. It could be a hard thing to negotiate with partners. You might
think, 'No way could I do that with my kids!'

So we want you to know, whenever we say 'Do this thing' or
'Don't do that thing', and 'Let me show you how easy it is to do
this thing on this special dentist chair' we are trying to communicate clearly, but what we really mean is 'If this works for you
and your family, you could try doing something like this, but it
doesn't have to look exactly the same.' You know your family
best. Do what works for you.

Because professionals everywhere say stuff like that dentist.
A screen time expert would definitely encourage us to reduce our
use of devices (grown-ups included!), an economist would roll
their eyes at my attempts at teaching financial literacy to my kids,
and while we're at it, a literacy expert would definitely waggle

her finger at the number of times we 'do our home readers'. Each expert is going to have their particular perspective and this can add so many layers to parenting. And it can make us feel shame to the point where we just give up altogether.

We don't want you to feel that sense of shame. We don't want you to feel like you've done anything wrong. Each of us is doing the best that we can, in our situation, and in every moment that we have, among aaaaaalll of the other things we have to do both at work and at home.

And if there's somewhere in this book where we say 'just do it this way', and you might have done the opposite in the past, here's a script. Repeat after us:

'I was just doing the best that I can. Now that I know better, I can do better.'

'I am constantly learning new things that help me.'

'This job is hard. And I'm doing what I can.'

We're hoping to bring on self-compassion, instead of shame.

Because even as the 'experts' writing this book, we learned new things while writing this book. And even some of the 'experts' we interviewed contradicted each other or admitted to doing things differently at home.

If in doubt, imagine that you are talking to a friend, saying: 'I just read this book, and they said I really shouldn't be commenting on my child's weight, but to be honest, I've done that before.' Think about what your friend would say in that situation. If they're any good kind of friend, they would probably say, 'Yeah, but you didn't know what you know now, then. Remember that your own parents were really critical of you, so you are breaking the cycle just by being aware of this. Actually, you've done so well to even fit in reading that book with your two part-time (but really full-time) jobs. I'm proud of you for learning more about this.'

And that's what we would say to you too.

8

Key messages for body confidence

YOU CAN'T JUST TELL KIDS to love their bodies and be done with it. If we could, this book would probably stop right here and you could head off into the sunset . . . but it's just not the way it works. There's a bit of a continuum – at one end is body shame, and then body dissatisfaction. In the middle you have body neutrality, and at the other end, body acceptance and body love.

Body image is a pretty complex thing. There are lots of influences, lots of processes, and lots going on in general.

So how do we try to move towards body acceptance and body love?

PROMOTING BODY ACCEPTANCE: KEY MESSAGES TO REMEMBER

Celebrate diversity
Focus on functionality
Be kind to yourself
Focus on real role models

Life is busy. Here is the shortcut: the top four messages, distilled from all of the research and all of the conversations we've had with parents. They are also the core messages of the *Embrace Kids* film. So if you forget everything else, here's what to focus on:

1. **Celebrate diversity.** Every body is worthy of love and respect. There are so many different types of people who look different and have different bodies, and it is these differences that make our world an exciting place to be. Reminding our kids that there are all different ways to look, and different ways to be in this world, is key to showing them that they fit in and they are accepted – they belong.

2. **Focus on functionality.** Our bodies are instruments, not ornaments. Our bodies are the vehicles to help us live out our dreams. Bodies are amazing – they help us to run, jump and play, to be creative, and interact with others through high fives and cuddles. Our bodies know what they are doing – they regulate our temperature, digest our food, and heal us when we are sick or have a cut or fall. We can see, smell, hear, taste and talk, thanks to our amazing bodies. Reminding our kids about the function of their bodies

will support them in reducing the emphasis on what their bodies look like.

3. **Be kind to yourself.** You are the person you will spend the most time with. Be nice! Everyone has challenges and everyone experiences pain. The key is in how you respond to that. You can be mean and critical to yourself, or you can be nice to yourself. The latter always ends well. The former rarely does. The greatest #hack or shortcut to having a body that you love is starting to accept, love and be proud of your own body. If we can encourage our kids to be less critical of themselves, and kinder to themselves, this can have a positive impact on their body image and mental health.

4. **Focus on real role models.** We know that the media, advertising and social media can be harmful to the way we feel about ourselves and the way we look. How can we still enjoy these things, but make sure we still feel good? Question the stereotypes and images used in the media. Encourage kids to watch media, and follow people on social media, who have a diverse range of body types and sizes – and, in particular, role models who look more like them. Encourage young people to seek out content that talks about more than just appearance – this could relate to their hobbies and interests, skills, talents, causes, careers, or plans for the future.

Your body is supposed to be proof that you have lived your life. Scars, smile lines and all, your body shows that you have lived a life that you should be proud of. So go on that adventure – eat that food. Because once you reach the end, you shouldn't be thinking about what you want to look like. Whatever you look like is enough – start focusing on who you are as a person.

SARAH, AGE 14

We gave you this brilliant quote in Part One, but we're going to say it again here in the context of the messages we want to give our kids. THIS is what we want them to understand:

Loving your body isn't believing your body looks good; it is knowing your body is good, regardless of how it looks. It isn't thinking you are beautiful; it is knowing you are more than beautiful. It is understanding that your body is an instrument for your use, not an ornament to be admired.

DR LINDSAY KITE AND DR LEXIE KITE
CO-AUTHORS OF *MORE THAN A BODY: YOUR BODY*
IS AN INSTRUMENT, NOT AN ORNAMENT

ACCEPTING YOUR CHILD'S BODY

By now, we hope we've made it pretty clear that making people feel body shame and body dissatisfaction doesn't motivate them to take up healthy behaviours. The key thing for us to remember as grown-ups is to try to encourage body confidence, and to accept our kids' bodies for the way they are, without trying to change them.

This is particularly the case for kids in larger bodies: making them feel bad about their weight and shape is unlikely to support them physically to lose weight, or psychologically in terms of their body image and mental health.

The case for not weighing kids

Health professionals, policymakers and governments around the world have discussed 'BMI report cards' and routine weighing in schools still happens in some places. The following provides a summary of the evidence in case you ever find those people, so you can sit them down and give them a good talking to.

1. Having a higher weight is a key risk factor for body dissatisfaction. Research from around the world confirms that those with a higher BMI are more likely to be dissatisfied with their bodies, have lower self-esteem, and a lower quality of life. This is found again and again in research studies in countries as diverse as Kuwait, Portugal, Lithuania and the United States. The people who want to weigh kids usually do so in order to tell them they are in a

high weight category, make them feel bad about that, and then try to tell them to engage in a range of behaviours so the kids will weigh less. But this research tells us that kids at a high weight are already experiencing high levels of body dissatisfaction – we don't need to add to this by weighing them and telling them to feel bad.

2. Body dissatisfaction also doesn't lead to weight loss. Instead, research from the US tells us that those who have high levels of body dissatisfaction and engage in disordered eating behaviours are more likely to *gain* weight over time, not lose it. This was shown to be true for adolescents over a five-year and ten-year follow-up period.

3. Body dissatisfaction can lead to disordered eating behaviours. Feeling dissatisfied with the body is not a benign thought – it is one of the strongest predictors of disordered eating behaviour.

4. Shame is a key factor. Adolescents who have high levels of dissatisfaction are much more likely to engage in disordered eating behaviours if they have high levels of body shame. In another study, body shame was the strongest significant predictor of eating disturbance. Although body shame has only received relatively recent research attention, the findings are quite convincing: adolescents with higher body shame report more disordered eating behaviours.

5. If we tell adolescents about their weight status and category (i.e., that they are in the 'overweight' or 'obese' range), they are more likely to be dissatisfied with their bodies, want to be thinner, be self-conscious about

their bodies, engage in disordered eating, and have low self-esteem. If those same kids are not told that they are in those categories, they are more likely to engage in physical activity, consume fruit and vegetables, and meet sleep guidelines. The ones who are advised that they are 'overweight' or 'too fat' end up exercising less. We don't need to weigh and shame kids by labelling them as being 'overweight' or 'obese'. It doesn't help them at all. In fact, it does the opposite. It can do harm.

The benefits of health professionals and governments knowing about and tracking weight simply don't outweigh the harm of labelling kids in these categories that make them feel shame.

As adolescent bodies are literally 'in progress', they don't grow at a predictable pace, or by the same amount each day: they grow in all directions, and in fits and starts. If a child or teenager looks a certain way at a certain point in time, that doesn't mean that they are going to look that way as an adult. But if they get it in their head that their body is 'wrong' or 'fat' or 'too big', it can start a downward spiral that is very hard to reverse.

THE 'F' WORD: FAT

So many of us are so scarred by this one word. It seems to be imprinted on our brains and we have a visceral, physical reaction to hearing it – especially if it is laden with all the judgement and intended as an insult. When we were young, 'fat' was the worst thing you could call someone, no matter what size they were.

When my oldest child was four and he started talking about 'fat' for the first time, I totally freaked out. I had no idea how to have a rational conversation with him about a word that had haunted me my whole life. A word that I seemed to have erased from my vocabulary, despite my research on body image. I immediately instituted a ban on the word 'fat' in the house. I now know that this wasn't a good idea – as it reinforces the power of the word. We can and should use the word 'fat' to describe pancakes, puppies and, yes, even people – if that's the way they describe themselves, as long as it's not negatively framed.

ZALI

Fat phobia is complex, and we won't go into this in this book – we encourage you to read others listed in the Resources section. Recently, fat activists and fat people have reclaimed the power of using 'fat' as a describing word, an adjective that can just be that – a word to describe their body, and not a source of shame – as part of the weight neutrality and body liberation movements.

We tend to suggest using the term 'people in larger bodies' in general. If someone calls themselves a 'fat person', you could ask 'I've noticed that you refer to yourself as fat – is that how you would like me to describe you?' When you talk to your kids about the word 'fat', try to treat it just like any other word that you use to describe people – like tall or short, brown or blonde hair, thin or fat. It's the way we *treat* that word that gives it its power. Let's make a subtle shift and see whether we can alleviate the next generation from a whole lot of unnecessary trauma.

Chevese Turner is an internationally recognised anti-weight stigma and discrimination activist and CEO of the Body Freedom Project. Chevese encourages all parents to:

Check yourself and your beliefs about fat people. Learn about internalized weight bias and how these beliefs can actually harm your children, those around you, and even you. Become an advocate for your child and make sure you establish boundaries with those in your child's life to make sure it is clear that body comments and shaming are not acceptable. You are modeling for your child and they need to see you rejecting diet culture and weight shaming.

You might need to practise talking about fat for a while without the kids there to see how you go. Try it now, say the word 'fat' out loud. How does that feel? What reaction do you have? Start using the word to describe other things, or talk about 'fat' in context. You want to practise so you're not left gasping when it inevitably comes to the conversation with your kids.

Fiona Sutherland @themindfuldietitian has come up with a name for this moment: Freeze and Regret. It's that situation where, when you're talking to someone, you freeze in the moment, and then later think of all the great things you should have and could have said. She writes, 'To avoid freeze and regret, I always say to parents, practice what you're going to say: practice it out loud, practice saying the word fat so that it rolls off your tongue, not like (covers mouth shyly) fat, but (more confidently) fat, people in larger bodies, people in bigger bodies or whatever.'

Questions or statements you might plan to respond to ahead of time are:

Am I fat?

That boy is so fat!

Why can't my legs be like Tahnyah's?

I want to eat healthier.

I need to lose weight.

My stomach is too big.

I've got cellulite everywhere.

Practising what you're going to say in these tricky moments can help you feel more steady than frozen, and supports you to stay open to what your young person might need in that moment. We've included lots of example responses in this book. Start by saying those out loud, and then change up the words to make it sound more like something you would say.

There are two main binaries to reject here: (1) There are no 'good' and 'bad' bodies, and (2) We don't need to be one or the other – thin *or* fat. Everyone has fat. All bodies are good bodies. Accepting all bodies as they are removes all of the shame of being 'bad', and frees us up to nourish and nurture our bodies. Fat is a really important part of our body, and it wouldn't work well without it. Fat doesn't just sit there doing nothing, either. Fat tissue insulates all of our organs and protects us from the cold. Our fat stores ensure that our brain will always have a steady supply of glucose in order to power our body functioning and our thinking. Fat helps us to metabolise a range of vitamins that can't be absorbed without it.

If everyone has fat, then the power of using the word as an insult starts to diminish. For the kids in smaller bodies, knowing that they have fat too might reduce the likelihood that they will call other kids 'fat' to try to hurt their feelings.

'AM I FAT?'

If your child asks you if they are fat, or tells you that someone called them fat, please, as we mentioned earlier, try to resist the urge to say 'You're not fat! You're beautiful', as this reinforces some of the power of the word. The aim is to keep your response as *neutral* as possible. Here's how you could respond – either at the time, or (if you freeze and regret) in a quiet chat afterwards.

1. Don't freak out. Be curious about what they have heard, and the context they have heard it in.

2. Empathise with them. You might talk about a time that you were called 'fat' as an insult at school or at home, and how it made you feel.

3. Explain that some people use the word 'fat' to make people feel bad about themselves, and it's not okay. In our family, we believe that all bodies are good bodies, and we know that all people have fat on their bodies, and it's really necessary for their body to work properly.

4. Emphasise the fact that it's quite a serious problem if people are teasing each other about the fat on their bodies. Just as we wouldn't tease someone who has a disability, or whose skin is a different colour, we shouldn't tease people about their size and shape.

5. Tell them that there is nothing wrong with their body, that you love them just as they are.

6. Brainstorm some of the things that their body can do that they are proud of.

7. Think of some of the kind things they can say to themselves to make them feel better. Empower them with things they can tell themselves and others if this happens again.

Your worth has nothing to do with your weight.
All bodies are good bodies.
Everyone is worthy of respect and love
regardless of how they look.

'THAT KID IS SO FAT'

What if your child calls another person 'fat'? There are many different options to respond to this, depending on the kid and the context. The aim is to try to reduce the power of 'fat', encourage empathy, and normalise the word.

For younger kids:
1. Explain that we all have fat: Fat is an important part of our bodies and keeps us healthy. It's important that we eat some fat as it keeps us full and makes things taste pretty good!
2. Neutralise the word: Fat is a describing word. We can use it to describe animals and things.
3. Talk about feelings: Calling people 'fat' can hurt their feelings. Have you seen anyone calling other people 'fat' at school? What could we do to help that person? How we treat each other matters. We need to accept each other and be kind to each other.

For tweens:
You can utilise all of the above strategies for young people, plus:
1. Encourage empathy: How would you feel if someone was talking about you like that?
2. Talk about stereotypes: By calling someone 'fat' are we also making other generalisations about them? You can also talk about these issues generally: Isn't it interesting that the people who made this show decided to use a person in a larger body to play a character who was lazy and not as

smart as the others – is that always true? What effect might this have?

3. What's the why: Ask your child why they think being called fat is a bad thing, and disconnect attributes from appearance. 'Someone isn't mean because they're fat. They're mean because they're not a nice person, and they don't treat others well.'

For teens, you can add the following:

1. Explain the biological necessity of fat: Fat is for insulation, an energy 'insurance policy', and for absorption of vitamins.

2. Take a social justice approach: Ask questions about why some people are treated differently because of their appearance, including people in larger bodies. Are any bodies really 'good' and 'bad'? What discrimination and judgement might people in larger bodies face? Is that really fair? How could we make our home, our school and our world fairer for everyone?

3. Ask them: How could we learn more about what life is like for people who are different or who look different to us?

'Fat' is just a word that we use to describe things. There are all different kinds of body shapes. Some people are bigger, and some people are smaller, and people can be healthy in any of these bodies. I just try to stop them from using 'fat' in a negative way, or as an insult, because I think that's when we start to attach a complex set of value judgements and health judgements to it.

GINGER GORMAN, JOURNALIST

**Enjoy your moments on this earth.
You only have one life.
You are enough.
It's time to focus more on living your life
and your hobbies, not your bodies.**

DION, AGE 11

We all want our kids to feel good about their bodies. To prevent them from developing depression and eating disorders that can come from feelings of shame and body dissatisfaction. The information in this chapter shows us that there is no one way forward; we have to meet our kids where they are at. But if we can just get them to be kind to themselves, to see their bodies as their vessels to experience the world, know that they fit in, and be inspired by what people do instead of how they look, it changes everything. Those four simple messages, repeated throughout their childhood, can create an environment of acceptance that can change everything. No, we're not being dramatic: everything!! Think about it – when we were young, there was one 'look' that we were told to achieve, everything and everyone was focused on the look and not on functionality or what people were doing, and we were actively conditioned to be critical of ourselves in order to push ourselves to try harder. We've seen how that went and we're now suggesting that we do quite the opposite. You can be that change for your kids, in your home.

FAQs

Q: My nine-year-old girl came to me asking whether she could 'chop off' her belly. What do I say to that?!

It's inevitable. At some point, your child is highly likely to say that they are fat. This could be just to see how you respond. It could be because they have heard something in the playground. This can happen regardless of the body size and shape they are in.

When our kids say they are fat it can be really triggering for us as parents, depending on what your experiences of childhood and adolescence were. Try to calm yourself . . . the whole idea is to neutralise the word 'fat' and take the power out of it rather than convince her that she is not 'fat'.

Start by helping her appreciate her body functionality. Talk about the fact that all bodies are good bodies, and we all have fat. Try to talk more about what her body helps her to do, and celebrate the range of bodies that we see out in the world. Remind her that the body is just the home for her self and her soul. Remind her to be kind to herself in the moments that she has these thoughts about her belly. Lots of people in the world have moments when they wish that parts of their bodies were different, but we need to remember that who we are is more important than what we look like.

Q: My sixteen-year-old daughter thinks she is ugly, and wants cosmetic surgery to 'fix' her face. She is watching a lot of things on social media, and I've heard her and her friends talk about it. I just want her to be happy. What should I say?

The desire for surgery doesn't usually come out of nowhere. Research shows that among adolescent and college women, wanting surgery is associated with higher levels of body dissatisfaction, higher body shame, disordered eating behaviours, and body 'checking' in mirrors and photos. However, surgery rarely improves satisfaction with appearance when there are underlying body image or mood disorders.

There are a few situations and procedures for which there are benefits (according to the research), including surgery for cleft lip, surgery for prominent ears, breast reduction in cases where breasts are very large and breast augmentation for severe asymmetry. Outside of these situations, it is best to delay and distract adolescents from seeking surgery.

Conversations here might centre around encouraging your daughter to focus on her own unique strengths, rather than comparing her appearance to others. Broadening interests and engagement in activities such as drama, sport and other groups might also facilitate meeting a wider range of peers that could be helpful. Show her examples of real role models with similar facial features. Encourage her to see and celebrate the diversity of appearance in people all over the world. Find ways for her to soothe and be kind to herself when she finds herself fixating on the parts of her appearance that she is worried about. If she is very distressed and insistent that surgery is the only option, seeing a psychologist would be helpful to gain strategies in managing anxiety related to appearance, lower expectations of surgery, and to rule out body dysmorphic disorder. Good surgeons would refer their patients to see a psychologist anyway, particularly for people under the age of eighteen.

Action

☑ Think about how you feel about 'fat' – what has your history been, and how do you talk about it at home? Talk about this with your partner and other people around you.

☑ Think about where and how you could incorporate conversations around modelling and celebrating diversity, valuing functionality, and self-compassion in your home.

9

Body image development in children and adolescents

FROM A VERY YOUNG AGE, children tell us that 'thin is good', and 'fat is bad'. When Zali interviewed three-year-olds for a study, over and over, they would show her the picture of a larger child as the kid who was 'naughty', 'mean' or 'lazy', and the picture of the thinner child as someone who was the one who was 'good' – or 'happy', 'nice' and 'active'. These attitudes, present from such an early age, pave the way for young people to be afraid of fat, and to start to be dissatisfied with their bodies if they don't think they align with what is 'normal'.

Body dissatisfaction is common in children and adolescents. Around 60 per cent of children aged five to eleven years, 60 per cent of adolescent boys, and 80 per cent of adolescent girls want to change something about their body. For girls, this tends to focus around losing weight, but for boys, it's split: 30 per cent want to gain muscle, and 30 per cent want to lose fat. These percentages vary slightly around the world, depending on the question that the researchers ask, but still, most young people say they want to change something about the way they look.

Every year, Mission Australia conducts a survey of young people, and body image consistently ranks in the top three issues of personal concern, alongside stress and mental health. Teenagers are more concerned about their body image than their physical health, bullying, financial security and drugs.

They are concerned for good reason – body image has an influence on so many other things in their lives, and research shows that there is a relationship between body image and pretty much every other aspect of physical and mental health. Body dissatisfaction directly predicts the development of depression for adolescent boys and girls. Adolescents who are dissatisfied with their bodies are more likely to engage in dieting, disordered eating, and to gain more weight over time, and boys are more likely to use steroids and muscle-building supplements. Body dissatisfaction is also related to other 'risky behaviours'. Dissatisfied teens are more likely to use alcohol and to smoke tobacco, have earlier first sexual intercourse, engage in self-harm, and experience depression and anxiety.

And then there are the academic outcomes, with studies showing that young people are less likely to put their hands up at school or put themselves forward for opportunities, and more likely to skip school, on days when they are not feeling confident about their appearance.

Sounds stressful, huh? We promise it gets better.

WHAT CONTRIBUTES TO BODY IMAGE AND BODY DISSATISFACTION?

As we mentioned in Chapter 2, there are three main influences on body image:

1. **Biological influences.** Things like your genetics, gender, Body Mass Index and the age at which young people go through puberty (pubertal timing) are really significant, and are pretty unchangeable influences on body image. Being female and being in a larger body are two of the major contributors to body dissatisfaction, and genetics influence both of these things in some way.

2. **Psychological and individual influences.** This involves things like the way our brains work and interpret the world around us. Anxiety and depression are highly related to body image – in fact, in one study, young people who were dissatisfied with their bodies were twenty-four times more likely to experience depression. The extent to which we do things such as compare ourselves with others, internalise that 'thin is good and fat is bad', and the strength of personality traits such as perfectionism all contribute to the development of body dissatisfaction and eating disorders.

3. **Social and cultural influences.** This is where peers, family and the media come in. These might be the influences most of us think about when it comes to body image. Most people assume that social media is the main influence, and research does show that it is important, but it depends what sort of social media people are exposed

to. Viewing people's bodies – particularly less-clothed bodies of the same gender – has more of an influence on body image than watching cat videos. Online, and in real life, friends and family can have direct and indirect influences on teens' body image, with the influence of family decreasing in early adolescence, when friends and peers become more important.

What does this mean for you and your family? The main messages here are:

1. There are many influences on body image, and
2. We can't control all of them.

Although this is scary to think about, we have to accept that we can do the best we can to create the most positive environment that we are able to, but in the end, some things are not up to us.

No-one is the same – we are all beautiful in our own way. We act different, look different, and feel different. So why compare yourself to someone else?

FLORENCE, AGE 12

BODY IMAGE IN TODDLERS
AND PRE-SCHOOLERS

At this early age, children already have firm ideas about bodies, and have clear ideas about what it means to be in a smaller or larger body. Many of these biases are innate – we are born with them – but many are also socialised by the conversations they hear, and the media they are exposed to. At this early age there aren't many opportunities for conversations about body image, but there are lots of lovely picture books that you can read that start to introduce the ideas of celebrating diversity, appreciating the function of our bodies, being kind to ourselves, and focusing on role models of people based on who they are and what they do rather than what they look like.

BODY IMAGE IN PRIMARY
SCHOOL-AGED CHILDREN

Children generally go through a period, when they are around four to six years old, where they have more rigid thinking about gender. This is often characterised by a desire for all of the sparkly pink things or all of the trucks, cars and dinosaurs – even when this hasn't been encouraged. At this age it is important that children have opportunities to express ideas about gender as they learn and explore through play.

At this age, you are likely to get a lot of questions about how the world works, why the way things are the way they are – and they might even listen to your answers! We usually get these questions when we're driving in double-windscreen-wiper-level rain, and they can catch you off-guard a bit, so it's worth having a think and a chat with your partner about the ways you want to talk about bodies, weight and health in your family. Keep reading those same picture books you read to them when they were little – they now take on a bit more meaning as your kids understand more complex concepts and have a deeper sense of moral judgement.

Emotion regulation is also developing throughout this time – and it is so important that we model positive responses to emotions and allow young people to practise these in safe environments. Studies have found that adolescents with body image concerns were more likely to experience bulimic and depressive symptoms if they engaged in social comparison, rumination, self-blame and suppression of their emotions. Developing more positive strategies now – like putting things into perspective, reframing, planning goals, expression and communication of feelings, seeking advice, physical activity, and focusing on pleasant activities – means that young people will be well practised at them when they need them.

The age of six and seven is usually when children start to gain the awareness that other people have thoughts and judgements about them. They can start to be aware of what other people think, and may start to dress and act accordingly. At this age, empathy is also developing, something that can be encouraged by considering different people's perspectives on things.

BODY IMAGE ACROSS THE TWEEN
AND EARLY TEEN YEARS

Puberty changes everything. Body, brain, hormones, identity – and it starts as young as eight and nine years old. The timing of puberty relative to peers is also very important – for girls, developing earlier can lead to increased levels of body dissatisfaction. For boys, it's the opposite: developing later can lead to increased body dissatisfaction. The age at which children progress through these stages does vary. Below, we've based the age and development information on population averages, but your child might be different – if in doubt, just find where you think your child is up to and follow on from there, without paying too much attention to the ages specified below. Development is a complex interplay of biology, environment and psychology, but it's helpful to have a sense of what might be happening at each stage, and what to expect at the next one!

8–9-year-olds

This is where it all begins. You might have thought you had a few years left before you had 'a teenager' but there are some shifts starting to happen and suddenly, your child isn't . . . well, a child all of the time any more.

This is the age where the hormonal shifts that will help your child's mind and body grow and change into an adult can start to happen. Alongside these hormonal changes comes a surge in growth. Children can suddenly become ravenous and seem to grow taller overnight! Sometimes height and weight don't always increase at the same pace at the same time, so children might store some weight around the middle to prepare for increases in height.

Cognitive development at this age means that young people develop the ability to compare themselves to others around the age of eight or nine. They might start to compare their colouring-in or running ability, but also their bodies, and we know that social comparisons are one of the bigger influences on body image.

At this age, it's important to discuss the functionality of bodies. Talk about the changes that are happening and why they are important. Whenever your children are doing things with their bodies, reinforce how amazing our bodies are that they can do those things. The idea is to continually remind our kids that our bodies are more than just something to look at. You can talk about body functionality in terms of the five senses, bodily processes (like regulating temperature and digesting food), doing physical things with our bodies, like running with strong legs, doing creative things like dance, art and craft, and interacting with others with our bodies – snuggling and hugging.

Encourage children to eat in relation to their appetite. Although you might have been used to being able to control your child's eating at predictable mealtimes in the past, it's okay if they want to eat snacks, or eat something else after dinner, if they are still hungry. Talk about the ways that we can listen to our body, and follow our body's messages for when we are hungry and when we are full, as well as what we want to eat.

According to parents we've spoken to around the world, this is the age when boys start talking about wanting 'muscles' or 'a six-pack', and girls might start saying they are 'fat'. Try not to freak out the first time your child tells you they are fat. Take a deep breath. Avoid your instinct to say, 'You're not fat! You're beautiful' as this reinforces some of the negative connotations of the word, and we want to keep it as neutral as possible. Explain gently that all people have fat on their bodies; it's really necessary for their body to work properly. Everyone has fat, and everyone has fingernails – but we don't go around calling people 'fingernails', do we?

Young boys might seem obsessed with having a six-pack, but they also might just be starting to notice that some grown-up men have muscles or a six-pack. Much of the time this desire for muscularity is tied to wanting to perform well in their sport, and noticing that their idols have these features. You can start to talk about how hard these professionals have to train in order to look like that, and what they have to miss out on while they engage in that much training.

10-11-year-olds

These pre-teen years are still full of tumultuous times. Young people's brains and bodies go through significant bursts and periods of growth during these years. Be warned that, if you are not already, this is the age where you might become 'so embarrassing'. Hey, it's good to be prepared, right?

At ten and eleven, kids become much more aware of the perspectives of others – particularly their peers. At this age, the influence of peers tends to overtake the influence of family in terms of what they want to wear, how they want to look, and what they want to spend their time doing. Friend groups and peer norms become very important in setting the standard for what is acceptable and desirable in their group. It's okay for young people to want to wear the same thing, do the same things, talk and act like their friends at this stage – that's how they show their friendship at this age and they have a strong drive for acceptance.

For girls, this is usually when the noticeable signs of puberty may start to take place. This usually begins with the development of breast buds under their nipples, and the areola begins to expand. Many parents and primary school teachers report that girls are starting to menstruate at this age, and the research shows that the age of first period has slowly decreased over time over the past 100 years (or since they started researching things!). Pubic hair may start to emerge for girls and boys, and boys' genitals may start to grow at around the age of eleven, beginning with the testes.

As kids start to seek more independence, it's a good idea to experiment with being able to offer them more time to be on their own with their friends, in safe and supported ways. Making sure that you are there to debrief, and help young people make sense of the complex peer environments and situations they find themselves in, is important in contributing to their learning and development at this time. This is also one of the key moments to focus on when having conversations with your young people. Make sure that they know they can come to talk to you about anything before they descend into adolescence.

12–13-year-olds

This is it – teenager-hood! Teens are also in a critical stage for developing identity, and their own unique characteristics and contributions to the world. For some teens, their appearance becomes an important part of their identity, or the way they explore and demonstrate who they are to the rest of the world.

Taryn

At the time of writing this book, I have two teenage boys and one tween girl. Honestly, I thought my house was only big enough to hold my monthly dose of raging hormones, but now I've got all these extra hormones flying around too! At times, I find my kids' behaviour is belligerent, moody, obnoxious, unreasonable, hostile and pugnacious. (Never used that word in my life. That's how serious these hormones are!) There are days I loathe parenting teens and tweens and then there are days like diamonds. We've just got to weather the storms, and hold on tight as each new phase ends and another begins.

Physical changes in girls

For girls, this is where the majority of obvious physical development will happen. Pubic hair will continue to grow, and acne may start to appear. The main thing that happens at this age is growth – girls at this age are at the peak level of growth for height and may grow up to 8 cm per year. At this age, girls need to start laying down fat stores on the hips and thighs in order to prepare for menstruation. This is the beginning of developing their adult female body. Girls need to be prepared for the fact that they will double their body weight between the age of nine and eighteen. Their body fat percentage needs to be 18 per cent to menstruate, and 22 per cent to have regular menstrual cycles. Of course, we wouldn't want anyone focusing on the numbers here, but we do need to talk to our girls about the purpose of fat, and to normalise this necessary weight gain in puberty.

Girls generally start to menstruate at this age, though it can happen earlier or later. Research from the early 2000s reported that girls had negative experiences of starting their period – including feeling embarrassment and shame, and needing secrecy around this topic. However, there has been a huge shift over the past ten to fifteen years towards empowerment and embracing this aspect of our bodies, and a lot more education for our children about menstruation. Some parents have started throwing 'period parties' and there are many mother–daughter 'positive period' workshops available to celebrate this time as a transition to womanhood. Despite this shift, similar research studies have found that girls still feel unprepared, ashamed and embarrassed. Girls can feel self-conscious about their bodies during this time – mostly because they have seen others being teased about menstruation or experienced this themselves.

The first period

I had already purchased a little gift bag, with the nice under-wear and the pads and a nice candle, some chocolates – just something to make it special for her. I wanted to de-shame it for her in a way that wasn't done for me.

MICHELLE, MUM OF TWO, USA

With all of my girls, we took part in 'Celebration Days for Girls', which created a really special space for the mothers and daughters to share and learn about their bodies and about periods in a really lovely, affirming way. At one point, we sewed a little felt heart, and the mums wrote a 'wish for their daughter' to put inside the heart that you don't show the girls at the time – I'm not a crafty person, so my sewing wasn't great, but I noticed that both the girls still have those and they keep them near their bed.

We've approached period management from an environmental perspective, so we have reusable pads and period undies. We don't have a separate laundry, because we never finished that part of the house, and with four of us menstruating, there's always a bucket with undies or pads soaking in the bathroom – and it's totally public. It's not hidden, they sit in the bathroom or in the bath, and so I think just bringing that sort of feeling like it's just really natural and there's nothing to hide helps to remove some of the shame as well.

SARA, MUM OF FOUR, MELBOURNE

She was like: 'Oh, yeah, I just put a tampon in', and I was like: 'You did what? Did you want to tell me beforehand? Did you need any help?' She was just walking out the door and was so nonchalant about this tampon. It was then that I realised that clearly, by this point, she's talking to friends about it, which is great, because I didn't even do that. I'm sure a friend was like, 'Yeah, here's one – it's no big deal', and so it wasn't a big deal. There was no sense of trauma at all, like I had, it was just a straightforward thing to her. Matter of fact.

EVA, MUM OF TWO, USA

The reproductive hormones that are surging in young women's bodies also have an impact on appetite. It can be helpful to talk with your daughter about the fact that her body knows what it needs at each point of her menstrual cycle and drives her to behave accordingly. If you are a woman, you may have noticed that you feel more and less hungry at different points of your cycle. Scientists have confirmed that this is true in animal studies with rats – they eat the least amounts of food after the peak of oestrogen in their cycle, and they eat the most just before they menstruate. If they take the rat's reproductive organs out, they eat consistent amounts every day. The only related research scientists have been able to do with actual human women is a study where they found that women looked (and probably salivated, let's be honest!) at pictures of high-energy foods longer when progesterone levels were high – typically between ovulation and menstruation.

Some girls might expect their bodies to stay the size and shape they were as children – but just taller and with breasts. It's important to talk to them about how their body is pre-programmed to increase in size, and to change shape in order to become an adult, and to be able to have babies (though that may not appeal right now!). The way that our bodies change throughout puberty is not because of what we are eating or how we are moving, but the result of powerful biological forces that change the way that fats are metabolised and stored in the body. Building up trust that our bodies are growing and changing as they are meant to is important at this age.

The opportunity for teasing and bullying about weight and shape is also at its peak during this key time of growth. As family members – including extended family, parents and siblings – start to notice that girls are getting larger and taller, they can tease them about their developing body parts or their weight. This might not sound like 'teasing' but it's the awkward 'Whoa, you've grown' comments that can have the same negative impact as teasing. Peers are also particularly good at singling out some of the first girls to develop in a year group at school, and making comments about them. All of this can be very hard to process for a hormonal, emotional teen girl, but one of the key things to reinforce is that they are not doing anything wrong and there is nothing wrong with their body. This is the way that their body is designed to be – as determined by their genetics and their hormones. Listening to her body and nourishing her body are really important at this time, to let it do what it needs to do.

Oh, and remember that drive to fit in? It's definitely still there. This is the age of 'But everyone is doing it' and 'I neeeeed this top – everyone else has one'. Don't worry too much if your girls look exactly like all of their friends at this stage – doing their hair the same, wearing the same thing – this is all part of the process. They need to shift their identity away from you to their friends first, and then they will start to explore their own individuality later. For now, they are likely to chameleon themselves in most ways to their friends.

My daughter is twelve and she's never been a person to compare herself or feel insecure – she's not really focused on her appearance – but she is starting to get slightly spotty skin. She will occasionally come

to me and say, 'Oh, I don't like these little spots.' And I just talk to her really openly and say it's hormonal, and that everybody her age or most people her age will experience it. I let her know that we will help her to deal with it the best way she can, and I remind her that she will come out of this space, it won't be like this forever.

ALINA, MUM OF TWO, UK

Physical changes in boys

Physical changes for boys tend to begin around the age of thirteen. They may grow 5–8 cm in a year, and have muscle growth, though they are not yet producing enough testosterone to actually 'bulk up' in ways they might like to.

At this age, boys will also develop armpit hair, their voices will deepen, and they may experience acne. At this age, the penis gets longer and testicles continue to grow. The first ejaculation typically occurs around age thirteen, and may occur at night (as a 'wet dream').

There is very little research or public awareness around boys' experiences of their first ejaculation. The one main study, now conducted over thirty years ago, found that, in the majority of cases, boys reported being 'surprised', and were not sure what was happening to them. Boys also reported being confused, embarrassed and scared, and many thought that they were wetting the bed when it happened. Although sex education does cover this topic, it is usually delivered too late for most boys. The boys who felt prepared for what was happening were more likely to report more positive experiences and feeling proud.

It would be helpful for parents to explain the nature and context of ejaculation to boys, and provide access to information about this so that boys are not so alone with their experience. All they need to know is that eventually, some liquid will come out of their penis that isn't wee – it's called semen and it has sperm in it that, combined with the egg of a woman, can make babies.

14–16-year-olds

At this age, the reproductive organs have grown and are now fully developed, and most other visible pubertal changes have taken place, such as the growth of pubic, armpit and facial hair (for boys). In this final stage of puberty, both boys and girls tend to continue to grow in terms of their size and shape – with boys developing their muscles, and girls laying down fat in their hips, thighs and bottom.

For boys, puberty takes them closer to societal 'ideals' for men's bodies, as they start to produce testosterone and can therefore grow muscles. We see increased body dissatisfaction in boys who develop later. For girls, we see the opposite – the necessary increase in fat to allow for menstruation actually takes girls away from the female 'ideals' that they may see on social media as they become women, and those who experience early pubertal growth tend to be teased more and have more body image concerns.

However, although their bodies are mostly 'finished', teen brains are still developing. It is both normal and essential for teens to 'hide away in their bedrooms' and create some distance from their parents from ages thirteen to fifteen. Their brains are literally evolving into the adult model, pruning back connections that are no longer required, and strengthening the ones that are used most. The part of the brain responsible for decision making and risk perception is the last to evolve – meaning that young people can struggle to think ahead and plan, or determine the consequences of their actions, even up until the age of twenty-four. While that section is 'under construction', the impulsive, emotive, instinctive and aggressive part of the brain is in charge – and this is why they react with grunting or getting very upset 'for no reason'. It's not about you and what you did or did not do – their brain has defaulted to fight/flight mode.

One of the other key developmental processes at this time that makes young people very self-conscious about their bodies is called 'egocentrism'. Remember back to being a teenager and feeling like everyone was looking at you all the time? That's egocentrism – best described as 'being in your own reality TV show'. This can be what makes adolescents particularly self-conscious about their bodies, and to feel dissatisfied with and want to change their bodies.

It's particularly important to talk to girls about the reasons why their bodies developed more fat, and to be aware of whether they are changing their diet in an effort to change their weight or shape. This is the age at which most girls start to ignore their hunger and satiety cues, and stop listening to their bodies. This is also the peak age for eating disorder onset (at 14.9 years – to be exact). This is the age where we should start encouraging young people to trust, accept and listen to their bodies, and follow intuitive eating.

It is critical that teens don't start training with weights at the gym too early. If boys go to the gym or use weights to try to build muscle before they have developed the testosterone that will allow their muscles to actually grow, they risk injuring themselves and permanently stunting their muscle growth. If they want to build strength and work out, encourage your teens to start with exercises that use their body weight first, and then move on to lighter weights.

At this age many boys will want to start to use muscle-building supplements. Another of Zali's research studies found that more than 50 per cent of boys in this age group in Australia were using protein powder, and even more intended to use it in the future. If this is the case, it is important to talk to them about what they are taking – not all of the supplements that are on the shelves are safe and effective, and none of them will have been tested with adolescents.

This is also the age at which so many teens are experimenting with their identity. Music choice, clothing, food, friend groups, sports and other hobbies can all change, dramatically, every few weeks or months. It might be hard to keep up, but they are just trying on different personas to see what 'fits'.

Yes, it's hard to go out to a family lunch with my daughter when she's dressed like a biker. You know, she used to be this gorgeous little affectionate girl who wouldn't even wear pants – she would say 'Princesses don't wear pants, Mum'. Now she comes out wearing hoodies, and black eyeliner, and big black boots – even if it's a hot day! I don't really want to go down the street with her looking like that. But it's not about me, it's about her. I have to set aside my desires, and also

be patient, because she's figuring out her identity. I need to let her go through those phases, so that she can work out who she is. I just try to go through those phases with her and I try not to actually scrutinise it too much.

JUSTINE, MUM OF TWO, BRISBANE

GENDER-FLUID TEENS AND PUBERTY

Most teens feel a little bit strange in their bodies, but when your body doesn't match your gender orientation, puberty can be a very difficult time. As bodies change physically, gender-fluid teens experience higher levels of dysphoria around the body, body dissatisfaction, poor mental health and distress. Transgender and gender-diverse teens in particular might engage in disordered eating behaviours in order to try to change their body to alleviate feelings of their body not being right or belonging to them, and align the body with their gender identity. Research with transgender teens and adults found that those who had undergone interventions such as hormone therapy then had improvements in their body image.

It is so great to see more people of all ages feeling comfortable and supported to express their gender in many and varied ways that feel most authentic to them. A psychologist at a girls' school reported:

We are seeing a big increase in the number of girls who identify as gender diverse in the past five years. I understand that presentations to transgender clinics around the world have skyrocketed. It used to be more males transitioning to female, but now it's increasingly adolescent girls presenting to gender clinics with gender dysphoria. We had a girl who came in Year Seven as Ashley. And then in Year Eight, she transitioned to a boy and was known as Max. Max would wear the sport uniform of shorts and everyone within the school community adjusted to him being Max. He had relationships with the other students. But after a year he moved to a co-ed school as that was what he wanted to do.

JANELLE, AUSTRALIA

Many of the parents and experts we spoke to were keen to discuss the fact that they thought that 'kids these days' were much more accepting of diversity, particularly in relation to gender fluidity and sexual orientation, much more so than 'back in our day'. Blake, a father of two, shares his experiences of teaching in primary schools:

I think kids are actually much more accepting these days – and parents too. We have someone in Grade Six who is transitioning to be a girl. The kids have been amazing – they've had some questions, and we've talked through all of that, but there has been no push back from parents at all. Not one parent has raised any issues at all. It's been amazing. There's quite a lot to consider, and they could easily have been unsure about her using the girls' toilets, and competing in the swimming carnival as a girl, but they've all been totally fine with it. My brother is a high school teacher and he's told me that they have a handful of students in any year level that are transitioning, but also a lot of bisexual kids too. He said there are girls kissing girls and boys will walk around holding hands; everything is fluid these days. It's very different to when we were at school.

A transitioning story

So I started out in the pandemic with two daughters, aged ten and fourteen, and now, I have one daughter, and a son . . .

One night, our daughter shared a letter with us that basically said 'I'm a boy.' We had been to a gay pride parade in our city that day, and we have always been very open about talking about being kind and inclusive, and we have a lot of pride in our family so we've always been really open about it. But in our heads, this was a kid who had long hair and played with stuffed animals and dolls, and had always presented as a pretty stereotypical gender consistent girl, so this was very confusing for us. So we knew there was something there, but I think he was figuring out what this meant – he just knew that he wasn't a girl, but he almost didn't quite know what he was. For a while we tried on different ideas – like that he might be non-binary or gender-fluid, but that didn't quite feel right. Finally, he said: 'No, I think I'm a boy' but it took a little while, maybe a year or two.

We got him into therapy pretty quickly just to help him figure out this process – and I read lots of books about it to try and figure out what's going on. I think your first instinct as a parent is that, when you're afraid, you want to try and control things as much as you can. But what became really clear is that we had no control over it. This was a process that was not happening to me or to my husband, it was happening to our child. Our child was living through this and experiencing this. The only thing that we did have control over was whether or not we were going to support our child through this process. And so I think once that became clear, our purpose in this was just to support our child, in whatever process they were going through, and to be okay with it, wherever it led them. My role was to help my kid get through this journey, feeling loved and supported and proud of themselves, so we can move through it and be in a healthy place. So if your goal is to have a healthy, happy, functioning kid, then, regardless of whatever gender designation they end up with, in the end, your goal is just to love the hell out of them as they're going through this process.

We were so scared about how the rest of the world would respond to our kid. We were so scared about how other people were going to perceive him. But what has happened, and I feel very lucky about this, is that I have not heard one negative thing about it, and he has not experienced any episodes of bullying or anything. We live in a community that's really progressive and very accepting – and luckily nothing bad has actually happened.

What did happen is that my son wears his identity with so much pride. He thinks that being transgender is just the most awesome and interesting thing about him – like it's his superpower. I'm actually really, really proud of him, because I think he's done a thing that's scary and hard to do, and the idea that you would know yourself well enough and feel confident enough in yourself, especially in your early teens, to be able to say 'This is who I am, and I recognise there might be social consequences, but I'm not gonna hide that part of me', I think that's really brave.

LARISSA, MUM OF TWO, USA

Try to wrap your head around the use of pronouns wherever you can – even when it feels grammatically incorrect!

When transgender adolescents are able to use their new chosen name and pronouns at school, at home, at work and with friends, research shows they experience much lower levels of depression (70 per cent less), a 34 per cent decrease in suicidal thoughts, and a 65 per cent decrease in suicide attempts. In other words, it's worth you potentially feeling a little awkward at first.

Aud Mason-Hyde, the incredible non-binary young person featured in *Embrace Kids*, sums it up with their wisdom:

I think what we need in general, in the world, is to understand that humans exist in such a multitude of ways – and I always like to say that there are as many genders as there are humans – because I think we all express our gender differently. And I think what we really need to combat that non-acceptance and that ignorance is just to talk about gender more openly.

Yes, Aud. Yes.

FAQs

Q: My child always chooses opposite-sex characters or action figures to dress up as. How do I support them?

This can be a challenging situation – even for those of us who are really open and accepting of different identities and sexualities. Although we might have friends and colleagues who are gay or trans, it can be hard to parent more inclusively around gender, mostly because it's so different from the societal context that existed when we were kids. We think that if we let boys take the pink drink bottle to pre-school, they will get teased for it because that's what happened when we were kids. Parents often also feel really alone in this, and it can be hard to know who they can talk to about this that will be supportive.

If you've seen the film *Embrace Kids*, you will have seen Scott Stuart's story. You would have seen him attending the *Frozen* movie with his son, both rocking their Elsa dresses. And you would have seen his fantastic storybook *My Shadow is Pink*. This book could be a really great way to open up a conversation about this with younger children. Having said that, this book explains things in such a unique way that we learned a few things while reading it, and Scott's Instagram @scottcreates has lots of comments from parents who report that this book helped their teens as well.

Carmelita Tiu, from Know Them, Be Them, Raise Them @knowberaisethem has some suggestions for older children. 'Talk about different things to pave a path so that your kids can step down it more easily. We talk about the fact that there are different combinations between your sex that was assigned at birth, gender identity, gender presentation and sexual orientation, and any combination of that is okay. Of course, I knew this and interacted with friends and colleagues like this, but we had never really explicitly addressed it as a family. Now, we make sure that the dialogue is "However you want to show up is fine. We love you no matter what. We will support you."'

Q My son is sixteen and still so small and slim. He is starting to worry that he will never develop muscle like his peers.

As much as you can, try to reassure him that it will happen.

There is literally nothing you can (safely) do to develop more muscle bulk before your body produces testosterone – but as boys are human, they hate thinking that they can't make progress when they really want to. Research tells us that boys can be more interested in strength and sports performance over the appearance of their body, so work with that. Focus on fuelling the body, and developing strength and skill, and the stuff on the inside.

Reassure him that his body knows what it is doing, and it will bring on the muscle when the time comes. There is nothing wrong with his body, nothing that needs changing, or to be worked on or worked out.

Q My daughter is lean and looks less developed than her peers. What can I say to reassure her?

Girls who are naturally lean can start to worry that they don't have any of the features that make their peers 'sexy'. It's enough that they are able to make those comparisons themselves and start to feel inferior, but then this is reinforced by hearing the positive attention that their developed friends get from boys, which can make them feel more insecure.

Girls get so many mixed messages through this time that can be hard to navigate. You can reassure them that everyone develops at their own pace, and that their body will grow and develop when it is ready. You can talk about the wide range of reasons why someone might be attracted to someone else, and that it's not always about the way they look.

They might not seem like they believe you. They might constantly argue back with 'Yes, but...' It might be completely frustrating to be saying these things that don't seem to 'work' to make them feel any better, but it's still important that you say these things to them. Having that support and encouragement, as biased as you are as their parent, is still going to be one of the critical building blocks of a strong foundation of confidence.

Action

We've covered a lot in this chapter. The main message is that kids' bodies and brains should literally have a sign that says 'in progress'.

Here are some conversation starters and guidance for action:

☑ **Prepare younger children for brain and body changes in puberty by having conversations earlier rather than later. Talking about how their brain and body need to grow to be the 'adult version' can be helpful.**

☑ **When talking about bodies and body changes remember to emphasise the fact that all bodies look different, that the way bodies function and the things our bodies do for us are more important than (and often unrelated to) how they look.**

☑ **Try to reduce the shame associated with periods, ejaculation and pleasure in relation to the body by talking about these things as being normal. Kids might think that hearing about your experiences in relation to these things is 'gross' or 'old fashioned', but you can talk about facts and information, or use stories of 'someone I know'.**

☑ **It is normal for young people to have concerns, worries and anxieties from time to time. If this is ongoing, persistent or debilitating, you can seek professional support from a psychologist.**

10

Feelings

THESE DAYS, PARENTING KIDS IS all about feelings.

But when we were growing up? We heard 'Don't cry', 'Suck it up, princess', 'Don't be a psycho'. In our homes, any of the negative emotions, like anger, sadness, loneliness, guilt, hurt, depression, anger, humiliation, fear, feeling threatened, rejected, anxious, insecure, lonely, vulnerable . . . were not 'allowed'.

There are a few reasons for this. Our parents were mostly parented by people who never talked about feelings (and their parents even less so). In the eighties and nineties, 'self-esteem' became the big thing, and our parents and teachers tried to protect us from the bad things that were going on in order to help us to be happy all of the time. It was all well intentioned. But you can't just be happy *all* the time. You need to be able to feel the negative emotions in order to experience the positive ones to the full. Of course, there isn't any research on this – science doesn't know how to capture these things very well.

Many researchers have tried to describe the 'basic' or 'core' emotions for a long time – since ancient Greek times. Of course they don't really agree on how many there are, or which ones should be included in the list, but Dr Paul Ekman proposed six basic emotions: fear, anger, enjoyment, disgust, sadness and surprise based on studying facial expressions and non-verbal communication. If these sound familiar, it's because he consulted to the filmmakers creating *Inside Out*. Dr Gloria Willcox articulated seventy-two emotions in groups of a beautiful 'Feelings Wheel'. And then there's Brené. Dr Brené Brown identifies and describes eighty-seven emotions and experiences in her book *Atlas of the Heart*.

Some people find it easier to name and feel their feelings than others. But people who have or previously had eating disorders tend to have lower levels of emotion recognition and emotion regulation. The inability to regulate emotions is associated with the development and maintenance of disordered thinking and disordered eating behaviours. People with eating disorders are known for suppressing negative emotions and – no surprises here – this often doesn't end well. Overeating and emotional eating are often used by people as pretty negative coping strategies for negative emotions. We feed our feelings when we can't – or don't want to – feel them. And some of these things hang around for a while, even after recovery.

So now we're trying to teach our kids to name and feel *all* of the emotions, but we might not be doing this intuitively ourselves. We've found that in teaching our kids this stuff – reading them all of the picture books about feelings, talking about all of the feelings – it's prompted us to learn more about this (and wonder why we didn't know any of this before!).

As adults who aren't used to talking about their needs and

emotions, 'I-statements' are a good place to start in asserting ourselves and our needs. Try practising this yourself, and you can also teach it to your kids.

The framework goes like this:

I feel [insert feeling],
because [x happened].
Next time [here's what I want you to do instead].

Pretty revolutionary, right? But when it comes to naming the feeling, try to go beyond 'angry' or 'frustrated' or 'upset'. For those wanting something visual, google the 'feelings wheel' and start to experiment with articulating exactly what you are feeling and why. For those wanting a narrative description, definitions and storytelling, *Atlas of the Heart* by Dr Brené Brown is recommended reading for you. Dr Brown writes: 'We have compelling research that shows that language does more than just communicate emotion, it actually shapes what we are feeling. Our understanding of our own and others' emotions is shaped by how we perceive, categorise, and describe emotional experiences – and these interpretations rely heavily on language.'

We are taught to eat our feelings. The classic movie cliché is that she breaks up with her boyfriend, and she's sitting there with a tub of ice cream. And there's nothing wrong with that, but that's how we're taught – to associate negative emotions with a reward, to make it go away. So then the cliché

continues and she feels even more unhappy and unattractive because she's gained weight. After a while she throws away the ice cream and gets on the treadmill. If we took all of that messaging away, I don't think we would have so many issues with our bodies. If you want to eat ice cream because you feel sad, happy, angry, whatever, you just do it – let's not get food all mixed up with our feelings, or fixing anything.

LAURA MAZZA, MUM OF THREE, AUSTRALIA

@ITSLAURAMAZZA

While comfort eating can have its place, it isn't really a long-term go-to strategy for emotion regulation. So next time you are feeling triggered, you can put down the chocolate, or whatever it is you are sneaking to the cupboard to eat without the kids seeing you. Here are some more positive mindset shifts to try yourself, and teach to your kids:

1. **Reframing.** Changing the way you feel about something by changing your interpretation of a situation. 'I'm not actually sure that she is angry at me. There could be another reason why she hasn't written back to me – maybe her phone is out of battery?'

2. **Acceptance.** What's done is done. To help yourself feel better about it, you can focus on planning what you are going to do now. 'I didn't get invited to that party. That's okay, my own birthday is coming up in two months, I could start planning my own party.'

3. **Growth.** This is an opportunity for learning. 'So I didn't get that job. I now know how I would have responded to those interview questions.'

4. **Perspective.** Weigh it up. 'Not making the A-grade team sucks, but at least I am lucky that I still have a chance to play in the social comp.'

We talk about being comfortable in our own skin, but sometimes you're meant to feel that sense of discomfort, because it's a warning sign to you that you're in a dangerous situation. I want my daughter to be able to feel a sense of comfort and confidence in her own body in different contexts, but I also would like her to be able to have an awareness of her body in a way that can tell her things about her social situation. Being able to read your own body and feel that is so important. For example, I want to teach her about feeling nervous, and to think through: how do I know I'm nervous? I'm breathing a bit shallow, I'm a bit sweaty, actually. It's exactly the same feeling as when you're excited, so maybe that's also a bit of a good thing.

RICHARD, DAD OF ONE, PERTH

RESPONDING INSTEAD OF REACTING

As we move towards learning about how to manage our own emotions, and how to best support our kids to manage and regulate theirs too, one of the key messages that came out from all the experts we spoke to was the need to respond rather than reacting to a situation.

Teachers and school psychologists we spoke to told us what they see often is that parents can find it difficult to contain their feelings, such as fear, sadness or disappointment when their kids are struggling. For example, when their kids don't get into a team, when they're not invited to a party or when they get grades they're not happy with. Given that the high school kids have phones on them now, the kids are contacting mum or dad straight away and dumping their distress onto them. The kids feel better, but the parent is left holding the distress. And what happens next isn't pretty . . .

The parents often then call the school and essentially dump their distress onto the school by getting upset or angry about what they think has happened. This can make the problem much bigger and prevent young people from developing their own resilience, self-regulation, and problem-solving abilities. However, if a parent can respond instead of reacting, by reframing the issue, putting the disappointment into perspective and asking questions of the child to prompt ideas around what to do, then this is a much better approach.

Dr Jody Forbes, school psychologist and mum of two teenage girls, explains the implications of this response, and what to do instead: 'When parents react and get caught up in their own distress, they can rob their child of having the opportunity to sit with their distress, to navigate their own problems and learn how to respond in a situation like this.'

What does responding, rather than reacting, mean in practice? It means that you:

1. **Listen.** Actually listen. Don't jump in. Hear them out. Ask probing questions like 'Tell me more about that', 'What did you think about that?' or 'How did that make you feel?' Resist offering a solution.

2. **Acknowledge and validate their distress, and name the feelings.** Ask questions such as: 'I can see that that's so disappointing for you', 'I'm really sorry that you didn't get included in the team. What do you think happened?', 'What was that fight with your friends all about?'

3. **Reframe and empower them to move towards problem solving.** To get some perspective, you could ask: 'Could there be another reason why you missed out on the invitation?', or 'Maybe this really isn't about you'. To encourage problem solving, you can ask them: 'What's your next step? Do you want to talk to the coach? What are you planning to do?' And then if you really can't resist getting involved, you can ask: 'What can I do to help?'

By doing it this way, you are teaching your kids to navigate problems themselves. For when you're not there. This is a core skill for adulthood.

Dr Forbes offers further encouragement: 'When you do this, you're building their self-regulation by teaching them to deal with disappointment, you're building their confidence by empowering them to manage their own problems. When you react, you risk sending a message that you don't think they are capable of managing their own problems because you are solving them for them, and this can also make it a much bigger deal than it is. Many of us jump in too early and are too quick to rescue, predominantly because we ourselves can't bear to see our children struggle.'

Resilience and confidence is really a DIY project; as parents, or educators, we can't just hand it to our children. They need to build it themselves.

DR JODY FORBES

TALKING ABOUT FEELINGS

So many of us are triggered by the absolute overwhelm and complete frustration that is trying to make small people do things they don't want to do, all day. And trying to get young people places within the structures of time and space that they don't yet comprehend, all day. 'Angry Mum' or 'Angry Dad' is not who we thought we would be as we daydreamed, pre-kids, about rocking a baby gently in a light-filled, perfectly decorated nursery, or walking slow motion through a field of wildflowers with our clean, happy, compliant children. Instead, when we have 'asked nicely' seventeen million times and they still haven't put their shoes on, aaaalll of the things our parents yelled at us come marching out of our mouths. And then because the expectations of parents are so high now, we feel ridiculously guilty about having a pretty human reaction to a very frustrating situation.

Laura Mazza, a mum of three, knows this situation well:

So I'm not a perfect parent, I struggle with my own mental health issues. I write about that all the time. If I have anxiety, I become angry, and I get frustrated, and I lose my patience. In the past I would get triggered and then yell and then I would hate myself for it, and think I'm a terrible parent, which in turn would mean I would withdraw from parenting. And that's not what my children need. So after a lot of therapy, and the 'Circle of Security' course, I am now aware enough to recognise these triggers, but I also know that when there's a rupture, it needs to be repaired.

So now I know that, if I feel anxious, I'll tell my children: 'I feel like I've got a short fuse today, this is not your fault. This is my issue. Let's do something that we can all benefit from. Let's go to the park or you guys play, just let me sit for a couple of minutes.' I try to verbalise what I'm going through.

And if I yell, I apologise. I explain that I was angry, and I shouldn't have yelled. The other day with my son, I told him that he needed to get dressed; he was on his iPad. And I said, 'If you don't get off your iPad, we're not gonna go anywhere because you're not dressed.' You know kids and technology. He flipped. He came up to me as if he was going to grab my arms. And I was like, 'Whoa, we do not put hands on each other. You reacted angry, and that scared me because I don't want you to grow up thinking it's okay to hit women. And this is because when Mummy was little, her dad used to always hit her and hit her mum. And that's not okay.' I said, 'You're such an amazing kid, but sometimes you have problems expressing your emotions, don't you?'. And then, it was funny because later on, he said: 'I'm having trouble expressing my emotions. Can you help me?' And I was like, Yessssss, that's good, because instead of being a toxic male who can't express their emotions, let's just talk about it.

Many mothers of boys we interviewed for this book talked about the responsibility in particular of raising boys who are emotionally intelligent. We now recognise the value of explicit teaching about emotions, of labelling feelings and of talking about how we feel all the time in normal conversation.

Okay, so we're sold on the need to respond rather than react, but part of us also kind of hopes that we don't have to do this every day. We're kind of hoping that it's all smooth sailing. Dr Forbes has other ideas: 'You also can't develop resilience or confidence when the path is smooth and everything is done for you. Just like we tell students that they get "smarter" by choosing the harder puzzle because it forces their brain to engage and develop, so too does confidence and resilience require a bit of a challenge.'

Jody has two girls herself, who are right in the deep end of adolescence. She says: 'With my kids, I work on staying as calm as possible and do a lot of reframing. Inside, I might be saying "That is so unfair, how dare she leave you out – I've never liked her!" But if I let that out, that's my reaction. That's my own fear and insecurity. And it is not what she needs right now. I mean, we're human.

So sometimes we will do that because we're not perfect. But it doesn't make the situation better.'

A few years ago, Jody gave a presentation of the 'listen, validate and reframe' approach to dads. A few weeks later, she got a phone call. 'One of the dads called me and said that he had put the notes from the session on his bedside table. So, when there was drama with his daughter, instead of telling his daughter to calm down and stop being irrational, and jumping in to offer a solution, he went and looked at the notes – calmed down for a second, then went to listen to his daughter, acknowledge what she was feeling, and reframe the situation. The result was a lot less "You're always telling me what to do", "You don't understand" and "You're not listening to me".'

The idea is that as adolescents mature they start to engage in this process themselves. Their prefrontal cortex continues to develop, and by the time they reach Year Eleven or Twelve, Jody sees the girls at her school develop the capacity to notice when they are feeling upset and start to put things into perspective themselves. 'I have heard girls reflect and say "Oh, yes, but I didn't actually study as much as I could have for that" and "It's just one exam, it's not going to ruin my whole life". They start to accept that they're disappointed, but it doesn't overwhelm them, they can tolerate the feeling and start to problem solve for themselves.'

DISCOMFORT IS OKAY

Children will experience unpleasant feelings, and it is not the parent's job to eliminate discomfort. The parent's job is to help their children tolerate discomfort.

DR JODY FORBES

Discomfort is something many of us avoid. But as a school psychologist, Dr Forbes hears about all of the uncomfortable things that are happening in girls' lives, all day long. She says:

Of the basic human emotions, most of them are unpleasant. This is a foreign concept to many of our young people as they can almost seem repelled by discomfort; they are desperate to avoid or escape the feeling. We need to tell our kids that this is a normal feeling. You're feeling that way because you're human, and you're supposed to feel that way. It will pass, it is normal.

As a parent, it's hard to see your child in distress: you want to take that away, you want to make things better. One of the hardest things I've ever had to do is manage my own discomfort when they're in distress, and not jump in and fix the problem.

One thing we are also seeing now is that young people have a lot more instant gratification, and this makes it easier for them to avoid discomfort. When I used to take a photo, I had to take the rest of the twenty-four pictures on the roll, take it down to the chemist, wait a week until they got developed. And only then would I see what I looked like in a photo. Now, adolescents can take fifty photos and upload them to social media for instant feedback, getting 'likes' or having friends comment about how 'beautiful' or 'hot' they are. Technology is great for connection, but it also enables instant gratification – if you are bored, you can be instantly entertained. If you are lonely, you can connect instantly with thousands of people. If you are feeling self-conscious, you can receive instant affirmation from peers. Social media and technology allow us to meet many of our needs instantly, therefore the negative feelings are avoided.

I have worked with girls in the midst of distress regarding a relationship issue or a disappointing grade and I think: 'Oh, wow, that is awful', and they are feeling awful and I am feeling awful, and they want me to take this awful feeling away from them. But the best thing I can do is help them to accept that what they are feeling is a completely normal feeling, and to sit with that discomfort, and to learn how to manage it, because otherwise they're going to spend their whole lives trying to escape distress.

Some of the girls I work with are incredibly capable and strive for perfection. At times I have said to these girls: 'I want you to fail, I want you to make a mistake, I want you to crash and burn.' I want them to experience this while the costs are not too significant and they are in an environment of support, because then they will see that it is not a catastrophe, and they can manage and bear it. If they can dip their toe into the experience of making a mistake or 'failing', this can help them to stop fearing it – to understand that it hurts, it feels awful and horrible, but it happens, and they are strong enough to bear it and learn from it. If young people are not reassured that mistakes or failure are normal and tolerable, then they can spend their whole lives trying to outrun them.

Dr Forbes' advice:

1. Explain to young people that learning, confidence and resilience can grow when they accept that it's okay to make mistakes.
2. Negative feelings don't feel good, but they are normal, and they are okay. They will pass.
3. Sit with distress: by fixing it, removing it or rescuing our kids, they don't learn.
4. Encourage young people to tolerate these feelings, and reassure them that they will come back from them.
5. Help kids to problem solve in terms of what they might need to do to manage this feeling. It might be physical activity, it might be talking to somebody, it might be distraction, or a mindfulness meditation. Ask them 'What do you think you need right now?'

I want you to fail, I want you to make a mistake, I want you to crash and burn.

DR JODY FORBES

STRATEGIES FOR DEALING WITH DISTRESS

Seeing a young person in full-on meltdown mode is quite something. We've talked through a number of frameworks and patterns of responding rather than reacting in this chapter and this book. You may have noticed some common threads. Empathise and validate concerns, actually listen to what is going on for them, and empower them to take action. Dr Lisa Damour even has her frameworks available on a PDF download of a bookmark so you can print one off for every room in the house (for the link, see the Resources at the end of the book).

The great news is that you don't need to remember each specific framework for each specific situation. If you remember the key steps (listen, empathise, reframe), you can get yourself out of most potential situations patting yourself on the back and feeling pretty good about yourself and your parenting smarts.

It's like when it's the middle of summer; it's incredibly hot, and you can never imagine being cold again. And then, six months later, we're freezing. And we can't imagine being hot. It's like waves – they roll over us, but they pass.

DR JODY FORBES

But those frameworks are more for us as parents than for our kids. They help *us* to deal with the situation. Sure, we are modelling a great response to our kids, but what about if you want to teach them something that they can use themselves? The answer is: self-compassion (it's always self-compassion!).

Dr Veya Seekis has trialled a high school self-compassion program, and we wanted to include one of its concepts in this book, because we think every young person should be taught this.

Dr Seekis teaches young people a 'traffic light' approach for when they are feeling upset, anxious, worried or concerned about something. The 'something' could be not knowing the answer to a question on a test, the fact that there is a test, the fact that they are worried about the pimple they got on the day of the test, or the fact that they didn't get many comments on their selfie they took before walking into the room where the test was held. The same framework applies. The idea is that you start on the 'red light' and move through to the 'green'.

Traffic light approach to turn down your inner critic and bring on self-kindness

Red: Be mindful. Stop and think about what you are feeling right now.

Orange: Not alone. Who else might be feeling this way?

Green: Go ahead and apply kindness to yourself.

We want young people to feel their feelings, recognise their distress, and sit with it. But we don't want them to spiral down into a pit of despair over things that they can learn to become more resilient to. Realising that they are not alone in feeling a certain way aligns with the idea of 'common humanity' in self-compassion. When we know we are not alone, it helps to reduce our suffering. Finally, applying some self-kindness can be in the form of words or actions. This could be a simple affirmation, like 'I'm doing my best right now', or something that a kind friend would say. It could also be what Dr Kristen Neff calls 'soothing touch', the name of which may or may not appeal to young people, but the idea is easy – putting your hand on your heart, or rubbing the back of your neck in a way that helps you feel calm, supported, cared for and safe.

This traffic light idea can be really quick to run through, and, when practised over time, could really help people to avoid the sort of self-criticism that leads to more serious depression, anxiety, and body image and eating concerns.

Taryn

I don't talk about my divorce often, but I really think sharing a little bit of my pain might save a little of yours.

When I separated from my ex-husband after being together for nineteen years, the *worst day of my life* (or at least I thought so at the time) was sitting down to tell the kids that we were no longer going to be together. 'The chat' was horrendous. It had it all: tears aplenty, lots of questions I didn't know how to answer, and the kids were devastated and shocked. Guilt ate me up in one mouthful that day. Never in my life had I done something harder than breaking the hearts of my beloved children.

'Oh, kids are so resilient,' people would say to me often, in an attempt to make me feel better. (Which it *never* did.) Fast forward a few months later, and guess what? The kids were okay. They were right, kids are resilient, but more to the point – we all are. We might whinge and complain about change, but we human beings are very adaptable and better at change than we give ourselves credit for.

For years and years I held onto a marriage that was over, in order to protect my kids from being hurt. But I learned the lesson that my kids are going to feel pain in their lifetime, and it's not my job to stop it from happening at all costs.

It's also not my role to pretend that everything is okay when it isn't. Or not cry or show sadness. And as much as we loved Emma Thompson for putting on a brave face in *Love Actually*, sometimes we've got to show our kids the reality of life too.

We all collect stories along the way in this thing called life, and some of our darkest days pave the way towards our most beautiful and joyous moments. It's the ebb and flow of life. It is okay to feel pain. It is okay for our kids to experience pain too.

Action

☑ Print out the 'feelings wheel' (see p. 390 in the Resources for link) and practise talking about how situations and events make you feel. Try to go beyond just 'happy', 'sad' and 'angry'.

☑ Trial using I-statements, and teach the framework to your kids.

☑ Trial 'responding rather than reacting'.

☑ Teach your kids the traffic light of self-compassionate responses to times of distress.

11

Food

FOOD, GLORIOUS FOOD. THE END. That's how this chapter should be written; a mic drop moment even. Food is glorious, and fun, and delicious. But somewhere along the way we got ourselves all tangled up in a complex web of food rules, guilt and restrictive eating. The good news is, we have an opportunity to break the cycle for our kids so they can enjoy a lifelong relationship with food that is without shame and filled with deliciousness.

Zali

I was so excited to feed my babies 'real' food. Of course, I jumped in like a proper Type-A Mum – went to a workshop, bought two books, made thousands of purees only to learn that 'family foods' were now the thing to do, then switched from spoon-feeding to the scraping-food-off-the-floor chaos that is having three kids under four at the dinner table. A friend at my twins' mums' group had the best #parentinghack – to

literally buy plastic paint scrapers for after-dinner clean up
best tip ever! Despite the endless cleaning, I was really
excited to share the joy that food brings me with the kids,
and to some extent, I still am.

It was a little overwhelming, though, knowing that you
were responsible for ensuring that they ate a wide variety
of foods, and needed to have their calcium intake, fruit and
vegetable consumption, and fluid intake on an invisible
constant register in your head. After forgetting a few finer
details on a work project and asking people to repeat things
they knew they'd repeated to me before, I burst out with 'I'm
sorry, but I'm all out of RAM [yes, as in computer memory],
I have to remember how much calcium all three kids have
had at any one time throughout the day.'

Of course, like most things, it feels hard at the start of the
process, when they're learning to use a spoon and aim it towards
their mouths, but trying to encourage kids to eat well and move
their bodies feels like it becomes even harder as they get older
and start getting their own ideas. Less messy, maybe, but harder.
There is a constant pull between what you know they 'should'
have or 'should' be doing, and what they 'want' to have or 'want'
to do. And every time you try to convince them to go to the
'should' side, it's hard to do so in a way that they understand, but
also without oversimplifying to the point of delivering up diet
culture on a plate to them: 'Eat it because it is healthy', and 'Do it
because it is good for you'.

As kids get older there is a subtle but ever-present loosening of the tight grip of control that we had over their nutrition and physical activity as we try to teach them to do things and make good choices on their own. And this loosening of control is wrapped up with a side serving of fear, as we worry that they might not be getting the adequate nutrition they need.

The thing is, if we threw out our rule book and the need to control everything, we would probably realise that we can in fact trust our kids to eat and move in ways that are good for them. Kids are born with the ability to regulate their food intake. It's some of the things that 'society' teaches them that starts to mess that up: that you need to have meals at three arbitrary times of day, that you need to eat the 'real' food before the 'treats', that you need to eat what is served up on your plate rather than let your body tell you that you are full.

We heard a common story from many of the women we spoke to. Emma, a mum of three from Melbourne, told us:

Growing up I was shamed when I was eating some things, or too much. I was told 'Don't eat this, don't eat that, you'll get too fat.' When I didn't eat those things it was like, 'Why aren't you eating? Why haven't you finished your food? You need to finish your plate.' So you're literally sitting in the middle where you're so confused – you're praised for eating and then you're also punished for it.

So now we're trying to unlearn all of those things, and make sure we don't pass them on to our kids. We're trying to stop our parents' voices of 'You need to finish everything on your plate or there won't be any dessert' and 'Well, maybe we should send that food to the starving kids in Africa' from coming out of our mouths. We're trying not to say 'healthy' and 'junk' foods, because we know that giving food moral value is a slippery slope for those with perfectionist tendencies.

But all of this is hard within a culture that is still banging on about an 'obesity epidemic' and shaming foods, like fat, and the new enemy – sugar – accordingly.

People tend to think that if they stopped taking this cognitive control over eating, they would eat all the chocolate in the world, and gain huge amounts of weight. But our bodies are actually very good at regulating this for us. And in truth, the only reason why we would binge on all of those 'forbidden' foods is because we've made them so appealing by telling ourselves that we can't have them!

There are lots of books about food and feeding kids, and all of them are written by fabulous dietitians and nutritionists and people who know more about food than we do. But we can't write a book about body image without mentioning food and activity. And to be honest, there is a *lot* of information out there, and it's a bit overwhelming even for us! So we've reached out to the best and curated the things you need to know here. We will bring you just a taste of the information here and you can go to the Resources for the full meal.

WHO DOES WHAT AT THE DINNER TABLE

The one model that is widely recommended by dietitians and psychologists is Ellyn Satter's 'Division of Responsibility' model. This approach to feeding children really focuses on parents trusting that their children can determine when they are hungry or full. This allows parents to have a structure that allows them to trust that their children will eat a wide range of foods, and meet their nutritional needs, while maintaining a positive relationship with food, and learning about their internal signals of hunger and fullness.

In this model:

1. The parent is responsible for *what*, *when* and *where* they eat.

2. The child is responsible for *how much* and *whether* they eat.

For example: The parent decides that dinner will be at 7 pm, at the table, and decides what the meal will be. In this approach, children are encouraged to select what items from the meal and how much they want to eat by serving themselves, and encouraged to try what is on their plate, but ultimately decide whether they want to eat or not. There are a few other guidelines around what parents and children should do, and you can look into the resources around this model if you want more than just the tasting-plate version of this approach.

Our aim here is to try to neutralise food and listen to our bodies. We don't want to attach moral value to food by talking about 'good' and 'bad' foods. Labelling 'junk' and 'good' and 'bad' foods, and even talking about 'healthy' and 'sometimes' foods can be problematic, as it places some judgement on the foods, but also relies on kids learning which foods are 'healthy' and which might not be 'healthy' – which is a cognitive rather than an intuitive process. Speaking of intuitive, we want to teach our children to self-regulate instead of us limiting access to foods. By limiting foods too much, we make them special, so they will want them even more.

In creating the 'Confident Body Confident Child' program for parents of two- to six-year-olds, researcher Dr Laura Hart conducted a study where she collated all of the advice given to parents and had experts choose the most important bits. The ones that were most strongly endorsed included:

- Role model consuming a variety of nutritious food and drinks.
- Make nutritious food options available.
- Avoid 'banning' foods or labelling some foods as 'bad'.
- Encourage kids to eat when they are hungry and stop when they are full.
- Be aware that kids have different food needs to adults and that these will change over time.
- Make mealtimes fun by focusing on family connection and conversation.

This program has been found to increase the knowledge and confidence of parents, and for parents to use significantly more positive parenting strategies in relation to food, movement and body image.

Dr Carolina Lunde has spent a lot of time interviewing adolescents about their bodies. After speaking about the 'ideal' food environment and talking about different ways of managing food in the house with so many other experts, Carolina, also a mother to four children (fourteen, eleven, eight and three years old), keeps it real:

The idea of sitting down and having a lovely dinner together where we are sitting and talking, it's a lovely idea, but it's really chaotic at our place, and there are a lot of other things going on. So we don't get to do that in everyday situations. It's probably more on the weekends that we get to all eat together.

She goes on to explain:

There are so many things that you're supposed to do as a parent. And so many things you need to know about, and learn, and manage. Mothers are really struggling with working full time, having two or three children, lots of activities, a partner . . . people struggle. There are so many ideas of how you're supposed to do things, including eating, including exercising, including your social activities. So, I'm not sure if it's that realistic, to follow mindful eating or intuitive eating all of the time. I think you just have to do what you need to do to make sure they are fed and happy. Sometimes even the bar of 'good enough' parenting is too high for us.

We 100 per cent agree.

MINDFUL EATING

Most of us have some experience of eating mindlessly – you reach your arm over without taking your eyes off the screen and when your fingers hit the cold hard bottom of the bowl of chips, you're like, what? Where did they all go?! Mindful eating involves paying a bit more attention to the body-related sensations (like feelings, hunger and fullness), and to thoughts and feelings around food. Similar to mindfulness in general, the idea is that we don't judge, compare or apply 'shoulds' to what our bodies are telling us about what we want to eat, how much, and when. Mindfulness and mindful eating have been associated with lower binge eating and disordered eating in general. There are a number of books and resources about raising kids to eat mindfully. In general, these approaches involve listening to hunger and satiety cues, paying attention to the body, trusting the body to know what it wants, focusing on what we are eating when we are eating it (not eating 'mindlessly'), and addressing our feelings and emotions (not eating them!).

> **When my kids were really young, I read that you shouldn't tell them to finish their plate – it was always 'Listen to your body', 'Pay attention to when you're hungry'. We try to talk to my daughter about needing the energy from her food to get through that soccer training – to connect it back to the things she cares about, and the importance of having energy to do those things.**
>
> **SHARON, MUM OF TWO, BOSTON**

INTUITIVE EATING

We talked a bit about intuitive eating in Part One, but we need to include it here as well. Although mindful eating is a good place to start with kids who have never considered dieting, intuitive eating is the place you go when you've noticed that they are falling into some dieting behaviours.

The ten principles of intuitive eating (see pp. 107–8 in Part One), as developed by Evelyn Tribole and Elyse Resch, mostly revolve around unlearning the dieting mentality and the judgement of 'good' and 'bad' foods. It includes learning to trust the signals from our bodies that tell us what and when to eat, and when we are full and satisfied. There are books and links relating to this in the resources section.

> **Children automatically eat intuitively. If you watch a child who has free rein of the kitchen, they will graze all day, if you let them. We do this at home. We have a drawer full of fruit in the bottom of the fridge, and we have a snack drawer with all the foods that he can eat.**
>
> **DR MEGAN LEE, BODY IMAGE RESEARCHER AND MUM OF ONE**
> **@MEGANLOVINGMEAGAIN**

Intuitive eating encourages us to feel our feelings but deal with our emotions somewhere other than the pantry and the chocolate stash. By meeting our body's needs, eating what and when we want, with no restrictions on certain foods, and therefore feeling satisfied, we avoid initiating our body's psychological and physiological mechanisms that drive us to binge on things, or crave things. Because we are never deprived, we are never compensating for that.

It sounds kind of simple, but what is really impressive about intuitive eating are the benefits. This way of eating has been studied by so many researchers around the world – all of whom confirm that eating intuitively is associated with positive physical and mental health outcomes. People who eat intuitively have better body image, self-esteem and wellbeing, and lower use of disordered eating behaviours like skipping meals, vomiting and binge eating. Most people assume that if they eat like this, they will go nuts eating all of the things, and gain a lot of weight. But the research shows that people who eat intuitively have a lower BMI and maintain a more stable weight over time, instead of fluctuating up and down from restricting and then compensating for the deprivation.

It's so important that we start to teach, model and encourage adolescents to eat intuitively at this critical developmental stage. Adolescence is pretty much the point where we solidify a lot of our ways of eating, and where a lot of people start to change their food intake in order to try to change their bodies. Girls in particular can start to experiment with controlling what they eat, and with dieting. It is important to try to fit in some modelling of, and conversations about, listening to and trusting your body wherever you can.

Zoë Bisbing, eating disorder psychotherapist and leader of the Full Bloom Project, adds:

The only way our kids can develop trust is if there's also a decent amount of structure around meals and feeding. I think that any time we talk about chilling out around food, we have to offer parents some steps to increase the structure and feel like they have some control, but also provide the kids with some boundaries. It's not about increasing the rules or the rigidity about what you're feeding, but it is about being very clear with yourself and with your family in terms of how things work in your home.

Some people think: 'Oh, but my kid will never stop eating cookies' – but where would your child get an unlimited supply of cookies? If you've got a plate of cookies, then they can experiment with how it feels in your body to eat two, three or four cookies and it gives you an opportunity to educate them around connecting the way their body feels with the food they've eaten, as well as starting to self-regulate around the foods that they love.

The thing about intuitive eating is that it offers a set of guidelines. Sometimes this is what teenagers are looking for – some boundaries around how to navigate some of the situations that they find themselves in. Intuitive eating gives these ten guidelines to follow, to think: what does my body need right now? What do I need right now? And what, from the choices available, is the best thing for me to eat? And when should I stop?

BODY POSITIVE FOOD AND EATING – RESPONSES TO EVERYDAY SITUATIONS

Managing food and mealtimes is a lot, and sometimes (hello school holidays) kids seem to be needing/wanting 17,654 meals a day . . . so how can you gently guide them towards eating the things that are good for them and listening to their body without this becoming a full-time job? We asked our experts for their input and have some suggestions here, but if in doubt, just remember to approach with curiosity.

Situation	What you can say
When you are suggesting foods and snacks to eat	'If you eat this, it will give you more energy for the game later on', or 'I wonder if your body needs some more fuel before we do XYZ?'
When you are suggesting healthier alternatives	'Tell me more about why you want [the food they want].' Then you can emphasise the nutrient content of healthier food: 'There are so many more good vitamins and minerals in this banana that will be great for your heart and muscles.'
When you are helping kids to regulate their intake	Instead of saying: 'Do you want more?', say 'Are you still hungry?' That way, you are connecting intake to the feeling rather than the wanting. You can say: 'So tell me how your stomach feels?' or 'Is your tummy full?'
When it's close to mealtimes and your kids want a snack	'Lunch/dinner will be ready in ten minutes and what I am cooking right now will give us much more energy and nutrients. Can you show me how you can wait until then?' or 'Here are some things I've chopped to go in the dinner, you can eat some of these.' Or you can try distracting them by getting them to join you with the cooking.
When they don't like something	You can model or encourage them to say, 'I don't like the way this is cooked', or 'My body doesn't feel like eating this today', rather than 'I don't like this', so that they stay open to trying that food when it is prepared differently in the future (and you don't feel so rejected when they dismiss your creations).

When they 'weren't hungry anymore' at dinner but want a snack before bed	You can try to talk to them about whether they were really full at dinner time, or if they were tired of eating the food, or didn't like the way the food was prepared. The response to this varies by child, but also depends on how much they are growing at the time. You can have a set range of foods (e.g., fruit, yoghurt, sandwich) they can have before bed, or have full access to snack and fruit drawers at all times.
When they are chowing down on their Easter eggs/ Halloween lollies/all the good stuff	Connect back to a past experience when they ate a lot and then got a tummy ache: 'I just want you to check in with your tummy, because remember last time when . . .' You can also encourage them to choose which ones they want to eat now, and ask: 'Which ones should we save for tomorrow?'
When they are asking for the 17,000th snack that day	'Are you actually feeling hungry? What else might you/your body be wanting?' Maybe they are hungry – or maybe they just want a cuddle.
When you are trying to avoid saying 'Eat it because it's healthy', because a certain body image book told you not to ☺	Try not to go on about 'Ooh, this is really healthy for us.' Instead say things like: 'Look at these beautiful greens' and 'This is so yum – I really love this dinner', or talk about how the food/meal makes you feel 'full of energy' or 'helped you focus' rather than attaching 'health' or 'good/bad' labels to certain foods.
When you feel like you want or need to improve what your kids are eating	Instead of focusing on what to remove, focus on fitting in more fruit and vegetables first. 'Let's see how many more colours we can get on our plate.'

TRY NOT TO PANIC ABOUT NUTRITION

Dr Stephanie Damiano is a body image researcher with a specific focus on childhood. She has developed programs for parents of young kids and kids in primary schools, and has two kids of her own. Stephanie is also the manager of the Butterfly Body Bright program at the Butterfly Foundation.

After speaking to so many parents, we've noticed that we all seem to have moved away from concepts we were raised on, like 'Finish everything on your plate' and 'Don't eat that, it will make you fat'. We've moved away from labelling foods 'good' and 'bad'. But in most cases, we have just moved to other labels, other dichotomies, like 'everyday' and 'sometimes' foods, or calling some foods 'treats'.

Stephanie has other ideas. 'We can just call food what it is,' she says. 'If you're going to kind of label food or categorise food in any way, then categorise it based on what it is.' So rather than calling things 'healthy foods', we call them a fruit, vegetable, potato or strawberry. As soon as we start to label things – even with the label of 'healthy' – we start to attach a moral association of good-ness to those foods, which automatically demonises the 'other' group. So rather than 'healthy foods help us grow', it can be 'fruits and vegetables help us grow', they help our brain to function, or whatever you are trying to convince your child at the time.

In giving workshops to parents, Stephanie reflects:

I still remember one parent saying, 'It just makes me so anxious that they won't eat their dinner because they're waiting for dessert!' I said, 'Okay, well, what's for dessert?' It was fruit and yogurt. Not a big deal. Pretty nutritious. So starting to change the language around food may be useful. e.g. maybe instead of saying that we're 'having dessert', we're having 'fruit and yogurt.'

It's the same with the word 'treat'. I say 'Isn't it a treat when we get to see our friends', or 'What a treat to go to the park and have a play'. I don't use it around food, but a lot of people in our lives do and so does the media children are exposed to. When my daughter says 'I feel like a treat', I will question, 'Well, what do you mean, a treat?' It turns out that she wants some chocolate. So I will say, 'Oh, you just want some chocolate. Okay, so tell me you want chocolate.' Introducing the idea of a 'treat' makes it seem special and forbidden, and restricting that is going to make them want it more. So let's call it what it is and normalise it a little.

And this is where we get to the hard part. Most of us are afraid that if we let our kids access whatever foods they want, and have as much as they want, that is all they will eat. It's really hard to let go of the habit of restricting certain foods for 'treats' and 'dessert' and 'special' times – particularly if that's what we grew up with. Here, Dr Damiano reminds us to think of the overall goal of health and wellbeing, and having a positive relationship with food and eating: 'If we're worried about their growth, eating some chips or chocolate every day is unlikely to stunt their growth, or make them malnourished in any way when they are eating other more nutritious foods as well.'

What it comes back to for a lot of people is a fear of fatness, and a fear of their child being 'unhealthy'. And that's it right there. When we were young? We were told 'Don't eat that, you'll get fat', or 'Don't eat that, it's unhealthy'. And then we've had twenty years of anti-obesity messaging that's really kind of reinforced the fear around that. Now we're evolved enough that we know we probably shouldn't say it to our kids. But the fear is still there.

And it's easy to be afraid. Most of us, at some level, feel like we are being judged about how good we are as parents, by how well we manage this whole food situation, as evidenced by our kids' bodies – by what they look like. It's so much more visible and obvious than getting good grades, and so much more constant than their behaviour.

Dr Damiano drops in with her wisdom here:

Children come in all sorts of different shapes and sizes, and there will be some variance in kids' height, weight, shape and size naturally as there is with adults. What parents need to know is that, as long as you feel comfortable that your child is eating a wide range of foods, enough nutrients to help their body grow and fuel their brain, and they're moving their body fairly regularly, there just has to be a level of acceptance that their child's body is going to do whatever it was naturally designed to do. I think that's really hard to accept, because we live in a society that doesn't make us feel like that's okay.

We see this coming out, in particular, in situations where parents have got a larger child and a smaller child, and the way they feed them is different. So when the smaller child wants a second piece of schnitzel they are like: 'Yeah, go for it.' When the larger one reaches for the tongs they will say, 'Oh, are you sure you're not full?' But we have to allow them to regulate how much they are eating, like we did when they were babies. Irrespective of size and weight, all children benefit from a range of foods and the opportunity to have a positive relationship with food and eating.

And then somewhere along the way parents seem to forget that we have this spectrum of sizes and start to think of their kids as 'doing okay' or 'overweight'. As we talk to parents around the world, we find that a lot of them classify their kids into these categories, just based on the way they look. Parents will say, 'Well, she is a little overweight.' Then they'll show us a picture. And what we see is this gorgeous kid who fits somewhere within the glorious spectrum of different shapes and sizes of people that we have on this planet and by the sounds of things, is perfectly healthy. So we tell these parents the best thing that you can do is just accept their body. Encourage them to move, doing things they love. Nourish their bodies with a wide variety of foods and listen to their bodies telling them when they are hungry or full. Trust that their bodies are still very much 'in progress' throughout puberty. And love them hard along the way.

The general advice here is to try and step back and play the 'long game'.

My oldest is ten next week – she's got a fast metabolism and usually, you just kind of can't fill her up. But throughout this period of being in lockdown, and higher stress, there's definitely been a change in her appetite and the way that she eats. Not removing food groups or things but there's just definitely

been a change. So my perspective initially was 'Ahhh, she's not getting enough energy and she's in a lighter body already, is that affecting her mood? Is she able to concentrate at school?' but then I took a step back and I looked at the bigger picture and thought, okay, there's a lot happening that's going to influence her eating patterns and her eating behaviours right now. I've tried to step out of the fear and worry and evaluating everything day by day and look at things a bit more broadly.

KYLIE, MUM OF TWO, MELBOURNE

WHAT TO DO IF YOU ARE WORRIED ABOUT EATING DISORDERS

Okay, so we just said 'Don't panic' – but what if you are really worried?

For this, we've called in the big guns. Danni Rowlands is the national manager for prevention services at the Butterfly Foundation, an organisation that provides body image and eating disorder resources. This isn't just her title. Danni embodies this role, and she's been in it for a long time, and there are so many resources around that just wouldn't exist if Danni hadn't advocated for them. Much of Danni's work is with schools and families, and she has her own two children, aged ten and eight.

One of the main things Danni is passionate about is educating parents so they know more about some of the very early signs and behaviours that might lead to eating disorders, and can arm themselves with information and resources to act. She told us:

It's not just that a child feels not great about themselves this morning, and then they diet in the afternoon, and end up with an eating disorder by bedtime – it doesn't work like that.

There are lots of things that will influence your child's body image along the way. And obviously, as a parent, you are one of those things – a very, very vital and important thing. But also, you're not the only thing. When young people become unwell, so many parents have that knee-jerk reaction and ask themselves 'What have I done as a parent to cause that?' We do see a lot of fear coming from parents in our parent sessions, where they ask: 'My child's decided to become a vegetarian, what does this mean?' Or, 'My child's friend has an eating disorder, are they going to catch one?' It's not that simple, and it's about more than just hating your body. There's a lot happening around a young person, and it's great if parents can be informed, be aware, also alert to different things, but not be alarmed or work in a way that is constantly in fear.

Danni describes four stages that are on a continuum or a pathway of eating disorder development:

1. **Healthy thriving:** Appreciating their body, enjoying food, engaging in exercise.
2. **Dieting:** Exploring diets, talking about themselves and their bodies, but also other people's bodies in more critical ways. Higher engagement with appearance-focused social media

and seeking out content online that might influence the way they feel about their body, typically in a negative way.

3. **Disordered eating behaviours:** Engaging in more extreme eating and exercise, removing food groups from the diet, language used is pretty critical and harsh of themselves, but also of others, competing and comparing bodies and appearance, low mood and anxiety or other mental health concerns may also present. Behaviours become more consistent.

4. **Eating disorders:** Disordered thinking and behaviours intensify and can present in a range of different ways, but in general the person's behaviours are interfering with their regular life; that is, they are affecting their school or social life.

When we have babies, feeding and weight is the one thing we have to know they are thriving. We learn to attach our kids' weight to how successful you're doing as a parent very early on. This is great when they are babies, but as they grow, we need to remember that they don't all grow at the same pace, and the graphs and percentiles and things don't consider all of the things that make up body size or health or wellbeing. I think as parents we have to give ourselves a lot of compassion around this because eating, weight and growth can be incredibly complex and challenging.

DANNI ROWLANDS, BUTTERFLY FOUNDATION

If you are concerned, one of the best resources is the Butterfly Foundation helpline. This is a webchat or phone line that you can call and talk through your concerns, ask whether things are normal or not, and get information about what the next steps might look like.

Danni tells us:

When people call the helpline, they are generally feeling nervous, maybe a bit confused, maybe incredibly stressed, or feeling like they are at a crisis point with what's happening in their home. An important thing to know is that the helpline isn't a crisis line. It's not like a 000 call where you're asked, 'What's the problem?' It's not like that at all. You will speak to someone highly trained in eating disorders who is a professional counsellor, so when you call, they will know what questions to ask so you can have a conversation. They're there to speak to you and chat, to support you, and can offer referral information and direct you to evidence informed resources.

Often parents will be thinking, 'Oh, I won't call, because it's not that bad yet, and I don't really have anything to report, but I'm a bit worried.' That's a perfect time to call because there may be some strategies or suggestions and referrals that could be offered that may prevent things going down that more serious path. So don't ever think you are overreacting. Trust your instinct as a parent, call up or use the email or webchat, and just have a conversation. You can be anonymous if you want to – you can just be seeking out some more information. The Butterfly Foundation website [see Resources, p. 391] also has a heap of resources and information as well.

Some of the things to look out for among young people and their friends include:

- Openly criticising their body.
- Spending a lot of time in front of the mirror, or checking their appearance.
- Talking about their own appearance in comparison to others.
- Withdrawing from the family, particularly around mealtimes.
- Becoming more secretive around food.

If you are starting to notice some red flags, here's your plan:

1. **Be kind to yourself.** Take a break from the worry. Relax. Do some self-compassion meditation. Realise that this is not your fault. Decompress a little.

2. **Know your role.** You are the parent. Even if you have a psychology degree or recovered from an eating disorder yourself, you are still the parent. You don't need to obsess over finding the 'right' things to say. You don't need to figure out how to fix this – there are trained professionals who have that job. Yours is to love and accept your kids unconditionally. Even if it's hard.

3. **Connect to services.** These experiences are common. There are support services available to guide you in terms of the pathways to take for help for your child, but there are also support services with other parents

who know what this particular type of stress feels like. Use them!

4. **Connect to each other.** You can't control everything, but you can do some nice things together to maintain your relationship with your child – particularly when there is so much tension around mealtimes. See if there is a craft activity you could do together, or meditation you could talk about to 'help them relax their brain'.

5. **Access help yourself first.** Call the Butterfly Foundation helpline, and get your questions answered and some ideas for where you need to go for help. If you can visit health professionals on your own first, do so, as it means you can speak openly without your child hearing you talk about them.

6. **Consider what your child is hearing.** Doctors and specialists often expect you to talk in front of your child – about your child – while they are listening. This is probably more relevant for younger children, but we've started taking devices and noise cancelling headphones to appointments and making it clear that if they want to talk to us about the details, they can do it while our children are distracted.

7. **Reframing help.** Although seeking help is essential, it can be challenging, as doctors and specialists have processes that you need to move through in order to access care – like weighing children, which could potentially be a trigger for further anxiety. You can talk about what to expect in ways that make it seem normal – and not like there is anything wrong, like: 'They might want to check how you

are growing', or 'You might need to jump on a scale, but they do this check with lots of [your child's age]-year-olds'. If you think that weight could be triggering, you can ask for your child to be 'blind weighed' where the actual number is covered.

TURNING POINTS FOR CHANGE

If your young people are showing signs of being really dissatisfied with their bodies, there are a few options for changing this.

There are a range of different programs and resources that are available to use with your child, in your home, and we've listed some of these in the Resources section at the end of the book. There are multiple evidence-based resources that can be implemented in schools, and in community group settings. Don't assume that your child's school already knows about these – you are allowed to pass programs on to them. And there are a range of things you can do to decrease exposure to potentially harmful comments and environments – we've already talked through many of these in this book.

But sometimes, focusing so much on the issue can make the issue more of an issue.

In a Swedish study conducted by Dr Holmqvist-Gattario, with adults who had a negative body image as teenagers but who now felt much better about their bodies, there were three key turning points identified. Individuals who now had a positive body image had found belonging and acceptance in peer groups, a sense of accomplishment in their unique achievements, and worked on their mindsets. This leads us to some guidance for how you can steer your young people in these directions.

- **Find your people.** Encourage your children to find friends and a peer group where they feel accepted and like they belong, or a romantic partner who supports and appreciates them, and move away from groups or contexts where they might be teased or bullied about appearance. So if there is some drama happening with their friend group from school, could you suggest they connect with a friend from an extra-curricular activity?

- **Feel good about other things.** Help your children feel a sense of accomplishment through hobbies and activities, or by having a part-time job. Could you seek out activities or community groups where your child could realise what their bodies can do and feel good about it? Like realising that they are actually great at singing, chess or mowing lawns?

- **Mindset.** Practise body acceptance, develop strategies to avoid or ignore negative body-related information (for example, curating, deleting, or setting limits to social media use). Help them realise that pursuing beauty 'ideals' means having to sacrifice other things in life.

Perhaps some of the easiest actions we can take to improve eating behaviours don't actually focus that much on food and eating at all.

FAQs

Q: I've noticed recently my husband will pack my daughter (aged thirteen) the same lunch that she used to have, but it will come back and she's eaten one thing out of there. I'm not sure whether she just isn't hungry, or if she is selectively eating less. At night, she eats a normal-sized dinner, and I've never heard her say: 'I want to lose weight', but I do wonder how much of this is her choosing not to eat things. Or is she just busy? I don't know.

We put this FAQ to a range of experts. Dietitian Carole MacGregor advises: 'If it's a one-off, I think I would get them to tune in and recognise how it feels in their body when they don't eat, and to realise that this might make them feel a bit cranky, or "hangry", and that they can't learn as well or have as much energy to play sport as if they had fuelled their body.'

If it's an ongoing situation, most of the experts suggest asking some really casual questions to find out what else is going on for her, and to listen (without judgement if possible!) to what else is going on. For example, are her friends also not eating their food? Is she too busy? Does she feel self-conscious eating in front of her peers? Have feelings of anxiety? Because if someone is continually not eating lunch, it's probably just a symptom of a bigger issue.

Danni Rowlands from the Butterfly Foundation says: 'In primary school settings, students don't always have sufficient time to actually eat. Eating at school is an important part of the school day, providing energy for their learning, movement and mood. One of the things that parents can do, if concerned their child isn't eating at school, is to talk to the school about what is happening at lunch time – it might be that more time is required, but it also might be that your child isn't eating at school and if that's the case, exploring that further and intervening early is important. And we also encourage parents to remind their children to keep their eyes on their own lunch box – lunch box shaming is a "thing" and it can impact the way a child eats at school.'

When it comes to teens, things can get a bit trickier because it depends on the reasons why they are not eating. They can also be busy with clubs and sports and extra-curricular activities. It's not always a break for them. 'Unfortunately, in many cases, eating just isn't cool – it's not the done thing, and they can get really self-conscious,' Danni says. 'I think we have to appreciate that, so we might offer a larger breakfast and a really solid snack after school so they can be getting the nutrients they need and the energy that they need to do their activities. Unfortunately, we do hear stories from schools about "diet clubs" and "health clubs" and things like that that happened among friendship groups and peer groups. Particularly in Year Seven and Eight, we are really seeing a lot of concern around eating (or not eating) lunch at school and while in the presence of friends.'

Q: My eleven- and thirteen-year-old girls seem to be eating a lot of sweet foods and have gained a lot of weight recently. I just want them to be healthy – how do I manage this?

Given the importance that society places on weight, appearance and attractiveness, it is natural that you would worry if your children do start to gain weight – particularly if you have had a challenging journey in relation to weight and body image yourself. However, weight gain throughout puberty is not linear: kids might store weight around their middle and then suddenly grow taller, or, for girls in particular, they might seem to gain a lot of weight on their thighs and bottom, completely changing their shape almost (what seems to be) overnight!

It's important to keep in mind that this weight gain is driven by hormones, and is biologically essential to puberty. You might see them eating lots of sweet foods that seem excessive to you as a rational adult, but teenagers do *lots* of things that don't make sense to adults, and this could be driven by their body seeking fuel for growth.

You might worry about their health, but also whether they will get teased if they are at a higher weight, which is possible. However, *all* of the research shows that making your child aware of, or focusing on their weight in any way, is really not a good idea – and that your opinion and acceptance of them, and the way they look is (deep down) more important than any throw-away comment that some kid says at school.

Rather than monitoring or changing what your child is eating, monitor and change what you think and say about it. As long as you are providing healthy, nutritious foods and opportunities to move, you are doing your job. It's time to trust the process, allow your teens some more independence and control, and know that everything will work out much better if your kids are kinder to themselves.

Q: At a barbecue, a friend's husband was visibly agitated at his daughter's eating behaviour, and what started out as 'I think you've had enough' turned to 'Do you really need a second helping of cake?' to 'That's disgusting – move away from the food table *now*.' What can I say to my friend to help her navigate this?

Zoë Bisbing reminds us to think about our overall goals. 'Often people are missing the forest for the trees – what they want is for their kids to be healthy, and have a positive relationship with food. But it's hard to control in that moment. What I want parents to know is that sometimes, the way they are behaving, in judging and commanding food rules, does not line up with their goals. I want people to understand that inducing shame, and signalling that foods are forbidden has almost the reverse effect, and is only going to make that kid want more without any connection to their hunger and satiety cues. In these situations, I recommend that parents try to relax – these sorts of environments are generally one-offs, it's not like they have access to a whole birthday-party buffet of foods every day.

You could try modelling a response to your own child as they approach the food table, and remind them to 'just check in with your tummy'. Zoë explains: 'At social gatherings where the feeding environment is less structured with my kids, I will say "You can have as many as you want – but I just want you to check in, because sometimes we can eat past the point of feeling comfortable, and then you might feel yucky." Reminding them to check in versus demanding that they stop eating is a totally different vibe altogether. It's no big deal to eat three cupcakes one day, but it is a big deal to have a positive relationship with food, which is what you're fostering in these moments.'

You could also mention to the parents that you've read a great book (this one!) and pass this on to them. Or try raising this later with the parents, maybe sharing some of your own stories about being shamed for eating as a kid, and the effect that it had on you. Or, you might choose not to say anything, but use the experience as a chance to learn and refine your own approach with your children.

It's a good idea for people to talk with their partners about what their food environment was like when they were kids and teenagers, but also how the environment, context and situation is different for your kids. Talk about the approach you want to take and why. Talk about whether you might think differently about a boy eating a whole loaf of bread after school to the way you might judge a girl eating a whole loaf of bread after school, because the way we expect people to eat is gendered. Talk about the things you remember your parents saying about food and bodies, and reflect on what that means for the way you will talk to your kids. You never know what comments might stick, and how the words you say about their food intake or weight and shape might become the voices in their head later. Make those voices have a positive impact by gently introducing teaching intuitive eating, appreciating body functionality, and acceptance.

Q: My daughter has started dieting – what do I do?

This is such a hard question. And a hard situation. Because many of us might have been through this before. We might have dieted in the past, we might have made changes that may or may not have been successful. Some of us might have progressed to trying to diet and then that didn't work, so we used more and more restrictive methods. And that may have led to bingeing and purging, or it may have led to more disordered eating behaviours. So a lot of us have some experience with this.

It's really common for teenage girls to start to try to exert some control over their life and their bodies, and to respond to some of the pressures that they feel around their bodies by manipulating their diet. They get a *lot* of messaging about this, of course, from social media and from peers and from family. Diet culture makes it sound and seem very easy for us to lose weight, when in fact, it's physiologically quite difficult to lose weight and maintain that weight.

So if this is something that you're starting to notice with your teenage girl, it could be worth having a conversation about fuelling her body. Ask questions about how she's feeling about her body, or just feeling about her weight, why she's making certain choices around food.

'Approach with curiosity,' advises Danni Rowlands from the Butterfly Foundation. Don't come in all, 'Oh my gosh, what are you doing?' Try probing gently. She says: 'Appetites fluctuate, things change, tastes change, activity and interests change. Change happens and that can be really confronting for parents. We think just because they were like that last year they're going to be the same this year, but the food they liked last year, or last week, changes all the time. Try to take a step back in that moment if you see something that's changed in your child's thinking. Try to understand and look at it in terms of what is happening in their body at that time for their age, what's happening in their peer groups, and whether there are any other mental health concerns.'

When you are worried?
Take a breath.
When you are triggered?
Take a breath.
When you are scared?
Take a breath.

All of the experts and clinicians we spoke to advised a calm approach. All of them mentioned that you need to put your fears aside, and approach with curiosity. They all visibly demonstrated this – moving from a 'freaking out parent' mode, to sitting back a bit, taking a breath, changing their tone of voice to 'curious parent' mode.

Q: My fourteen-year-old son has started asking me to buy protein powder so that he can bulk up – is this okay?

Muscle-building supplement use is really common now – around 50 per cent of boys reported using some sort of supplements in our Australian study. Twenty years ago, when we asked boys what they were doing to gain weight, they would say they were eating more meat and eggs, and drinking more milk. Now they name the specific brand of the big tub of mass gainer, and pre- or post-workout formula. The supplement industry is huge and extremely profitable, and now very well embedded with specific stores in gyms and shopping centres.

Supplement use in adolescents is concerning for many reasons, partly because there is very loose 'regulation' of these products. It is possible for some products to fall through regulation loopholes because they are classified as a 'food' instead of a 'medicine'. The system is based on people reporting negative side effects or outcomes – and there are instances of this – with people reporting liver failure, heart attacks and death from seemingly innocuous products like 'green tea tablets'. As soon as one deadly ingredient is banned, another is created that is very similar but fractionally different. These products are often contaminated, or intentionally 'spiked' with illegal unapproved ingredients, and even then, they are not always withdrawn from sale. Claims on the packaging may be untested, so you may not be fully aware of what's in there, what can hurt them, and what could get them banned from competing in their sport.

We understand that boys want to use these things – they want to improve their sports performance and they want to be more muscular. So how can you use this safely? A standard whey-protein based powder from the supermarket is going to be very different from a jacked-up monster tub that might be being pushed on your son by the 'personal trainers' at the gym, or recommended by a sports coach. You can use the Informed Sport or ASADA (Australian Sports Anti-Doping Authority) Clean Sport Apps to check the relative safety, and whether there are any banned ingredients in the products they are interested in.

The two main ingredients to be concerned about are caffeine, present in huge amounts in 'pre-workout' formulas that are becoming more common, and anything that will be converted to testosterone in the body.

Zali was involved in the Goodform project, designed to help people feel better about their appearance so that they don't take supplements or steroids. As part of the project, they came up with a traffic light system. In general, if you look at the ingredient list and it looks like food – and perhaps some milk powder, flavours, colours etc., it should be okay: green light. If you look at the ingredient list and there are lots of long, chemical-sounding words that you can't say out loud because you did everything you could to avoid chemistry in high school, exercise caution: that's an orange light. And if there are numbers in the chains of long chemical-sounding words, that's probably going to get a red light. Anything injected into the body is absolutely a red light.

Rather than banning kids from using supplements, try to see this as a great opportunity for some teaching moments. Deconstruct the messages they are getting in the advertising, such as: 'Why do you think they've included a picture or an actual hulk-man on there?' and make sure that you reassure them that they will naturally develop muscle when their body starts producing its own (free!) testosterone. Talk about the instructions, dose and recommended use, and ensure that they are not exceeding the recommended doses. Suggest that you can buy more foods that naturally have protein for snacks, like cans of tuna, milk, and eggs. Use the quick opportunities to discuss things before their eyes glaze over. It might take multiple attempts, but in general, the longer you can keep them away from these supplements, the better.

And if you really have to get something, get the powder at the supermarket that is basically just 'milk powder that you add to milk' – the further towards the green end of the traffic light system, the longer it could be before they're going for the harder stuff.

Action

☑ Access and read up about intuitive eating. Reflect on what comes up for you as you read about this approach.

☑ Have a conversation with your partner about the food environment in your home. Reflect together on what the food situation was like in your houses growing up, what that meant for you, and how you would like to create a similar or different approach with your kids. Come up with some guidelines that you will follow, talk about the parts that are hard for you, and support each other as you learn to parent in ways that you might not have been parented.

☑ Inform yourself about disordered eating behaviours, muscle-building supplement use and eating disorders. Know what to look out for and where to go if you need further information or support.

12

Media

MOST PARENTS WE TALK TO will mention social media as 'problematic', and it is. The reason why we feel bad when we look at images of these models, celebrities, and even peers, is because our brain makes automatic comparisons with these people. We look at them, determine that we are not as thin/muscular/attractive/worthy as them, and it makes us feel bad. Decades of research has proven this. There is nothing about seeing these images that motivates us, inspires us or helps us to change our behaviour. Nothing.

Some people follow social media accounts because they think that if they look at the images long enough, it will help them to become more like that. It's just not the case. It's not how our brains work. When we compare ourselves (remember – automated process – thanks a lot, brain!) to other people, we feel bad, and that initiates shame and depression. Not exactly the best and most motivating starting point for your new exercise routine!

But to give you some good news, social media is only problematic if people are looking at certain things, and engaging in certain behaviours. So here's the upside: viewing images of average-sized models has been found to enhance body appreciation, or positive body image. Seeing more diverse body sizes and shapes, ethnicities, abilities, and so on, on social media, can improve your body image. Viewing action shots, where people are doing things instead of just posing, can help you feel better. Seeing fewer bodies in general – and more #funnydogvideos – can make you feel better. We can control what we see on our feeds, so let's encourage our kids to see the good stuff.

Remember *Dolly* magazine? We were never able to unfollow any of the photo contributors. Never able to report an ad at the click of a button. We now have so much more control over what we are exposed to, and there is no place where we have more control than on social media, where we can follow and unfollow with the click of a button. Sure, there is 'the algorithm' (say this like 'Oooh, it's a ghoooost'), but you can tame the algorithm a little to show more positive things. It's still a wild beast, and things will creep in, but you can shape it to some extent.

We can think of what we see in the media (and on social media) as what our brains are consuming each day. We want to nourish our brains with things that inspire us, interest us, educate us and make us laugh. It's okay to see some images of 'idealised bodies' every now and then. As long as they're not the only things we are looking at.

So here's how we are going to help your kids navigate this complex media landscape and still feel good about themselves. First, if they are still little, we can talk about how you control what they see. If they're a bit bigger, we're going to share some strategies for starting out on socials, and dealing with what comes up there. And then at any age, we can start to teach our children to be more 'critical' consumers of the media and see through what they see on screen or online so that it doesn't have so much of an impact. It's not easy. None of this is easy. But we don't need to panic about it.

We know that social media is probably making a huge impact on your life. So stop following that person you are comparing yourself to, stop looking at mean comments, and stop making yourself a person you are not. Life is about so much more than other people's opinions! Focus on other things – your dream career or trying something new. Enjoy your life – you only have one.

ALLY, AGE 14

MODELLING MEDIA LITERACY

We will never be able to fully protect our children from the impact of the media. Screens are everywhere. Even those of us who tried not to put our (first) kid in front of the screen, and didn't let them have sugar until they were two, eventually relent and then bask in the sweet, sweet relief of five minutes of peace while *Peppa Pig* or *Bluey* is on.

So they are going to have screens, and they are probably going to use social media. What we can do is encourage a healthy amount of scepticism about the reality and nature of what they are seeing so that they don't just drink it all in unfiltered.

Adolescents who have higher levels of media literacy generally have lower levels of body dissatisfaction. They are able to be more critical consumers of the media that they see, so it doesn't have so much of a negative impact. As parents, we can encourage our children to develop this skill by watching with them and questioning them about what they see.

It's easiest to start with advertising. After a funny or silly ad, you can ask primary school-aged children questions like 'What do you think they are really selling here?', 'Why do you think they used that person to sell that product?' or 'What are they trying to tell us?' Usually, in the case of TV commercials, advertisers are trying to link product consumption (let's say, for a popular brand of soft drink or large fast-food chain) with happiness, success and having a great time. So they use very attractive models, and show them having a great time so that we think that will happen if we buy the product. But did that same result happen the last time we stopped off at Maccas on our road trip? No. Will it happen next time? Probably not. They are showing us this because they want us to buy their product and then they will have more money.

Of course, asking these questions assumes that you are watching with them, and often, we are doing our own work while they are watching. It's pretty exasperating to have to watch YouTube videos of people unboxing and unwrapping things. It's not how we want to spend our time. But occasionally, if you're in there telling them that it's time to turn off their screens for a while, you can stop and watch for a bit and ask them questions about it. Most of the time, they don't realise that those women, or those kids, are showing us their toys because they want us to buy something. They think that 'ads' are the bits that interrupt their show. But when they watch unboxing videos, they don't realise that the whole show is an ad.

As kids get older, they can be exposed to a whole range of things through the shows, YouTube videos, games and movies they watch. Sometimes we don't even know they've seen something. Sometimes we do. They are going to see stuff. It's our job to help them interpret those images and messages, and to constantly remind them that what they see isn't actually real. They might have some of these conversations at school too, but when you do it at home, in relation to what they are already watching, it's more relevant.

Media literacy: Key questions to ask

- **Who created this message?** We're trying to get them to realise that what they see isn't happening for real. Someone 'constructed' this situation and this message, and they spent lots of money creating this message to try to tell you something.
- **What are we being sold here?** Sometimes it's hard to tell. By constantly asking this question, kids start to realise that even the subtle things are advertising, and even the social media they consume is sending a message or selling something.
- **Why might they have done that?** Did they use something to get our attention? Did some characters in a movie do something that reinforces gender stereotypes? Or break other stereotypes?

- **Why might they have chosen those people?** The key outcome here is to get kids to realise that what they see in the media isn't like real life. They might have chosen those people because of the way they look and they want us to associate being good-looking with a product. Those people on the screen were chosen because they look a certain way.
- **Is that what we think or do in our family?** If a character is doing something mean, or saying things that don't align with your values (hello, every kids' film made in the nineties!), you can relate this back to your own family and remind them of your values. What we watch is just for fun and entertainment – it doesn't show us how to be in real life.

We're not saying that you need to interrupt movie night with a PowerPoint presentation and a lecture about corporate media giants. You can use just a few questions, here and there. Sometimes during the show, sometimes after.

Dr Kristina Holmqvist-Gattario, a positive body image expert in Sweden, tells us about how movie night goes down at her place with her two boys, aged ten and twelve.

We know from body image research that criticism against appearance ideals, or having a more sceptical view, in terms of the importance of appearance, is protective of body image. If my kids and I watch a TV show or a film together, and I see something where they are showing 'idealised images' or where the characters are commenting on each other's appearance, I would say to my kids, 'Ooh, isn't that strange?' and ask questions like: 'Why do you think they comment on appearance as the first thing they do, why is that so important?' Last week for example, we watched *Grease*, which was a favourite movie of mine when I was younger. I was so shocked to watch it again as an adult – it's terrible in terms of body image! But it was a good movie to talk about stereotypes: gender stereotypes and appearance stereotypes. So I don't stop them from watching those things, but I try to watch with them, and we talk about it as we watch, or afterwards.

They've actually started questioning for themselves now, which is nice. So they will say, 'Mum, wasn't that strange that they did that?' But it takes time, you need to do it many times. Many, many times.

Here's what other parents from around the world say about modelling this media literacy:

My son loves Japanese anime – and while I can appreciate the style and the hair, there can be a lot of swords and violence and things. Sometimes I will ask about why they are fighting, and usually it's for a purpose. 'Ooh, that's interesting, do you think they are just doing that because they enjoy beating people up or killing?' It's usually not to try to really harm somebody, it's to protect something.

JOCELYN, USA

There are often deeper ideals or morals of fairness, of community, of loyalty, of what it really means to connect with people, a bigger theme. You could ask 'What do you think [character name] has realised here? What do they know now that they didn't at the start?'

MEGAN, TASMANIA

Be mindful of how female characters are treated. Women's bodies are often more exposed than men's, but rather than getting overly caught up in what they look like, we can ask: 'What are they trying to do? What are they trying to accomplish?'

SKYE, SYDNEY

You can model media literacy on socials, too. Teenagers are generally pretty into social justice. They seem to be programmed for fairness, and they really enjoy getting on top of a cause and just being like, 'That's not right. That's not fair. I'm going to do something about that.'

Let's work with that. Intuitive eating encourages young people to actively reject diet culture. And if you can start that process and make beauty standards or diet culture the bad guy, you're on to a winner.

So, say you see some celebs promoting a 'juice cleanse' on social media. Some of the questions you can ask:

- Does this cost us in terms of money? Is it expensive?
- Does this cost us in terms of our social health, because we're not going out to dinner and joining in with our friends?
- Does it cost us in terms of our psychological health, because we're worrying about what we are eating and what we look like rather than having good mental health?

- Does it cost us in terms of our physical health, because we're doing things that aren't actually good for our bodies? We might be getting injured at the gym, or we might be realising that we're feeling like fainting all the time, from the juice cleanse or something that they might be doing.
- Who benefits from these insecurities? Let's look up who owns this brand/company. How much are they making from preying on people's insecurities? Are we okay with this? Should we try to do something about this?

If we can get young people interested in taking an active role campaigning against diet culture, then that's probably the most protective thing we can do to prevent body image problems and disordered eating.

Taryn

My secret weapon in helping my kids get a handle on media literacy is Celeste Barber. If you don't know her and you're on socials, get her in your life immediately! Celeste Barber is an Australian comedian and media personality who is best known for recreating celebrity Instagram photos and videos. She is the queen of celebrity parody and has amassed a following of over 10 million people, including the people she takes the piss out of!

She'll take a video of a 'hot' Cindy Crawford sexily and provocatively drinking Pepsi in a TV commercial and do the same, with a lot less sexy and a heap more funny.

Over the years I've shown my kids a variety of her comical parodies. Not only do they think she is hilarious, these moments of lightness and laughter have created a space for us to have important conversations about advertising. For example, why did the model drink her Pepsi in the way she did? Do you think drinking Pepsi actually makes people feel that good? What do her looks have to do with a can of drink?

Celeste's powerful work came to a head recently. I was walking through a shopping mall with my daughter Mikaela and she pointed out an advertisement of a man and woman selling swimwear. The woman was posing in her bikini while the man was surfing some big waves. The woman's image had been heavily photoshopped and she was looking 'sexy' and 'pouty' in her bikini. Mikaela turned to me and said, 'Hey, Mum, Celeste should "do" this photo.' Instead of Mikalea seeing the woman as someone she aspired to be, she saw through it, and even went as far as to say, let's make some fun of the ridiculousness (and fakeness) of the image. As Celeste says, hate the game, don't hate the player. It's not about giving the model a hard time, it's just about getting our kids to understand that what they see isn't always reality.

STARTING OUT ON SOCIALS

Some of the biggest parenting questions of our time are: at what point do we let our kids have phones? And at what point do we allow them on social media? And what type of social media? When we know how addicted we are to our phones, and how social media makes us feel about ourselves, it's hard to imagine allowing that influence on our kids.

> When my girls were eight and eleven, there was this very early, very kid-friendly social media app where they made little music videos, an early version of TikTok. It was all very safe and parent-controlled, so I thought we would give it a go. My girls made these little music videos and did these dances and then strangers would like them, and they were just intoxicated by the idea that three other people, or maybe six other people, liked their little videos. It was like they were celebrities. So they kept checking it constantly and talking about '(squeal) how many people like us now' and '(excited squeal) look, someone has left a comment', and it was the most exciting thing in the world. But then they would check it and if there were no likes or comments they would be heartbroken and start to question whether the video was any good, and they would start to feel shame. Watching it happen in front of me so quickly – it was probably only three days after they had got an account or something like that – I was like 'Hold on, time out, we have to stop and have a conversation about this right away.' Seeing the power of it, that feeling of being liked and accepted online, and seeing how quickly they started to connect that to their self-worth was scary to me. I had to call time out on it, to go back and have some conversations, and to prepare myself for those conversations too, because it had all happened so quickly.

> **LEANNE, MUM OF TWO, USA**

In the discussions we've had with parents around the world, many of them seemed to be having some very smart conversations with and setting good guidelines for teens entering the social media world. This is a slow and progressive educative process, just like teaching them to walk or sending them off to school. It didn't just happen one day. You prepared for it, and talked about it, and it took a while to practise or get it right. Professor Linda Lin, Professor of Psychology and mum of two, has seen this in her research and in her home. Here's her advice on having some structure around social media.

1. **Chat early, chat often.** Make sure that you've had conversations about how images on social media don't represent real life; they are a highlight reel. Talk about how photos are edited, lit well, and posed in order to be the best possible version of what happened, and that people only usually share 'the good stuff'– not the times when their hair was a mess and they were upset about something.

2. **Friend them**. In the early days, you will want to have your kids add you as a friend on the account so that you can see what they are posting, what other people are commenting, etc. This acts as an opportunity for you to have a reminder to check in on what they are posting, but also, the fact that you are there might make them think about what they are posting and saying.

3. **Check-in.** Part of 'the deal' to allow social media is to agree to check in with them often regarding how they are going, and how it makes them feel. Open up regular conversations about what they have seen and how they feel that is good, like 'Do you feel more connected with your friends?',

'What have you seen lately that is funny?' and so on. As well as the not so good: 'Have you seen anything that made you feel bad, or like you need to change who you are or what you look like?', 'How do you feel after you've been on there for a while?', and 'How do you feel after you've taken a break from social media, or seen your friends in real life?'.

4. **Active consumption.** Encourage your kids to curate their account and to be active consumers of the content rather than passive. This is where you enable them to take the power that they have to make decisions about what they are seeing and who they are engaging with. Some families have 'Unfollow Fridays' – where they go through and take notice of what makes them feel good versus stuff that makes them feel bad, and then unfollow accordingly. Modelling this, and doing it on your own accounts alongside them, can help you have the sorts of conversations that can help them critique and contain the influences of these images on their body image.

5. **Keep talking.** Professor Lin suggests we say to kids, 'Come to me to talk through things that are confusing' so that they know we will welcome these discussions. The conversations don't stop once kids are off and away on social media. We need to keep the doors open to helping our young people interpret the world around them – particularly the advertising or more adult things that they might be exposed to. Tina, a mother of two in the United States recounts: 'I also told them that there's nothing that they can see on there that is ever going to shock me. They can come to me without shame about what they see – there's going to be a

lot of stuff that they can't control that's going to be coming in, it's going to be confusing, it's going to make them feel bad and good (sometimes at the same time). I want them to know that they'll never get in trouble for coming to me to talk about something that they have seen. I won't take their social media or their phones away from them. We can just talk about it so they can know what is going on.'

So how does this go down with the teens? Audrey, mum of two from the United States, reflected:

When I first started talking about all this stuff, I think they kind of were like, 'Yeah, yeah, yeah.' Especially in the beginning, when they didn't kind of realise how it was affecting them. I think they were like, 'Yeah, yeah, whatever, Mum, we will do whatever you say to allow us to have it.' Then with a little bit more time, I think they realised that sometimes it doesn't feel so good, and sometimes the way their friends are posting does actually make them feel bad. So then we started having more complex conversations around it, but we could only have those complex conversations because of some of the early conversations, that allowed for the more complex conversations down the line.

TOUCHY TOUCHY

According to the experts, some of the most problematic social media behaviours are around retouching, editing, filtering and photoshopping our own images, and being exposed to images that have been altered.

Many young women now feel that it is essential that they digitally alter the images of themselves on photo editing apps, or use filters provided by social media platforms if they are to post images of themselves. Researchers are still trying to figure out whether it is the photo editing that drives high body image concerns, or if it is the adolescents who are most concerned who are likely to edit their images, but the relationship is definitely there.

For some young people, it's always been possible to edit the way you present yourself online. It's completely normal to them. This seems to have prompted concerns among parents of young kids, as they worry that these behaviours are being normalised, as Simone, mum of two, explains:

When my family comes over they will take selfies with my daughter with all of the filters on and suddenly she has these cute bunny ears, or eyeliner and lipstick. I overhear her say, 'Oh, I look beautiful', seeing herself with computer-generated make-up on, and I cringe! I try to expose the kids to more diverse media, for example, but then also ways of thinking about themselves. So we talk about the fact that what really makes a person beautiful is what's on the inside, and that she is beautiful because she is kind to her brother, and beautiful all of the time, not just when she's dressed up.

I feel like it's my job to empower her to be critical of those messages, because she's going to be bombarded with them. I can tell her right now at the age of six that her beauty is within, but as she gets older, the world is going to tell her something very different to that. I feel like it's about trying to then just build her body appreciation and resilience to that.

Retouching has been around for ages – there are some dodgy cut-and-paste jobs of Oprah in the eighties, and many situations where photo editors accidentally added an extra hand or foot in the process of combining a few photos together. But the fact that this can now be done by anyone, on your own phone, without needing fancy photo developing equipment or a fancy computer program, is a bit of a concern – particularly when cosmetic surgeons report that people are turning up for surgery wanting to be made to look in real life like they appear online!

Retouching has been the focus of many legislative and public policy efforts, where countries like Israel, France and Norway have passed laws requiring disclaimers for digitally altered images. Unfortunately, the research (much of it led by Professor Marika Tiggemann, an Australian body image researcher featured in the first *Embrace* film) has found that regardless of the type or wording of the warning, disclaimers on retouched images did not reduce the negative impact of exposure to images that had been retouched.

If you notice a lot of editing or filter use on your kids' own images, or the ones they are looking at, what can you do? Gently probe to ask what has changed about the image, or why they are editing it. Try going #filterfree and give positive encouragement and reinforcement around that. You could explore hashtags and challenges like #nomakeupselfie or #instagramvsreality and take note of the reels showing filters versus real life faces. Dr Jasmine Fardouley's research has confirmed that viewing these images has less harmful effects than viewing images where women wear makeup and are edited. Could we encourage young people to push back against filters too?

LEAVE A COMMENT

Much of our understanding about what goes on when adolescents use social media comes from our own experiences, or the brief glimpses we get over a teen's shoulder. So we were both excited when Dr Beth Bell and Dannielle Paddock agreed to speak to us from York in the UK. They had just spent a lot of time interviewing adolescents about their social media experiences.

There are quite a few differences between social media platforms, but it turns out that the types of comments that young people give on social media depend a lot on whether people are identified or anonymous. When anonymous, they are much harsher than when they are identified. The negative impact of the comments on teens' posts isn't just because someone might say something negative about them, it's more that young people get upset if they don't get *as many*, or the type of positive comments they expected on an image that they post. On platforms like Instagram, where you know who people are, positive comments and compliments are common, but there's an element of quantifying how many positive comments you might have got. Beth explains:

If they post a picture of themselves and only got ten comments, whereas another post has got fifty comments, they kind of compare and use that as evidence as to why they look good, or what they have to do to get that positive reinforcement.

When you give a compliment face-to-face, it happens, and then it is just kind of gone. Whereas with social media, you can always go back and look through those interactions again. There's a fair bit of rumination about the things that people have said to them about their appearance and judging whether they fit in and the strength of their friendships along-side the evidence about how other people think they look.

Danielle goes on to add:

There's an aspect of those comments where it's self-deprecating, so girls might post a caption such as 'felt cute, might delete later'. By posting that, with a really great photo, they are seeking out these positive comments to then make them feel good.

The challenge here, particularly for girls, is that there is still this idea that they have to appear modest, because if you appear too confident, then that's also not good – people will think you're too cocky. For some reason, confidence with appearance is seen as a bad thing.

Girls are quite serious about it whereas with boys, there is a lot more banter, and the comments about each other could have been interpreted as negative, but were gener-ally intended in more of a humorous way. One example is posting the 'sick' emoji in response to someone's photo. As a researcher you would expect that to mean something quite horrible, but they interpret that as a joke.

The 'just joking' stuff is some of the hardest. Everyone knows how it can feel for someone to be 'joking' but actually be cut quite deep over something they are already insecure about. Over the past two years, Beth and Danielle have trialled a few different interventions to try to reduce the impact of body talk and comments about appearance on social media. Because we know that the extent to which young people are talking about appearance is connected to their feelings about how they look, especially on social media where they are also exposed to lots of images that they will automatically be comparing themselves to.

The tempting, 'grown-up' answer here is 'Just tell them not to spend so much time on social media', or 'Just don't post selfies or pictures of yourself in a bikini' – don't invite the positive or negative commentary. But it's not really that simple.

So, can we instead encourage young people to comment on things other than appearance on social media? Danielle continued: 'In our intervention program, we discussed what you could do. For example, if someone posts a picture of themselves, how can you comment about things that are not related to appearance? They were just like, "Well, you just can't because then you would look weird." Doing that would come at the cost of how they would then be viewed by their friends.'

In her interviews with young people, Danielle asked them to go back through their feeds and talk to her about what they were doing. 'That was a big thing, how they present themselves in the comment section. They talked about needing to post nice things to their friends, and most of the time, that was an appearance-related compliment. If you don't do that, then you're seen as kind of a bad friend or not a nice person.'

Even in the midst of all of this pressure to comment, there are lots of great things that teens can learn from more body positive, size or weight inclusive, or body liberation groups and accounts on social media. Following along, and observing the more positive and accepting ways that people speak about their bodies or counter fatphobia online, can be incredibly informative for young people.

AND THEN THERE WAS COVID . . .

So most of us were pretty anxious about, and had some sort of boundaries around, screen time back in 2019. Some of us were already worried about the amount of media and screen time our kids were exposed to. And then a very tiny virus shut down the world. Suddenly, so many of us were juggling not just the jobs of parent and our actual work role, but now adding 'teacher' to that as well. And many of us had to relax all of the rules and boundaries we had around screen time so that we could, you know, survive a pandemic without our brain exploding from being interrupted with requests for snacks and entertainment every seventeen seconds of our Zoom call.

This blowing-up of our perfectly well thought out digital access plans is perfectly captured here in an interview with Shelley, a mum of two from Boston:

My daughter got her phone when she was eleven. We started out with a contract, and all these rules about when you can use it and what you can use it for. The idea was that she was basically borrowing the phone from us, so if she broke the rules, we would just take it back. At first, she just used it for texting. She didn't have apps and things, it was more about communication. Over time, it was like, 'Can I get this app?' I would talk to other mums that I knew and would ask them, 'What is this app? What does it do? Is it okay for this age?' I would check and approve every little thing.

I think the real hard part for us was when the pandemic hit, and I lost all control. It was like, 'I have to get work done. You're home, you have basically half a school day of work to do, and you can't be with your friends.' We used to limit hours and have rules and that all got blown up. We let her have her phone and be on social media because it was the one thing she's had where she could stay connected with friends, and I just didn't want her to lose that. I thought the worst thing that could happen while she was in isolation was to lose connections to other peers – when you are a teenager that's the most important thing. So I just let it go – it's pretty free rein now. We take it away at ten o'clock at night, and we've got parental controls, but that's about it now.

You probably don't need us to cite the research on just how much kids' screen time increased over the pandemic and lock-down periods. Safe to say 'a lot'. A Canadian study that was already tracking screen time by surveying parents about their kids' media use each year pre-COVID reported a doubling in screen time hours for eight-year-olds – from eleven hours a week to twenty-three hours a week once the pandemic hit eighteen months later (excluding time spent on screens for schoolwork).

The impact of this additional time in front of devices depends a lot on what kids are doing on them. When young people are engaging in more appearance-focused social media use – taking selfies, using filters, being on Instagram, or watching YouTube content that relates to beauty, diet or physical activity – it can have a more negative impact than if they are watching videos of cats.

That seems kind of obvious, but adolescents are wired to compare with their friends, all day, every day, to see if they are fitting in. In the absence of the ability to do that in person, where people are a bit more real, they have had to do it online where only the best, most edited versions of images are usually shared.

This was explained so beautifully by Leanne:

I think the pandemic may have exacerbated these anxieties a little bit more, at least for my kids. They're seeing their peers less, but they are getting social media, so what they see of their friends and peers is edited and perfect. Those images have, in some ways, even more power, because they represent more of a share of their interaction with their peers. Their social world got really small, and a lot of their interactions with the world are happening by texting or through social media. We need to let them do it right now, because otherwise, they won't see their friends, but it is scary as a parent to watch this happening.

We all did this. We all had to do this. But the question is: what do we do now? When we realise that our kids are a bit too obsessed with a show that has some not-great role models in it, or when we know that they are having too much screen time, how do we claw things back?

We're no experts on digital parenting, but here are some ideas for when we lose our way:

- **Put on your oxygen mask first.** There's a bit of decompression that we, as parents, need to do before we can start doing hard things like reintroducing rules and boundaries around screen time. What do you need to do for yourself first so that you can take these actions? A week at a silent meditation retreat? A night out for dinner with your friends? A sleep in? One uninterrupted hour? It's important. Do this first.

- **Slowly, slowly.** Remember when the kids were toddlers and you planned a week ahead for daylight savings time and moved their bedtime in fifteen-minute increments so they wouldn't realise they were going to bed with daylight outside? Nope? Just us? Anyway, this is a bit the same. It's so tempting to go in guns blazing with a new plan-for-improved-life and change everything at once. But that rarely ends well. Usually, we give up after two days because it's too hard. We've learned the hard way that slower is better. Try making changes to one part of the day per week: like mornings, after school, after dinner. You could suggest pruning back the apps they have on their devices, 'trading' a new app they want for the deletion of one you would rather they don't use, or culling who they follow on social media to open up a conversation about what they are engaging with, what they are enjoying, and what might be having a negative influence.

- **Replace screen time with face-to-face time**. The easiest way to down the devices is to organise some major distractions. A day at the beach, waterslides, bushwalking, playdates and sleepovers. The more fun they are having in real life, the more they will forget that they aren't playing their favourite games online.

IT'S NOT ALL BAD

Most experts talk about media and screens being bad for body image. But sometimes, books, toys, games, screens and media also offer really nice opportunities to open their minds to some things that they might not have considered before. Their eyes might glaze over at the whiff of a 'mum lecture', but when they experience your 'teachable moment' in the form of a book or on screen, they might actually appreciate it and take it in. The key is to expose them to things that celebrate diversity, functionality of our bodies, and are counter-stereotypical. Exactly what this looks like varies across age and interests and what you do in your family, but those are the key things you are looking for.

BOOKS

Picture storybooks are such a great place to start instilling positive body image, and a whole range of positive attitudes and behaviours, for younger kids. Under the age of eight or nine, kids are unlikely to bring up this topic themselves, so reading these books gives you a good chance to talk about it. Researchers found that reading the picture book *Shapesville* by Andy Mills to girls in the first few years of primary school was effective in improving body image. There are now a whole range of beautiful and lovely kids' books that help to celebrate diversity and encourage young children to appreciate their body for what it does for them. We've included a list in the Resources at the end of this book.

As kids move to chapter books, it can be a bit harder to know that the books have the good stuff in there. Young adult fiction in the 'body image' category can sometimes focus on weight and weight loss, or being bullied about appearance. In general, it can assist kids to read things that help them feel less alone. If they can identify with the main character, and if the main character ends up accepting their body, realising what their body can do, and being kind to themselves, then that's the sort of book that might be helpful. Non-fiction books can be really helpful in explaining all of the things they might not believe when you say them. Just make sure that they are specifically designed for the age group of young people, as some of these books can almost give too much information that, to a vulnerable young person, might exacerbate some issues.

It's okay not to like something about yourself. Try not to focus on that. Focus on other things that you like about yourself and things that make you happy. For example, I like that my body works well so I can play sports. I like that my mind is creative. You know, stuff like that.

LILY, AGE 10

TOYS

This wouldn't be a book about body image without mentioning Barbie. And most feminist, progressive parents have probably had that moment where they are confronted with one of those plastic dolls in the sickly pink packaging and wondered whether they are setting up their kids for body image hell by giving in to their whining demands for this new toy.

There's a whole other book to be written about whether Barbie might be bad for body image. There have actually been a few studies on this and, in general, playing with Barbies doesn't seem to damage girls' body image, but looking at the still images of Barbies wasn't so positive. People without kids might say, 'Well, I just won't let my kids watch *Barbie*, have any Barbie merchandise, and I won't let them have the dolls, just in case.' But our small people have their own ideas, and there's not a lot of 'letting' happening. They go through phases where all they want to watch is *Barbie* and it's hard not to 'let' that happen.

Dr Jennifer Webb, a clinical health psychologist and researcher who has done some studies about Barbie, explains: 'I don't think it's a black and white issue. I think a lot of it does have to do with how children are accessing these toys, how caregivers might be trying to help frame the context or nature of the play with some of these toys as well, in the school or home environment.'

Now that Barbies come in a wider range of sizes, shapes and colours, one of the situations that could unfold is that 'regular' Barbie might start teasing some of the other, more diverse, Barbies. Children learn and express things through play in the same way we process things through conversations with other adults, so there is no need to be worried that this is what they would do in real life. They might have seen this played out on some of the things that they are watching. Dr Webb recommends one option is to come into this with curiosity: "'Oh, I noticed that this Barbie is saying some unkind things to that Barbie. Can you tell me a little bit more about why they're saying this? How might that make [the teased] Barbie feel? What could she do in this situation?" You can either play out or talk through potential resolutions to the scenario that represent more prosocial options.'

CHILDREN'S MEDIA

Most parents of girls have also had that moment where they wonder if 'Disney princess' culture is doing any damage. Rewatch any of the Disney favourites from your youth and they remind us how bad things were in terms of racism, sexism, and a general lack of acceptance of diversity and empowerment of women. When every movie ends with a wedding to a prince and every princess would meet the BMI cut-offs for an eating disorder, it's pretty easy to find reasons to get worried.

This can become a concern, particularly when girls don't see themselves represented within these stories. Take Ryan's example:

My niece is Aboriginal and Indian, and she's quite dark skinned, with lots of curly hair. When she was three, she would be observing and saying: 'I have the same skin as Nanna and the same skin as Dad, and Mum has different skin.' She was just observing it, but she wasn't judging.

Whereas now she's four, and she's right in the middle of the princess phase, dressing up and all of that. So she's just started saying, 'When I grow up, I'm going to have straight hair.' I feel like she's started observing her hair, and knowing that it's curly, but she's starting to judge it for what it's not, at four. If this is what it's like now, what will it be like when she's fourteen?!

This is where it can be helpful for children to see examples of main characters that look like them – a bit tricky when we still don't have a lot of diversity in the media. But as much as possible, we can try to help point it out and help them to see the people who have the curly hair. The freckles. The skin colour. And to open up conversations about how the characters might look different to you, but that's what makes the world pretty awesome – to have diversity and difference and so many types of people making the world more interesting.

Thankfully, most of the more recent films present the female characters as capable, brave, not in need of rescue, and, for the most part, pretty disinterested in marriage. But the majority of children's media still has characters that are generally quite thin. Of course there are now some really notable and lovely examples of where this is not the case – the characters in *Moana*, *Turning Red* and *Encanto* being our recent favourites. There were still some fatphobic lines in the films, but at least the characters are a little more diverse and not so unrealistically thin. The male characters have also improved. They are now much more in touch with their emotions and solve problems without resorting to violence.

But back to princesses. Because the 'official' Disney princesses are still featured on aaaaaaalll of the merch like a standard line-up of the 'big five' supermodels from the nineties, even though many kids don't even know the stories behind Snow White, Cinderella, Aurora and Tiana, they still *know* them from all of the toys, dress ups, lunch boxes, books and so on. Researcher Dr Sarah Coyne has conducted several studies of the impact of 'princess culture'. Her latest research has followed children over a period of five years, from the ages of four to five to the ages of nine to ten, and found that engagement with 'princess culture' actually had a small positive effect over time. The kids who saw and engaged with more princess culture were not necessarily more stereotypically 'girly' or 'masculine' – even if they did watch the old-school movies. Also, and unexpectedly, the kids who were more engaged with princess culture actually had a more positive body image than those who weren't. This surprised everyone, but it is possible that the kids were actually learning more from the story – where the protagonists had to work really hard, show incredible bravery, overcome challenges and pursue their dreams, and where their bodies had function, value and purpose beyond their appearance. All of these things align with the key messages of body acceptance. In summary: we don't need to worry so much about The Princesses as we might have thought.

USING THE MEDIA FOR GOOD

Once our kids get beyond the age of dressing up as princesses, we can still use the media as a force for good. Many parents we spoke to talked about the conversations that they had about TV shows, films, books and toys that benefited their children in a range of ways. Others spoke more directly about the potential to improve body image using the media. One of the most powerful examples of this came from one mother we interviewed, below.

You can be what you can see

I've got polycystic ovary syndrome, so I'm very hairy, and I've always struggled with that. One of my children, even though she's very little, she's always been hairy from birth, and she still is, and she started to say to me: 'I want to get rid of this hair.' I nearly burst into tears when she said she needed to shave it and get rid of it. She's little, only eight years old. It was upsetting but I didn't want her to get bullied, so I bought her a home laser hair removal device.

Initially I was really psychologically resistant. I just did not want to assist in helping her conform to society's unrealistic and damaging beauty norms. But then I thought about it deeply and remembered being mercilessly bullied and teased for having pubic hair when I was ten years old at school. And my mother just wouldn't help. She said, 'I am *not* having my ten-year-old shave.' It was a response about my mum's needs, not mine. And I was really thrown to the wolves in terms of school bullying.

So, with my own kid, I just had this moment where I thought: what is the thing that I would have liked my mother to do in this situation? I would have wanted her to help me resolve the great body shame and bullying directed at me by others. And I would have wanted her to help me normalise hair on women.

I took two steps. Firstly, I found this *Vogue* article about really beautiful women who are really hairy, and I printed out fifteen pictures of these women in colour – beautiful models with really hairy arms, hairy faces. I gave them all to her and she just loved it. She asked for a special scrapbook to put them all in, and she wanted me to help her find more. She was like: 'But I've got hairy legs. Can we find someone with really hairy legs?' So we went online looking for women with hairy legs and printed them out. It was just beautiful to watch her realising that it was okay to be like her. She was saying, 'Wow, this is amazing, these women are so beautiful – I could be like them.'

The second action I took was that a few days ago she was talking again about her moustache and so I offered to help her use the hair removal device I'd recently purchased. I tested it on my own legs in front of her. She thought about it for a while and said, 'No, I don't think I need it, Mum.' All she wanted and needed was to feel accepted, just the way that she was. And that's all I had ever wanted from my mum, too, it just never came.

GENEVA, MUM OF TWO, ACT

WHAT'S WORKING

Some of the things parents have tried:

I found a video that had girls their own age talking about their bodies and body image concerns, so it broke that taboo. I played it to them and asked them what they thought. They organically started a conversation about the video once it ended, openly discussing their own thoughts about body image.

GENEVA, ACT

One of the things that I've actually appreciated about the Japanese anime is that there's all sorts of different hairstyles and colours – there's a lot of diversity of how they wear their hair, and a diverse range of skin tones. It's an empowered sort of self-expression.

JASMINE, USA

My girls started to use the word 'fat' a lot and were comparing themselves (negatively) to others. I think it was happening because they'd started watching a lot of music videos where women's bodies are portrayed as sex objects. So I found a playlist of body positive songs, and whenever we hear songs like this now they will say: 'Mum, you'd like this song! It's about how our bodies are strong!

GABRIELLA, ACT

So screens and media are here to stay. But with so much content out there, we can guide our kids to watch and engage with the things that might be good for them. There is now research that shows that engaging with body positive social media accounts, such as those found on TikTok or Instagram, can be helpful. Listening to songs about how all bodies are good bodies is better for kids than the music that objectifies women's bodies. Watching TV shows and YouTube videos where there are characters who are more diverse and who aren't conforming to the thin ideal might also be helpful, as are videos where there aren't any human bodies depicted at all!

**Being who you are is better
than being all fake . . .
You don't have to be that girl in the magazine.
The best person to be is yourself.**

ISLA, AGE 11

**Dear people over the age of eighteen,
you need to accept your body.
You need to realise that those bodies you
want to look like are unattainable, and a
complete waste of your own unique body.
You need to embrace every part of you.
The way you look should not control
how you behave, what you wear, or what
communities you are a part of. Your
body isn't a cage, it's your key to life.
Your appearance doesn't define you
and shouldn't restrict you. And you**

shouldn't place restrictions on others
based on their appearance.
Just let kids be free. Love your body.
And most of all, don't let how others perceive
your body define who you choose to be.

A LETTER FROM JOSH, AGE 15

FAQs

Q: What do I do when my kids have seen a movie or YouTube video that I wouldn't let them see at home, and they have potentially been exposed to hypersexualised imagery or more mature concepts?

You can't control everything, and even if you do have really strong boundaries over what your kids can watch at home, this might not be the case everywhere they go, and they will eventually see things that you wouldn't want them to see. The key here is to mediate that experience with a discussion that helps them to think critically about what they have seen, and introduce some media literacy to the situation.

At a good time to chat, you might start with:

- I know you've seen that movie, what did you think about it? Did you like it?
- In the movie [there are a lot of girls in thin bodies/there is a lot of talk about sex], how did the people feel (and why might they have felt this way)? Why do you think they might put this in a movie?

- In my experience, high school was nothing like that. The movies are really fun to watch, but that's mostly because they are a fantasy and very different from real life.
- None of those things happened to me or any of my friends in high school, so you shouldn't feel bad if this isn't what your experience is like.
- Do you have any questions about anything you saw? You can talk to me about it whenever you like.
- Here's what I hope your experience is like: talk in relation to body acceptance (e.g., that you go through high school with a fun group of friends who like you because of your personality, you don't all need to be the popular girls, or look a certain way), or in relation to sex (e.g., whenever it happens, it's just important that you are doing it with someone who likes and respects you, and who your feel comfortable with, and the timing is right for you. It's not necessary that this will happen 'at prom', like in the movies).

Q: My daughter (aged thirteen) will say: 'I don't know what to say when my best friend says: "I'm fat" or "I don't like my thighs".' I think she just doesn't know how to respond to that. What can I do to help?

There has been so much research that shows that this sort of appearance talk with friends can reinforce some negative body image pressures, and reinforce the importance of appearance (and usually, the importance of thinness) among friends.

Dr Beth Bell advises that we avoid being too prescriptive in our advice, as her work with adolescents has found that there isn't necessarily one solution that works for everybody. One option is to acknowledge and validate concerns, but also change the topic. This could be done in a combination of public and less public ways; for example, posting a 'hug' emoji in the comments, but then sending a DM or calling to connect with the friend who posted that negative comment. 'You can encourage your daughter to think about how they can potentially demonstrate that they are being a good friend in other ways' suggests Danielle Paddock, from the research team.

In certain situations, young people might feel comfortable actually challenging some of these ideas and ideals, on or off the public forum, with things that might come from multiple perspectives:

1. A broader social justice perspective: 'Isn't it awful that we sit here tearing ourselves down.'
2. A feminist perspective: 'I wonder if boys would spend time worrying about these things?' or
3. A body acceptance space: 'We are all beautiful in our own ways. Let's try to remind ourselves of that.'

However, Dr Bell is quick to remind us that this is in context, and under the right circumstances, 'you can also just take a break from appearance-related content – you don't have to be fighting to change things all of the time, you can just take a break.'

In their research, Danielle and Beth noted that sometimes, just questioning things can be helpful: 'When girls were made aware of how much of what they were talking about online was related to appearance, and how that could have a negative impact, they suddenly realised, "Oh, wow. Yeah, we do that we do that a lot." After a while they told us that they were reducing their appearance commentary, so awareness of it could lead to some attempts to pull back a bit from the culture because of how they might be affecting other people, and also themselves.'

We're not going to hold our breath for social media platforms to realise the errors of their ways and alter their systems to improve wellbeing instead of making lots of cash.

If we can't change the tech, we can at least make our young people realise how toxic it is.

Professor Linda Lin teaches psychology, conducts body image research, and she is also a mum of two (twelve and fifteen years old). So she's pretty qualified. Here's her perspective: 'My goal for my children is to explain that, when you feel like you don't measure up, many people feel shame, like there's something wrong with them, or that they did not measure up in some way. What I want to teach them is that the standard is toxic – every time you feel like you don't measure up, it's not that you are missing something, or that you are insufficient in some way. It's the fact that there's a really unrealistic standard that sets the bar unrealistically high. So every time you feel that way, don't feel bad about yourself, don't feel shame, be angry that these messages exist and mobilise and externalise that blame. It's not you. It's not your fault. It's these standards and messages.'

Action

Conversations:

☑ Talk to your kids about the sort of media they like to engage with and why. What sort of bodies are represented? What stereotypes are perpetuated? Why might they have done things this way?

☑ Talk about the sorts of comments they see about their friends on social media. How do these comments make them feel? How could they shift the conversation away from weight and appearance?

To do together:

☑ Challenge each other to scroll through socials and unfollow five people who make you feel bad about your body. Talk about your rationale and reasons why, or model critique along the way.

☑ Watch a film or TV show together and talk through the media literacy questions on pp. 253–4.

13

Friends

PEER GROUPS EXERT A STRONG overall influence on young people, particularly in relation to their body image, eating and movement. This happens through direct and indirect means, all wrapped up in developmental processes. It's complicated. The key areas where peers influence young people are through the establishment of norms and reinforcement of societal ideals through 'peer pressure', social comparisons, appearance-based conversations, and teasing, bullying or body shaming.

FITTING IN

Making friends with kids is not something we ever thought parents had much to do with – until we became said parents. Surprise! You have to do everything! When kids are young, proximity is the biggest factor in determining their friend groups – as in: you're here, I'm here, let's be friends! So we have a lot of influence as parents, taking them to playgrounds where they meet kids, arranging playdates, awkwardly asking for strangers' phone numbers so we can set up a time for the kids to get together. We're all in it together until the kids reach pre-teen stage.

In the pre-teen stage, common interests and activities are the driving force in friendships. Again, we can control aspects of this by signing kids up to the same sports as their friends.

And then they get to high school and everything changes. In adolescence, female friendships in particular become more complex and involve considerable emotional investment. As kids get older, they have increasing expectations of loyalty, trust, self-disclosure, and intimacy. It is so much harder for us as the parents to really know what is going on, and to help with friendship challenges as our kids enter the teens.

Adolescence is such a confusing and challenging time. Not only are kids moving away from the certainty of the family towards peers, they become obsessed with 'fitting in', and yet also need to develop their own sense of identity. What follows seems to be five to six years of trial and error – figuring themselves out and seeing where they fit in the world. One of the ways that we do this is by comparing ourselves to others.

Comparisons happen automatically. We all compare ourselves to others around us, but girls have been found to do this more than boys, and some girls do it more than others. After observing and comparing, two other processes come into play here. One is that young people will engage in 'mirroring', which is imitating attitudes and behaviours of their friends and peers. Suddenly they are all dressing the same, and talking the same with similar eyerolls and dismissive hand gestures. All conversations that they have with their friends create, explain and reinforce the 'social norms' for their particular friendship group and broader peer group. Young people learn vicariously through the experiences of others. So, for example, a group of girls might exclude someone from the preparations for a dance performance because of her size. This directly and indirectly communicates the group norms that might go unsaid but are very well understood: that thinness is important, you need to conform to a certain weight and shape to be a part of the group, and that it is okay to discriminate against people in larger bodies. There is so much learning going on about 'the way things are' from seemingly minor events and conversations that happen in friendship groups. This is where the 'need' to do things because 'everyone is doing it' comes in. They know what the negative consequences can be – they have seen them happen to others who don't conform to the norms.

In our conversations with mums of girls who were struggling with their body image, the one thing many said was 'She thinks she is the biggest one in her group'. Jillian, a school psychologist and mum of two girls aged fifteen and eighteen, suggests that this is one of the first red flags that starts to indicate a potential problem: 'Girls will refer to themselves as the biggest in the class. They'll say things like, "I know I'm not good at sport", "I know that I'm bigger than other girls", "Everyone else is so skinny" and things like that. They have compared themselves and decided that they are the biggest. But the comparison is not realistic. It's completely skewed.'

The need for acceptance from peers can be particularly strong in early adolescence when identity formation is still in progress. While teens are figuring themselves out, they defer to the likes, dislikes, and attitudes of their friends or their group. At this developmental stage, it can be hard for teens to assert that '*I* don't like this or that' – and much easier to talk about how '*We* don't like those things':

> My daughter [aged thirteen] has one friend in particular who is extremely influential on her, but I think it's almost an unhealthy relationship. I can't tell whether there's intent by this other girl to manipulate her but all I hear when we're shopping is 'I need to take a picture of these shorts. If Billie says that they're okay, then I'll get them.' Even to the point where I bought a new lamp for my daughter's bedroom and she was like, 'Oh, no, Billie doesn't like it. You have to return it.' It's so hard because I know she just wants to fit in and belong, but I also want her to know that there are going to be things that people are going to want you to do, or not do, to buy or not buy, but you need to decide those things for yourself too – it has to come from within and inside of you and be what you care about as well.
>
> It's not just physical items: sometimes she'll text me and say 'Billie wants me to sleep over at her house, but I don't really want to. Can you say no?' I did, and I told her: 'I will do this for you, but I want you to know, you can say no.' Of course that makes me worry: particularly when you get into consent and boys and sex – how she's going to find her voice and her courage to say: 'No, I don't want to' in a respectful way where they can still stay friends and she can feel good about it.
>
> **DANA, USA**

This level of desire to fit in, and this sort of control over what friends think and do, can be a cause for concern when it comes to food and eating. It's one thing when teen girls want to dress like each other. But when one starts dieting, this can lead to others in the group questioning their eating habits. Research shows that high levels of dieting in a friend group lead to increases in dieting and disordered behaviours over time. In other words, it's not contagious in the viral kind of way. But it is kind of 'catchy'. It's a good idea to be aware of what's going on in terms of food, dieting and movement in your young people's peer groups, and if you notice any red flags, you can call the Butterfly Foundation hotline to seek information about helping a friend. Depending on the age of the kids, your own child might have noticed something and want to help too. Involving them in helping their friend can be beneficial for all.

FRIEND DRAMA

Girls, (yes, it's mostly girls) can be so mean to each other. Where does all of the friend drama come from?

Kate has some ideas. As a primary school teacher, she's observed a lot of 'mean girl' behaviour. 'I think it comes from a culture of having to "be a lady" about things,' she says.

'The boys and men could fight on the streets, out in the open, and have it all be done with. The girls had to stifle their anger, repress their emotions, and find other ways to express it. Girls have to be a bit more sneaky about it. They have figured out how to really hurt each other, and it's in going behind each other's backs to cut them down.

'And when we look at the role models that are around right now, like reality TV "stars", they are horrible to each other and they say such awful things, because they know they will get a reaction, but this is what young girls are watching, thinking that this is a normal way to treat your sisters and your friends.'

It's easy to feel a little powerless in the midst of the teen girl friend dramas. We can be triggered by our own experiences, and it can be hard to remember how life-threatening those things seemed at the time, when they just aren't part of our life anymore as adults.

One thing we can have agency over, as parents, is supporting our kids to create and maintain friendships outside of school. Research indicates that encouraging playdates and catch-ups and spending time developing relationships with kids away from the school setting can help to reduce the impact of friend drama – and you can always prompt a reconnection with one of these other friends in tough emotional times. Tina, mum of two in the United States explains:

> What I have found to be particularly important is having different sources of friendships, and different circles of friendships. Little pockets of people her age who care about her. The circle of friends she has at school can get really hard to navigate – one minute they're in one group, and then someone gets kicked out or moves on, and there's this breaking up of friendships, it's just part of what happens. In those moments, or on a really tough night when there is drama with her school friends, or she didn't get invited to something, she can connect with someone from her other little support group outside the drama – her group of friends from summer camp, her cousins, or good family friends that live in other places. It's that sense of knowing there are

people who know her, and that care about her. No matter what happens with the drama at school, she's got pockets of those all over the place. And I just feel like that's been such a wonderful buffer for her.

Fitting in is everything for adolescents. Many parents of teens explained that they had forgotten that feeling, and then it came back with force. As the parent it can be hard not to be dismissive: it's long enough ago for us to go, 'Oh, that was a very bad, but very short time in my life, and it just got better from there.' But for kids who are in it, it is their whole world. So if you are saying things like: 'Oh, well they're not good friends to you', or 'Just don't worry about what you look like', they feel like you don't understand anything.

When it comes to helping your kids – particularly girls – through drama and conflict within friend and peer groups, we can listen, validate and empathise with our children, but often there isn't anything we can do to 'fix' the situation. Dr Jody Forbes sees this often as a psychologist at a girls' school, and a mother of two teenage girls: 'When a girl has done something wrong to upset a friend, maybe by body shaming her or making her feel bad about her appearance, we need to be able to say to them, you might have offended a friend, a friend is angry and upset with you, but you have done all that you can. You have apologised, but they're still angry, so you've got to sit there with that painful, sick feeling that you've offended somebody, and you know that they'll get over it. But it takes time, and you have to wait.'

Jody continues: 'This is where some people can't bear it, and they have to try to fix it. But this is where we have to remind ourselves – and our kids – that you just have to wait now for that person to process things, and for time to pass. We have to remind them that this is a normal feeling, and it's a hideous, horrible feeling. And the horribleness of this feeling tells you that your friend matters to you. But in order for this friendship to continue, you now need to sit and wait.'

FAT TALK AND BODY TALK

In Chapter 2 we talked about how research has shown that 'fat talk' or 'body talk' – which is when we say negative things about our own appearance – has a really significant negative impact on our body image.

This fat talk starts early. When researchers ask teens to report how often they engage in conversations like this about their appearance, they find that the teens who talk more are also more dissatisfied with their bodies. Participating in fat talk has been found to be worse for body image, but even listening to fat talk can have an impact.

Let's take an example. Izzy is in a larger body, and hasn't really thought about her body that much. But when her friends start to talk about the things they don't like about their bodies, this makes Izzy feel like she shouldn't like hers either. When her friend Abby, who is a few sizes smaller than Izzy, says that she doesn't like her thighs, Izzy looks at her own thighs and worries that she shouldn't like them either. Izzy jumps in saying that she doesn't like her arms, seeking feedback and reassurance from her friends, but all she hears are others complaining about the parts of them they think are too big. The cumulative impact of these conversations just reinforces societal beauty standards, the norms for the group, and the importance of weight and appearance to our friends and peers – it kind of sets the standard for what that peer group will 'accept' in terms of thinness and appearance.

Boys tend to do more than talk, but some of the key activities they engage in socially are physical and movement based – sports and in weightlifting. These activities naturally mean that there are opportunities for lots of body commentary about how they and others look, and lots of comparisons. Male body talk often presents as fun, harmless banter, when it's actually really hurtful.

These same conversations can also take place online. Focus groups with girls and boys eleven to fourteen years old in the UK revealed that the conversations changed depending on how public, private and permanent the social media platform was. So a platform like Instagram, where everyone can see each other's comments and who made them, and they are there to refer back to, is different to private messages in Snapchat that disappear after a time, or comments that can be made anonymously. In this research, adolescent girls explained that, despite investing time and effort trying to appear physically attractive, there was a need to appear modest in your own comments about yourself, and this was a strategy to avoid appearing too confident or 'full of yourself', and a strategy to gain compliments and reassurance about one's appearance.

If you have a chat to your young people and find out that there's a fair bit of fat talk happening, you can talk to them about the fact that it's not such a great thing to be doing, for their mental health, and encourage them to try to stop it when it is happening with their friends. You could encourage your child to either divert the conversation, or confront the situation head on. The easiest option is to change the subject. However, it can mean that the same thing happens the next day. Other options are to say something like 'I don't think this is very helpful for me/us. Can we talk about something else?' This can be challenging for teens, who are really focused on fitting in, but having the conversation with them about it, and letting them know that these chats aren't helpful, could neutralise the effects.

> **When I was talking with friends and peers and they would start saying negative things about their bodies, I would be thinking – what should I say? I need to say something that I don't like about my body. And it was a really unusual thing for me.**
>
> **TINA, MUM OF TWO, USA**

TEASING, BULLYING, AND BODY SHAMING

Appearance-based teasing, bullying and body shaming happens so often that many people don't even recognise it anymore. You would bristle and intervene if you saw a child at the park saying things about someone who had a disability, or someone from a different ethnic group to them, but what about if someone got called 'porky', 'chubby' or 'fat' in the kind of way that tells you they are using it as an insult and not in an enlightened, reclaimed kind of way?

Studies about appearance-based teasing find its occurrence to be relatively common. Around one third of adolescents say that they are teased about their weight. Young people who think they are at either end of the weight spectrum – at either a low or a high weight – are more likely to report teasing, and the teasing was particularly common around the point at which adolescents' bodies were growing and changing during puberty.

Research suggests that the majority (up to 60 per cent) of teasing comes from peers, 36 per cent from siblings, and 19 per cent from parents. But what is also happening, in a way that can't really be measured, is that body shaming goes largely unnoticed in schools, and is underreported by adolescents, because people think that they just have to accept it.

When people say awful, judgemental things about our bodies it sometimes doesn't sink in for a while. 'Are you sure you want that second helping?', 'Goodness, you've grown so much more than when I last saw you', 'I think you've had enough sweet things for today' – we try to brush it off. And they come back at us much later, branded across our brains, and into our flesh. Young people in larger bodies have been subjected to so much weight-based discrimination – much of which is from medical settings – that some think they actually deserve to have these comments made about them. There is so much conflation of weight and health that some people think they are being helpful by making comments about young people's weight: 'I can help you lose that muffin top', 'People will like you if you are thinner', and 'You can help your netball team win if you lose weight'. In reality, these things that people say about young people's bodies all imply that there is something wrong with their body, that they need to control and change it in order to be loved, and they all lead to a feeling of shame.

One woman we spoke to called them the 'daggers' – the things that people said to us twenty or thirty years ago that we can recall like it was yesterday. The words and names from our peers and, more often than not, the adults around us: 'Katie can't play this game because she's too fat', to 'Okay, Miss Piggy, let's slow down or you will get even bigger'.

Those of us who have felt the daggers know how damaging they are. Whether online or in real life, teasing about appearance can lead to young people feeling stigma and shame around their bodies and is associated with poor body image, low self-esteem, and disordered eating behaviours as well as depression, anxiety and suicide ideation, so it's not just harmless name-calling or a bit of 'banter'. The impact of teasing is still relevant up to twenty years later; research with adults has found that their level of body dissatisfaction and disordered eating in their thirties is related to how they were teased about their weight as a child. More daggers means adolescents and young adults are more likely to be depressed and engaging in disordered eating.

An athlete's perspective

There was a lot of pressure and comments from the older (male) coaches, who were certainly not educated in this space. The message was basically just that smaller was better, at any cost. I remember being told that I was looking a bit top-heavy one day, bigger chested than others, and there were comments that other girls were 'a bit soft around the edges' or that someone's butt was 'as wide as a windscreen'. Even the positive comments were damaging as they would reinforce the connection between thinness and performance and being a worthy or deserving person. The coaches seemed to put thin bodies on a pedestal and anyone who deviated from that was made to feel as though their bodies were not okay – not for athletic performance, but also, not okay at all. These comments have stayed with me and many of the girls I grew up training with, continuing to impact our thoughts to this day. It was never 'just a comment'. It always had this really negative value judgement to it. Like, she performed poorly, and she looked overweight, and she was lazy. You want to say something and call them out but you don't even know where to start because they come from this generation where commenting on women athletes' bodies was an 'acceptable' part of their job.

MELISSA, 23, ATHLETE

Teasing has changed a little over the years. Young people being interviewed told the researchers in one study: 'It's not the stereotypical 1980s movie bullying.' You know, the kind where the kid with the glasses gets held up by his shirt onto the row of metal lockers, and then has to walk in slow motion through a cafeteria where kids throw things at him, and someone puts their foot out to trip him over. Things have changed even in the US where the schools actually look like that. Yes, there is the obvious emergence of online trolls and negative comments, but most of the time now teasing can look like harmless banter, but it still cuts deep.

Research from Dr Beth Bell in the UK, who interviewed adolescents about social media, found that negative appearance comments are common and problematic, but not always intentionally harmful. Teens indicated that they would not intentionally make negative comments on platforms where they were named or identifiable, because that would make them look like a bad person or a bad friend. However, particularly among boys, adolescents described 'joking around' or 'just having some fun', but the examples given indicated that the commentary reinforced appearance ideals, and could be harmful to those on the receiving end.

Appearance-based teasing and bullying sends young people the message that they, their bodies and their appearance are not 'right' and not accepted by the people around them. This presents a problem for adolescents, who are in a developmental stage where everything is all about fitting in and being accepted by their friends and peers.

You don't even need to be on the receiving end for comments to be harmful. Seeing people make negative comments about or to others can have a similar effect. When we see the level of scrutiny, judgement and vicious comments that are made about others behind their backs it makes us wonder, 'Well, if they are saying that about her, what are they saying about me?'

SO, WHAT CAN WE DO ABOUT IT?

Most advice about teasing and bullying is about what you can do at the systems level, or how you can jump into 'fixer' mode. Yes, it's important that we report teasing, speak to the other child, and follow up with parents and the teachers and the school or setting that it's happening in. But one of the main things that we can forget in this process is what to say to the young person who has just had those daggers thrown at them.

'We don't realise how injurious these moments are. You need to behave as though you just saw a child cut someone else with an object they didn't realise was sharp. And this child is bleeding metaphorically.' That's Zoë Bisbing, mum of three, and licensed New York-based psychotherapist and founder of the Full Bloom Project, a podcast and resource for body positive parenting. There hasn't been any research done in terms of what we can say to young people who have just been on the receiving end of weight-based comments and teasing, and we've tried asking various experts in the past. But Zoë blew us away with her three-step process to respond:

1. **'Something serious just happened.'** Take it seriously. Make sure your child, and the person who said something, both know that what was said is not okay, and that commenting on other people's bodies is not allowed. So many people, particularly those people who already believe that their body isn't 'ideal', think they just have to accept these negative comments because they are to blame for having a body that isn't like everyone else's. It's your job to disrupt this.

2. **'There is nothing wrong with your body.'** *Most* importantly, make sure that your child knows that this was not their fault, that there is nothing wrong with their body, and that you love and accept them exactly as they are. You don't have to tell them they are pretty, or that they are 'not fat'. What they need to know is that they will be accepted, by you, and by others. They need to know that they will find their people (eventually) who will love and accept their bodies and themselves exactly as they are – people who

won't say these awful things to them – but that this can take time. Until then, they just need to know that there is nothing wrong with them.

3. **'How can you be kind to yourself in this moment?'** Self-compassion is the antidote to shame. We want to encourage our young people to be kind to themselves in these moments. Other people might not say kind words, but we can be kind to ourselves. Talk through how the comments made them feel, sit with the feelings, feel the feelings. Help them know they are not alone in feeling that way, and maybe empathise by talking through how you felt when this happened to you, or tell a story of how this might have happened to others. Then encourage them to think of some things they can say to themselves right now. These words might be what a kind friend would say in this situation – they might talk about your strengths and inner qualities, your personality or achievements – try encouraging your child to say those things to themselves. Things like 'They might have said mean things to me but I am a kind and strong person, and a great friend'. Encourage them to say these things to themselves that they might also use again at other times.

It's what we wish our parents had said to us when those people said those things about our bodies that made us feel shame. It's what we wish our friends had said to stick up for us.

Not 'You're not fat, you're beautiful'.

Not 'I'm going to call their parents'.

It's 'There is nothing wrong with your body. You are perfect just as you are'.

And *then* you can start to figure out who you need to tell, whether you need to call the school, what you need to do, how you can prepare them for this if it happens again. All of the 'fixing' can wait.

When Zoë shared a similar framework on her Full Bloom Project social media, the overwhelming response was that everybody wished they could have had some trusted adults say this to them. To say 'There's nothing wrong with you'. To still understand and validate their pain, but to essentially say 'Your body is fine as it is, no matter what'. It can be hard if your own body is not quite what you wanted it to be, and not quite what the beauty standards say. It's even harder if it's fat, but that doesn't mean there's anything wrong. The main response to this framework has been, 'Can we please go back in time and have this be what my parents said to me?' and 'If one person could have just said something like that, to me, it would have changed my life'. It's what people have been desperate for.

It's the reason why we are so excited you are reading this book, because by applying the principles of this book together with using your voice, we can create big, meaningful change together.

Zoë knows: she treats people with eating disorders in her practice: 'I can tell you on that back end, working with really traumatised people, their trauma is related to a lifetime of trying to change their body. Often they say: "Had someone just said to me, you don't have to change your body, you can just be big, and that's okay, that would have changed my life." A lot of people don't recognise that deep trauma and that deep pain, because people only open up about it in those really safe spaces like therapy.'

Using your voice, we can create big, meaningful change together.

Responding to an incident might also form a part of a larger conversation, or series of conversations. 'Maybe this is also an important moment, especially if your kid is in a bigger body. Maybe we need to start sitting down and saying it: "You are in a bigger body. We haven't talked about that yet (or, remember how we talked about that?). People out there in the world might try to make you feel inferior because you have a body that they think it's okay to make fun of,' Zoë says. 'We want our children to understand that they can't change their body size, not if they don't want to mess up their metabolism, and mess with their head, and not if you don't want to gain weight because that's the science. I think it helps to say "Something bad happened to you, there's nothing wrong with you, but yes, let's talk about how you're going to handle that next time, because it will happen again, this is a cruel and unusual world when it comes to weight-based teasing, it's wrong. We're trying to change that, and you can be a big part of changing that, but it will take time."'

Many parents panic about their child's size, and almost have judgement about their child's body, even if it is similar to their own. We've evolved to the point where we know not to say anything to their face, but we still worry about it. We want our children to be healthy, and we will do anything to avoid them getting teased and bullied. So what do we do?

We ask Zoë. She says, 'I tell parents it's really natural to not want your child to be ostracised, not want them to be bullied for being different in any way. But the best way to empower your kid is to make sure they hear from you that the solution is not going to be to change themselves to fit in, it's going to be to figure out a way to survive the toxic environments and to find their people, because they do exist. You tell them yes, it's hard, but we're not afraid of hard things. You can't invalidate the pain, but you also can't shrink the pain away – we need to make parents really understand that it is not worth it to try to change their kid's body, because if the goal of that intentional body change is weight loss, that's not what's going to happen.'

TAKING ACTION IN EDUCATION

Much of the peer stuff happens while the kids are at school. We're not seeing everything while we're pushing them endlessly on the swings. We see it when our kids come home withdrawn, or we get that distressed text message from our teens. Now that you are more aware of all of the things that impact on body image, you might also start to notice that some of the things that come home from school might be problematic in terms of the peer interactions and body shaming, and in terms of the content of the lessons or homework.

Fiona Sutherland @themindfuldietitian writes a blog for dietitians and parents, and this issue often comes up in her Facebook group. There are some things that happen in schools that are well-intentioned, but quite triggering, such as weighing kids in class to teach them maths (like Jameela Jamil's story in the *Embrace Kids* film), or doing skin fold tests and fitness tests in PE. Home readers and library books that are focused on food and weight, watching *That Sugar Film* or *Super Size Me*, recording all of the foods they eat in a day, calculating calories. Ugh. The list could go on. Many of these things turn up in psychologists' offices as the triggers for eating disorders. They don't *cause* an eating disorder on their own, but they contribute.

Schools are complex places, and teachers are amazing: often overworked, under-resourced and under-appreciated. They often don't get the chance to learn about body image in their training, so they are doing their best. But there are a lot of things that happen in schools that shouldn't be happening if we really care about our young people's wellbeing.

Here's what Fiona suggests you do if you want to take action on something kids bring home or tell you about.

1. **Don't lose your shit.** Sleep on it. Don't do a rage email, or get on the phone. Just slow down and think about it.

2. **Don't do nothing.** Because if you are worried about it, and you've picked that up, it could be really problematic, and you're probably not the only one who is worried.

3. **Approach the teacher.** Don't go storming up to the principal's office as it could make things worse.

4. **Approach with curiosity and ask them a little bit about the peer issue or rationale for the activity.** Is it part of the curriculum, or their idea that they've come up with? For example, 'My child came home and told me about [insert conversation/activity] and I'm hoping we can talk about it. Can you help me understand a little more about the conversation/activity for context?'

5. **Ask them if they're open to understanding a little bit about some alternative ways that we can talk about bodies and food and healthy eating or nutrition.**

For example, 'I'm wondering if I can share with you some concerns I have about this. I know you care about the kids and I also understand this was just part of the curriculum. I've just read a book about body image/I've been doing some learning in this area and I am aware of the potential for the food/eating/body image messages that kids receive during their school years to really affect their relationship with food for life. Are you open to hearing more?'

6. **If they are open to it, you can then offer them some information.** Lend them this book – or send the links to some of the resources mentioned at the end of this book.

After seeing that six-step process about taking action, your first thought might be: 'But I don't want to be *that* parent.' But we have to be *that* parent about stuff that matters, otherwise nothing gets done. If you've noticed it, and if it's made you think, 'Wait, they're doing what?' then it's worth having a chat with the teacher about it. They are usually so focused on the educational outcomes that they might forget to think about how things could be interpreted by kids in different bodies.

Fiona has been there and had these conversations: 'The couple of times I have done this, it's mostly been around books that have been sent home, and the teachers have been so receptive. They've said, "You know what? Yes. I didn't notice that. I didn't see that. I didn't think about it in that way. I appreciate you bringing this to my attention." Maybe I was lucky, but I think if you approach it with curiosity, and assume that the teacher didn't mean to do any harm, then I have found it quite okay.'

STRATEGIES FOR YOUR TOOLBOX

1. Tell stories

One of the most effective ways we can help our kids to understand themselves is to help them to identify emotions, and figure out how to act accordingly – and one of the most effective ways of doing this is modelling and explaining how we might have done that. Psychologists call this 'reflective listening'; we just think about it as 'telling stories'. Either way, this is one of the most foolproof strategies you can have in your parenting toolbox.

Here is a step-by-step approach to reflective listening using the 'validation of feelings' sandwich:

1. **Validate:** 'That must be so hard for you. How does it make you feel?'
2. **Empathise:** 'I felt [x] when a similar thing happened to me.' (*Tell the story.*)
3. **Reflect:** 'It's okay to feel [x] right now.'

The key here is to try to support young people in recognising their emotions and relate them to the experiences they have had, and model how we might have done this in our lives. What we like about this strategy is that it comes so naturally to us as parents to tell our kids stories of 'the olden days' (as our kids call them) – when we were young.

Dr Robert Wood knows a lot about the power of stories. He founded the Centre for Stories in Perth. In his perfectly calm, easy way, Robert explains his use of reflective listening, or 'telling stories' from his own experiences to help his daughter, or his niece, to understand their own worlds: 'My niece was a bit self-conscious about her broken arm, so I just started telling her my own stories about my body, from when I was a kid and had really bad allergies. I was talking about how I always had rashes, and my allergies meant I couldn't eat eggs or cake or chocolate. She was just like listening to this story and I could see her thinking, "Oh, other people have things that go wrong with their bodies too" and "Oh, that's so much worse than having this thing on my arm." It's about connecting through the imperfections of the body.'

2. Anchoring

Professor Linda Lin explained the concept of anchoring in relation to parenting her own teens. She says it can be so hard as a rational, fully formed adult to remember the ups and downs of peer interaction in your teens, and how life-shattering singular comments and events can be. Again, it's hard not to be dismissive and say, 'Just get over it, we all did!' gesturing to all of the adults around you. It might be true, but it's not that helpful.

The reason why we got over it is because we learned perspective from sorting our experiences and anchoring them according to our own sorting system. Professor Lin says:

A lot of times, and particularly on social media, when someone does or doesn't comment, or they do or don't get the likes, or someone says something really nice or mean, kids will react to the extreme, and go straight to 'I feel great' or 'This is the worst thing ever.' Rather than trying to make them feel better about that particular scenario, we want to put it into perspective, and to get them thinking about all of the things in their lives that they do that are hard, or wonderful, or worthy of pride and feelings of accomplishment.

The concept of anchoring gives kids a reference point that helps them to gain perspective, and ensure that any one thing doesn't impact the way that they feel about themselves too much.

To do this, we want to create 'anchors', or scores from 0–100 in terms of how much effort they put into something, and how much they let things influence their sense of achievement or self-worth. It can be good to introduce this idea when you are not 'in the heat of the moment' or at a crisis point.

1. Start by getting your child thinking about something they have done that was really hard for them, like public speaking, or doing a test, or competing in a sport. Ask: 'How hard was doing that thing for you, on a scale from 0–100?' (The score should be high.)

2. Then get them to realise that the difficulty should relate to the sense of achievement. 'And so how proud did that make you feel about yourself, from 0–100?' (The score should be high again.)

3. Now compare this to the smaller things that usually cause their worlds to come crashing down. 'That post that someone made that negative comment on, how hard was that for you to make that? How much effort did it take?' (The score should be low!)

4. And then bring in the perspective: 'So how much should that affect the way you feel about yourself?' (The score should be low again.)

The whole idea is to praise progress over perfection, and effort over achievement.

Even though kids move away from the parents and family as the central influence on body image and identity, and towards the influence of their friends and peers, there's still a lot of support that we can offer our young people as they navigate these complex and challenging relationships, environments and developmental stages. Being informed about the extent and nature of the influences is more than half of the battle, so you're doing well already.

As parents, we can't underestimate the importance for kids of fitting in and feeling like they belong. And even though a lot of it feels toxic, for them it's like air. They *need* that feeling of belonging with their peers, in a way that we don't, and I think we can't discount that. Society has all of these toxic scripts and expectations and narratives about what it means to be a good girl, a valuable girl, a girl who is worthy. The intensity of those scripts can be different by gender, racial differences, visible differences, etc. But they are all internalising all of these really toxic messages. Our goal isn't to shield them from all of these messages, because that would be unrealistic, but it is to help them to understand that they don't have to accept those messages as true and follow

them blindly. They should be critical of all the messages they are receiving from society.

LEANNE, MUM OF TWO, USA

FAQs

Q: What do I say when my daughter complains that she is the biggest one in her friend group?

Dr Jody Forbes advises that the thing to do here is try to provide some perspective. The frontal lobes of teens are not developed, so they're not able to think things through rationally. So if your daughter says to you: 'Oh, my God, I hate myself, my stomach is so repulsive, and all of my friends are so skinny, it's not fair', start by reflecting what you hear, empathising, and validating her feelings and reminding her of the functionalilty of her body. 'Oh, it sounds like you're feeling really down about your body. I'm really sorry that you're feeling that way, I think you are so beautiful, I think you've got a gorgeous body and it's healthy, and it's fit, and it's strong. Your body helps you play netball and go swimming.'

Then start to question to make her curious about why she might be feeling that way, and bring in your own experiences: 'I wonder if it has been more difficult for you as you've developed curves, has that been hard for you, because your body's changing? I can remember when my body was growing and changing, I was feeling really uncomfortable in my skin around that time.'

You can try to push back against the idea that she is 'the biggest': 'I know your friends, and when I see you all together, you have all different shapes and sizes. I know sometimes you feel like everybody's skinnier than you, but all of the bodies around you are different – and they are all growing and developing and changing so much that it doesn't make sense to focus on how it is right now. But the fact is, that's absolutely not true.'

Finish by really trying to deflect from the need to compare her body with others. 'I try to talk about the other things she should be really proud of, and remind her that your weight doesn't define you, and that it's not really important anyway,' Dr Forbes says.

This perspective can extend out to other areas too. Jody says that sometimes it's a matter of being curious and asking questions:

- How do you know?
- What are the facts?
- What makes you think you are the 'dumbest' in the class?
- How do you know everyone else got a better result than you?
- How do you know everyone else was invited to the party?
- Could you have been left out for a different reason?

Asking these questions gets them to think through things more clearly and brings it back to the facts, without so much emotion behind it.

Then we could start to talk through what might make them feel better, and ask: what can I do to help? Would you feel healthier if we all cut down on soft drink? Would you like a tutor to support you with your maths? Is there something that would help you to actually feel more confident about your grades? This way, you are helping them to do some problem solving around what they can do, rather than saying to them, 'You're not fat', or 'You're not stupid', or 'Don't be ridiculous, just ignore this or that'. Often they are catastrophising, or they're seeing things in black and white, they're 'reading people's minds'. We want to gently support them in moving away from this to put those sorts of things in perspective, and empower them to move forward. It's so much more powerful than saying 'You need to do this, this and this' and 'fixing' the problem for them.

Q: My thirteen-year-old boy is a lot bigger than his peers, and his friends (always in a joking way) are talking about his 'man boobs' since they did swimming in PE. I just want to make sure he is healthy, and I would love to protect him from the bullying and teasing he gets every day. Should we encourage him to lose weight?

Ugh, kids are horrible to each other, aren't they? We know that you just want the absolute best for your boy. In general, it's best not to say anything about his weight. All the research suggests that when we tell young people they are in any of the larger bodies categories (like 'overweight' or 'obese'), it leads to increased body dissatisfaction, eating disorders, and weight gain. This is from multiple studies following kids over five-, ten- and fifteen-year time periods.

Your role here as the parent is to show that you accept your child and their body unconditionally. You may be the only person in their life who shows this acceptance – so make it known and say it loud and clear. Reassure him that there is nothing wrong with his body. It is totally normal, special and powerful in its own unique ways. Help him appreciate what his body can do, and help him feel strong.

It's better to try to change the situation and stop the teasing rather than changing your child's body. Depending on his personality, you could workshop some equally 'banter-like' responses that might put a stop to the man-boob talk. Or, you could work on creating something that he might say to himself to show himself some kindness that he is not getting from his friends right now.

If you want your child to be healthy, try to encourage them to engage in health behaviours, but present these as things that the whole family are doing to be healthy, not just something that he has to do because of his weight. Examples might be doing an 'eating more fruits and vegetables per day' challenge, or getting in thirty minutes of movement after school. If the thing you need to do is reduce or give up soft drink, make it apply to everyone in the family, and make it about the chemicals rather than the sugar.

Action

☑ Help your kids to broaden their friend group to have separate family friends, friends in different places, or for different activities. This helps to give a sense that someone always has their back, and that they belong – even when there is drama with their school friends.

☑ Have a conversation about body talk or fat talk with your kids. Have them come up with some ideas about how to avoid this in person or online. Follow up and ask how things are going.

☑ Practise reflective listening using the 'validation of feelings' sandwich:

Validate: 'That must be so hard for you. How does it make you feel?'

Empathise: 'I felt [x] when a similar thing happened to me.' (*Tell the story.*)

Reflect: 'It's okay to feel [x] right now.'

☑ Practise using anchoring to give perspective.

14

Families

Taryn

When my daughter Mikaela was about five, I took her to get her first proper haircut and blowdry at the hair salon. Before we arrived at the appointment, I rang the hairdresser to request that no-one was to make comments to Mikaela along the lines of 'You're so pretty.' You see, I was taught growing up that being pretty was really important, and it skewed my perception of what was important and what wasn't, so I was damned if I was going to let Miki think the same. The hair appointment went as smoothly as Miki's fresh hair and our next stop was a department store to get her a new outfit. As I lay the new clothes down on the counter, the attendant gushed at Mikaela, 'Aren't you just the prettiest girl!' She clearly missed my cues of dissatisfaction because she went on to say, 'Pretty like your mum. Are you having a girls' day out together?' In my head I was like, *Yes we're just two giddy and giggly girls shopping, getting our hair done, you know all the things, sugar and spice and everything nice, that's what little girls are made of.* Insert eyeroll.

Now, I know that she meant well, and to be honest if anyone deserves an eye roll in this story it's the control-freak mum, phoning people to request they don't compliment their daughter. I soon learned that I was not able to control every situation, and no matter how much thought or planning I put into a situation, whatever was going to unfold and be said was going to happen, regardless of anything I did.

At home, we often talk about attitudes towards appearance and behaviours around food, eating and physical activity because they form part of daily life as a family. This means that there are many opportunities to influence the thoughts and feelings that our teens have in relation to bodies, what appearance means, and how to look after ourselves.

One of the main influences here is comments from parents about their own insecurities or dissatisfaction about appearance, or comments about other people's bodies. Saying these things models what women should think about their bodies, or the value of thinness to our kids.

This means, as we said in Chapter 7, cutting back on saying unkind things about yourself like 'Ugh, I'm feeling so fat today' or 'I really shouldn't have that piece of cake', and 'I just need to lose five kilos, then I'll be happy'. The things we say to others, like 'You look great, have you lost weight?' are sending the same message.

Research shows that this 'weight talk' is one of the key influences from parents. For mothers, the effect of their dieting behaviours seems to be the strongest influence on kids. For fathers, it is the impact of teasing or making comments about bodies that have the strongest influence. All of these things are consistently found to relate to, and result in, body dissatisfaction, and increased use of unhealthy and extreme weight control behaviours, especially bingeing and purging.

COMMENTS ABOUT BODIES

One of the things that crushes our little optimistic spirits faster than ever is when we hear stories from young people saying that their parents comment about or tease them about their weight, shape and body in general. Yes, it still does happen.

Now, I'm pretty sure that if you are reading this book, you might already know that we shouldn't be teasing our own kids about what they look like. And if you, or others around you, have said things to your kids in the past, possibly without thinking, or probably with good intentions, we need to forgive those others and forgive ourselves, and move on.

But young people do report that their parents make comments about their weight, and report being teased, more often by fathers than mothers. Research shows that girls who report being teased by parents (mostly fathers) had higher levels of depression, body dissatisfaction, dieting and bulimic eating behaviours and lower levels of self-esteem than girls who reported that they were not teased. In addition, girls who were teased by fathers reported that they were also teased by siblings, as the fact that the dads were doing it kind of made it okay for others to say these sorts of things in the home. Teasing from fathers and older brothers was associated with the most negative outcomes in that study.

We want to be clear. Making comments about your child's body to them is harmful.

As Taryn says in the *Embrace Kids* documentary: Okay, parents, this one's for you. For all of the things that have changed in the world, there is one thing that hasn't, and that is: what we say and do in front of our kids matters. We must stop talking negatively about our bodies in front of our kids, and instead pave the way for them to move, nourish, respect and enjoy theirs.

Yes, we needed to put that in big bold writing, because it's very important.

Sometimes this teasing looks a bit like saying things in a 'joking' way, or having cute-but-kind-of-mean nicknames like 'Tubby' or 'Muffin-top'. Sometimes these comments are direct suggestions to diet or try to lose weight, or jokes or 'teasing' to suggest the same thing. The overall advice from the research in this area is that, whether you are talking about yourself, your children or other people, you should not say anything. And if you do need to say something, you can focus on health behaviours for health outcomes, rather than weight. If someone in your family is making comments to your kids, you can ask them to stop, or 'throw the book at them'. As in literally. This book.

Things to say to shut down body shaming

1. Please don't talk about my child's body like that. Saying those things can be really damaging – please don't do it again.
2. Research shows that shaming people doesn't improve their health behaviour. Please stop.
3. I know you are trying to help, but it's not helpful when you . . .
4. We don't talk about bodies like that in our family. I would appreciate it if you respect this.

Teasing from siblings is also really common, and potentially pretty damaging. Many of the mothers we spoke to connected their daughters' body image concerns with comments made to them by their sons. Kara, mum of two from the United States, said:

The first time I saw her start to notice something about her body that she wasn't happy with was because of criticism from her brother. She was nine at the time, and he said something about her thighs being fat. I put a quick stop to it, and said: 'Girls have enough issues with their bodies and body image, we don't need their brothers criticising them!' and he hasn't said anything since. But after that, I saw her from that time start to fixate a little bit on her thighs – just from that one comment. I noticed that when putting on her bathing suit or looking in the mirror, you could tell that she was worried about her thighs.

It also seems to be particularly important that siblings don't make unkind comments about parts of their brothers and sisters that are growing and changing because of puberty. It's usually the more obvious bits – breasts, thighs and bottoms getting bigger for girls, and being shorter or less muscular for boys. Teasing about acne, hair and other features is also off-limits. Young people are insecure and self-conscious enough about those things as it is!

Now that my three girls (eighteen, fifteen and twelve) have started sharing clothes, they're observing the differences between each other, the way they look, and their body types, and wondering why they look so different when they come from the same gene pool. Even with their two cousins, there's a fair bit of talk about some of them being bigger or taller than the others, and why some look different to the rest of the family.

The conversation last night actually got a bit teary and emotional. We were about to eat dinner and everything seemed fine, and then the next minute, one of the girls became upset and left the table in tears. She generally feels incredibly confident in her body but last night, she felt a sense of wanting her body to be thinner like her little sister, who is really skinny (and deeply self-conscious about that!). It's just really interesting, observing them observing each other. With sisters, there seems to be a deep connection, but also a sense that maybe the genetic lottery isn't fair.

I don't think jealousy is the right word, but here is someone who is so like you, yet so different, and you have to figure out how you feel about yourself, in relation to them. I didn't have sisters myself, so it's really interesting to observe that.

SARA, MUM OF FOUR, MELBOURNE

So we're about to suggest something here that might sound like hard work, but it's something that, if you do it early on, could actually prevent a lot of issues. We want you to sit down and write up a family agreement. If you can talk openly about it, and set a standard in your home, or draw up an agreement, or a list of rules – to say that you will respect your own and each other's bodies – it can prevent a lot of problems. These things generally work better when the suggestions for what to put in the agreement come from the kids, but you might want to come to this with some ideas.

Family agreement

We will respect our own and each other's bodies. We don't talk about the way our bodies look in negative ways. We are kind to ourselves and our bodies. We focus on what our bodies can do, and how unique and different and amazing they are. We celebrate diversity.

In addition to the framework outlined by Zoë Bisbing (see pp. 301–2) in the previous chapter, there are a few other things you need to be aware of when responding to a sibling issue – mostly because you're responsible for helping the one who was hurt as well as the one who did the hurting.

In order to respond to weight-based comments or teasing between siblings or extended family, it's important to jump in straight away and let them know that it's not okay. Something like 'Saying [what they said] can be really hurtful and harmful, and is unacceptable. It's really serious. We don't speak to each other like this in our home.'

The problem is that the most common response back to this will be: 'Yeah, but I was just joking.' If this happens, it's important to go further by saying something along the lines of: 'It's easy to say "Just joking" as an excuse to get away with this kind of comment.' This is a powerful statement, and works in lots of different contexts where kids might be bantering and teasing each other. Then remind them of the expectations again: 'In our house, we have agreed to avoid saying negative things to each other and ourselves about the way we look.'

There are also conversations that we can have when it's not the heat of the moment. Even though it might be awkward to raise the topic of bias about appearance, it is important that you reflect your family values of acceptance of diversity through active discussion. So when some things come up – maybe something has happened at school, or they see something in a movie – you can open up a conversation and ask: 'Why do you think some people might tease or bully, or be teased or bullied about the way they look?' This creates an opportunity to talk about the fact that some people do experience really hurtful comments, or negative experiences, based on the way they look, and this can be related to their size and shape, the colour of their skin, or whether they have a visible difference, disability or appearance-altering condition. Talking more broadly about appearance-related teasing and bullying, as well as stigma, discrimination and bias in relation to appearance, might help your teens to decipher some of the messages they see when they are out there in the world.

RESPONDING TO COMMENTS ABOUT YOUR OWN WEIGHT OR SHAPE

Talking about how harmful appearance-based comments can be within your family can help you to navigate this space, and hopefully prevent siblings from making appearance-based comments and teasing. Dealing with appearance-based comments at home can seem really tricky – and we know, as parents, that this seems to come up when we're least prepared and ready for it, but it is important to shut it down.

Talking about this within your family can also help your kids to be the people who can stand up for others. Who can start to spread the resistance to appearance-related teasing. So that the next generation of young people don't have to accept the comments; they can accept their bodies.

We've pre-prepared a few responses to the well-meaning-but-completely-inappropriate things some people say about each other's bodies – positive and negative. Take your pick and insert them into conversation as needed. You can model these yourself, or teach your kids to respond in these ways, or both!

Actually, I'd prefer we don't talk about my weight today.

I'm really comfortable with how healthy I am at the moment.

We don't talk about our bodies like that in our family.

My body is feeling really good, actually.

I feel uncomfortable with you saying that about me.

Actually, my weight isn't important. Could we talk about how school is going, my new job, my hobbies – anything other than my size?

Back up, did you really just say that about me?

So, what should we say about our kids' bodies?

Should we comment on appearance at all? It's a tough question – and one that we put to many of the experts and parents we spoke to. Here's what they had to say:

I think we should because I think our kids need to know that they look good the way they are.

JESSICA, MUM OF TWO, TASMANIA

In our family, their appearance also connects them to their cultural identity – their dad is from Argentina, so it's a big part of them – the Latin part – so we often talk about how they look being connected to who they are.

ANNA, MUM OF TWO, SWEDEN

I think it would actually be really unnatural for us to never say anything about their appearance – as long as it's not the only thing you are saying, it's fine – having a balance of comments across appearance, achievement at school, sport, being kind, all of the things, means that it is all in context.

RACHEL, MUM OF TWO, USA

In general, and much broader than just focusing on bodies, the advice is generally to praise effort over achievement, and process over product. You praise the fact that they worked hard at something rather than praising them for getting an award for it. We think the same thing applies here.

Other ways to praise your kids

Instead of this	Say this
'What a beautiful painting.'	'I love how you worked so hard on all of the colours here.'
'Well done – you got an A on the test!'	'See what happens when you study so hard – are you proud of yourself for that?'
'You look so pretty.'	'I like how you put that outfit together.'
'You look great.'	'You've got such a glow about you – are you feeling good inside?'

IT'S NOT ABOUT YOU

As parents, we are used to our kids being a little extension of us when they are small, and we are used to feeling like our child's appearance and behaviour is a reflection of our parenting ability. Part of the shame and fear when they are young and having a tantrum in a supermarket is about 'What does this say about me as a parent?' The exact same feelings can creep up when your teenager is presenting themselves and acting in a certain way.

As a parent, you have to be able to identify your own 'stuff', and then contain yourself. And that's with everything, not just body image – that's with grades and letting kids make mistakes and all sorts of stuff. But it is becoming increasingly difficult for parents to be able to separate themselves from their kids. They are so invested in their child's performance, their sporting and academic achievements, their popularity and their child's happiness. It makes it hard for the child to develop their own identity and their own interests when they have this pressure from the parents.

JENNY, MUM OF TWO, BRISBANE

So how do we separate ourselves, and let our kids do their own thing?

It's about recognising who they are, what their strengths, skills, personality, hopes and dreams are, and accepting that. You might not like it. You might journal about it to get all of your feelings out, and you might talk about it – a lot – with your therapist or psychologist. But accepting them – all of them – is good for everyone in the long run.

THE IMPORTANCE OF CONNECTION

One of the key themes that emerges from the research in this area is that young people are more likely to thrive when they have more positive and strong relationships with their parents. One really large study across twenty-four countries found that 'difficulty talking to mothers or fathers' was associated with body dissatisfaction. This finding was stronger among girls, but still there in most cases for boys. This made us curious about how exactly we maintain this 'strong relationship' and 'open communication' that sounds easy when you write it down, and yet so, so hard to do in practice, when they are, well, human, and, well, teenagers!

Dr Jody Forbes is a school psychologist at an independent girls' secondary school, and a mother of two girls herself. In her work, she sees girls about all of the things that trouble them, and delivers a number of presentations to parents. One of the main things she tries to teach is about the process of identity formation, and how necessary it is for adolescents to develop identities that are separate from their parents. She says:

> I talk to parents about holding on while letting go. I explain to them that the whole reason for adolescence is to form your identity. They need to go through these journeys,

to work out who they are, physically, socially, sexuality-wise, gender-wise. They're all exploring every single part of their identity.

So it's all normal. As a parent, you need to contain your fear, and not overreact, while they explore their identity. They're not always going to come out with the big black boots and eyeliner. Just like they might not always like the music they are into right now. They have to try on and explore these identities to work out who they are. They're going through that identity formation, and they will go through all of these phases and explore things.

If we react to that, if we're critical, if we draw our attention to certain things, or try to stifle that part of them, we mess with the process. We need to pick our battles and realise that it's not actually about winning.

What we need to do is renegotiate your relationship with them, put aside your 'stuff' compared to their stuff, so that you can continue to be supportive, and available, and close. As they get older, they do pull away. They need that autonomy, but parents find it so difficult. When I talk to parents I try to reframe that and help parents understand that the final phase of identity formation is that they need to pull away from you. So they can work out who they are separate from you. That's why they go in the bedroom and close the door. That's okay, that's quite normal. They need to be behind closed doors for a year or two to experience that time on their own, away from you, so that they know they can actually function.

So that's where we are holding on while letting go – letting them do certain things, letting them have their freedom and explore their identity, letting them voice their opinions, letting them argue with you at the dinner table, giving them those experiences of how to do those things within the safe structures of the family. Knowing that you always love them, you'll always be here. So then they can come out the other end, knowing themselves and who they really are, but also feeling capable and confident and still connected.

Professor Linda Lin tells us:

A lot of parents want it all done. Like, want every problem fixed in one conversation. And their kids, especially in middle school, are so awkward, they don't actually want to have these conversations with you all the time. Rather than thinking that you can 'fix' everything, and 'tick it off' in one conversation, we need to think of it more like planting little seeds, in nice little conversations. It's being proactive and mentioning things ahead of time, not bringing it up in the heat of a moment. Instead have a brief, quick conversation about the topic to plant the seed and circle back to that a few weeks or months later. You never know when they're going to be ready to talk to you about it. But if you can mention these things in small doses, they start to seep in.

The teen years are all about gaining independence to move out into the world, but they still need you to come back to every now and again to make sense of their experiences. As teens experience and experiment, it's important for you to be able to help them navigate this, and keep coming back to you for support and guidance. If you get angry at them for some of the things they have done that you don't approve of, it may mean that they are still doing those things, but have just stopped telling you about it, which isn't the best outcome!

Carmelita (Cat) Tiu, mother of two aged nine and eleven, producer and host of 'Know Them, Be Them, Raise Them', a podcast all about raising tween and teenage daughters, has a clear goal: 'My intention is really to be in the position of ally and cheerleader. I come from the position of "As long as it is safe, I will support you in whatever you want to do – it's us versus the issue, not me versus you".' Cat advises that you tell your kids that you want them to come to you, and talk to you no matter what. Instead of 'Oh, we're in trouble, better not tell Mum', it should be 'Oh, we're in trouble – let's call Mum'.

It can be a good idea to notice the times that they seem to open up. Most parents mention a few key times this happens, such as when you are doing some simultaneous activity where you aren't looking at each other (like driving or walking together) or doing something with your hands (like craft or folding laundry – if your kids help you with things like that; ours don't!). The other time is right before bed, when the lights are dimmed and they are a little sleepy. Ask them: 'I wanted to ask you about [X].' The darkness and sleepiness can encourage them to open up and can facilitate the feelings of intimacy and vulnerability required to deepen connection. You have an opportunity to put their minds at ease right before they process everything in their sleep. Despite the fact that this might just be them stalling their bedtime, it's a great chance to connect!

Families are all different, and complex, and special. The one thing you need to remember here is that teasing, and anything else that makes kids feel shame in the family environment, is to be avoided. That's it. Focus on coming together to move, nourish, respect and enjoy being together. Always.

Action

☑ Develop a family agreement with the people that live in your home, or with your extended family included.

☑ Have a hard conversation with someone in your extended family about body commentary, teasing and body shaming.

☑ Experiment with times when both you and your kids are up for a chat (e.g., in the car) and have a go at talking to them about how they can talk to you about anything.

15

Sexy time

WE'VE TALKED TO PARENT AFTER parent about the things that are going on with their kids right now in relation to their bodies. And we noticed that a lot of conversations also related to sexuality and sexiness, and the difficulty balancing these issues with encouraging teens to be confident about their bodies. We're not actually going to talk about relationships, sex and sexuality, as this book would be about twice its size if we did – and there are other books for that. But there are lots of situations where sexuality and bodies overlap in adolescence, so we want to dive in to talk fashion, sexting and showering.

SHE WEARS SHORT SHORTS

I struggle to know how to talk to her about modesty and getting untoward attention. This is the first time she's actually gone out wearing something other than baggy

jeans and jumpers. All of a sudden, I've got this little girl with these huge boobs who is wearing singlet tops. I've tried not to comment and just hope she works it out.

JANELLE, MUM OF TWO, QUEENSLAND

It's easy to dismiss clothing and fashion as something that's not that serious. But as we heard the struggles of parent after parent navigating this challenging topic, we realised that clothing is actually one of the most tangible and relevant topics in relation to body image – it just hasn't been studied that much in the research.

We have to wear clothes, right? Every day. There's a choice in how we put things on our bodies. There's the feeling – the comfort (or not) factor, and the identity factor, and the 'fitting in' factor. To choose what to wear, you generally look on social media or in magazines – both of which have been blamed for body image issues – and then you go into a store or online, where you see even more idealised bodies and social comparisons. And that's just the beginning. Fashion is marketed to be all about aspiration, and usually, all about thinness. We try to wear things that are fashionable and new and fit our bodies. Young people – and in particular, young girls – are just trying to figure all of this out.

Mothers of young adolescent girls explain:

I'm starting to see that she's so much more about the clothing and the fashion, it's suddenly really important to her. This tends to be about fitting in or impressing other girls – it's not about the boys yet – it's much more about girls accepting her or being included, and feeling like she's part of something by virtue of wearing certain clothes or brands. She will say: 'I really need that brand of sweatshirt', or a particular pair of shoes. It's mostly driven by her friends and peers but I'm sure social media is part of that, too.

JILL, MUM OF TWO, SYDNEY

But the girls all look the same with the ripped jeans, and the crop tops. I sound like the middle-aged person that I am, but their clothes are just more and more revealing. My daughter was crazy about this hot pink dress that was so short and low cut. When she came out of the changeroom my reaction was like 'Whoah – that's way too much'. She said: 'Don't you want me to feel confident in my body? Don't you want me to feel empowered?' She was using those words. It's hard, because I do want her to feel confident, but I also know that when I see girls wearing those sorts of clothes, they're not comfortable, and they're always pulling them up or down, or super conscious of how it looks. I talked to her about balance. I said, 'I know I sound like an old lady, and I want you to feel confident, but also there's things that are appropriate, and things that are not'. I used the word 'appropriate', whatever that means.

MONICA, MUM OF TWO, USA

There is this growing sense of outrage (mostly from teen girls themselves) that we require teen girls to be 'modest' and to censor their clothing choices 'for their protection' when technically, what we are talking about here is that men can't control their actions when women wear less clothing. The problem is with the men, not the women.

The younger generation are also seeing mixed messages in the media.

There's such a fine balance between empowerment and exploitation. I think our girls are seeing a lot of women who are owning that empowerment to be sexual. We see celebrities use it, and music artists, and my daughter watches some of these. These women seem to be saying, you know what, I'm going to own it. But there's another part of me that feels like, yes, they are empowered, but they're also still using their bodies like objects. I get confused and don't really know how to talk to my daughter about that.

CELESTE, MUM OF TWO, USA

Many of the experts in parenting teen girls suggest that our reaction here is driven mostly by our own discomfort. In some cases, the feeling that we can't quite put our finger on is that we are grieving the little girl that we've lost and thinking: 'Geez, that went quickly.' But when we open our mouths, everything that was said to us about our clothing choices, and about our bodies – either directly or indirectly – comes marching right out, even if that's not what we planned.

So, how do we help young girls to feel the power of being confident in their bodies while still staying safe as we navigate this transition from child to adult? We don't want to make girls feel ashamed or self-conscious of their bodies. Ever. At all. But sometimes, what they do and what they wear trigger us, the adults, to feel uncomfortable about things. We bring our older, middle-aged, understanding of sexuality and sexual cues to the situation, along with our own baggage from our own experiences, our judgement, and our fears about their safety. The outfits make us uncomfortable for so many reasons, but judging or reacting strongly to that outfit won't be that helpful. We blurt out 'You can't go out wearing that', when that's not really what we are trying to say.

The kinds of clothes they are wearing now as teenagers – the really short shorts, and the crop shirts, and the g-string bikinis – there are a lot of choices they're making. I want my daughter to feel empowered to make her choice, and I don't want her to feel ashamed of her body, but I also want her to be aware of how some people might perceive that.

ELSA, MUM OF TWO, USA

In an interview on the *Raising Good Humans* podcast, Dr Lisa Damour encourages us to consider this from their developmental level. At twelve and thirteen, young girls don't understand the way that sex and intimacy works, and what it means to actually be 'sexy' in the ways we do as adults. They don't understand anything about what it actually means to initiate sex. They are just wearing the outfit that everyone else is wearing, that they have seen online or seen the 'cool kids' wearing. They are trying to wear that outfit to look good and impress their friends. They are just doing the dance moves that they have seen other people doing that they think looks good. They are just trying to do what is 'cool' and what they feel they need to do to fit in. These outfits mean something completely different to teenagers than they do to us.

But what do most parents say? 'Oh my god, you are not going out like that!'

Cue shame.

Cue argument.

Dr Damour encourages us to think about opening up a conversation about clothing like this: 'That looks really cute on you. I know you're just wearing what everyone else is wearing. Here's where I'm struggling – those shorts are really short. Clothes send a message, and you want to be aware of the messages you are sending. I'm not sure if I'm ready for you to have to deal with the reactions that might come your way.'

It's about finding the words that aren't shamey and don't imply that it's your daughter's 'fault' for making other people (parents, men, boys) feel uncomfortable because of what they're wearing. It's best not to use words like 'slutty' or 'tramp' and avoid ultimatums – they're a great way of making your teen dig their heels in!

A young woman we spoke to shared her experience: 'If I was wearing something that Dad didn't like, he would ask me "What's your reason – why are you dressing like that? Is it just for the likes, and the reaction? Or is it because you feel comfortable being yourself in that?" We could make our own choices, but he made us explain those choices.' She told us this strategy worked, as this approach did actually make her slowly realise and question whether her outfits, and eventually her actions, were to please others or herself. So if you can't quite remember what Dr Damour recommends, just ask 'Why?'

It's about opening a conversation. Over time, you can talk to her about what did happen when she wore certain things, the reactions that people had, and whether those reactions reflected her true value. You can have a discussion about the sorts of names that other girls might have been called when they wore certain things, and how wrong it is to judge and label people or make assumptions in this way.

Dr Damour has two teen girls herself, and has written two books about parenting adolescent girls. She is quick to explain that teen girls will roll their eyes and come back with something along the lines of being confident in her body, comfortable with her sexuality, and feeling empowered. She suggests that you position yourself as a curious ally – someone who wants to know 'how kids think and talk these days' as though you are some alien who has come from space on a mission to understand things, but ultimately has her best interests at heart. From there, you can prompt her thinking, questioning and consideration of how she wants to walk out into the world.

The other side of this is, of course, the experience of the boys around them. It's not about changing what the girls wear – we want girls to be able to express themselves and wear what they want to wear, so let's teach boys about this too. Talk about the fact that they have a strong role to play in creating change, supporting girls and women and calling out disrespectful behaviour among their friends. Let's have these conversations with them, in front of them, or around them. Question why people might have certain attitudes and opinions about what girls wear, and what 'signals' clothing might or might not be sending. We want to talk them through the fact that yes, bodies can be very distracting, but in the end, it all comes down to respect. Teach boys *and* girls to respect women enough not to treat them like objects. Whether they are in front of you or on social media, or you are out with your mates and they are way over there. We act with respect. And it's about teaching boys and girls to respect themselves, and not treat *themselves* as objects. To value themselves more than a reaction, a look, or a 'like' that they get. To know their worth beyond their weight and appearance.

One size does not fit all

While we're still on clothes and shopping, though, it can be hard for kids who don't feel like they 'fit' into the 'standard sizes' in stores. This is something that we're hoping to shift and change with more dialogue and advocacy with brands and retailers – to create an environment where everyone feels comfortable and able to express themselves through what they wear.

Katrina, a mum of two who lives in Sydney, told us:

I think it is a problem for girls in Australia in that, when you are above a size 14, you can't find anything that fits you in mainstream shops, so you start to think there's something really wrong with you. In England, the regular stores have all of the sizes, so you feel a bit more normal being able to choose things in the same shops as everyone else. You just feel like you're not represented when nothing fits you.

It makes me sad that there are young girls trying to work out where they fit in the world, and are being labelled with a number that you can't even find in the shops. If you're going to go out there and change the world, you need to be able to feel like you're covered - clotheswise.

It's slowly changing. There are brands now that have larger sizes and more diverse models. But a lot of it still involves online shopping. To really have that confidence, you need to be able to walk into a shop, and just buy everything - underwear, bras, swimsuits. I've never bought swimwear in the shops, it's always online. And that makes it feel secret, shameful, like I should be hiding something, or hidden away.

That's what I would want to see changing by the time my daughter goes shopping. If she ends up with big boobs like me, or curvy because that's in her genes, I want her to be able to go into a shop and buy anything anywhere. To feel included.

So, brands, if you're listening. Let's increase the size range. Let's have it in stores, all in the same area together, so you don't have to go to the back corner to find anything above a size 12. Let's design for a wider range of body types. Let's use images in your store and online marketing that depict a wide range of bodies in your clothing. Let's have sizing information and change rooms that make everyone feel welcomed in the vulnerable moment of trying on jeans and swimsuits. Let's encourage your retail assistants to be inclusive and supportive. Oh, and pockets, please - while we're dreaming up a wish list, we want pockets.

SEX IN A TEXT

Sexting is something that most of us weren't able to do when we were kids. Fast forward twenty years and kids are now able to Snapchat a picture of themselves to anyone they like. Sexting can therefore seem pretty scary to us adults. As parents, when we are scared of something, we can try to control it or to ban it, but this isn't always effective in achieving the best outcomes.

Dr Kristina Holmqvist-Gattario has conducted research on sexting among teenagers and has this advice: 'In Sweden, the emphasis in sex education at school is on sexual safety rather than abstinence, and so I think we need to treat sexting in a similar way. We need to talk with our children about the privacy risks, and about images being used for other purposes, going viral, or staying on the internet forever. If we talk about the risks but say they are not allowed to do it, that might be the end of important discussions further on.'

So yes, it's awkward, but it is important to start – and keep having – these conversations with your kids, so that they have a chance to hear your perspective, to think about their perspective, and to know that they can come to you to talk about these things – especially if things go wrong.

Dr Carolina Lunde, who collaborated on the study, adds: 'Young people have just integrated and incorporated the digital world into every aspect of their lives – including exploring their sexuality online. The privacy of the digital arena allows for trying out stuff that you maybe wouldn't be able to try otherwise.'

Young people want to do this to explore their sexual curiosity or sexual enjoyment, but there is also an element of seeking positive reinforcement and validation about their body and appearance. Carolina adds: 'I think that could be an empowering way to get that validation or approval of how you look. But on the other hand, we wouldn't want people to be too invested in appearance and for this to be the only messages they receive about their body.'

There are lots of resources to guide parents and young people around this – check them out in the Resources section.

PERSONAL HYGIENE

Many parents asked about the delicate balance between encouraging hygiene and grooming without shame or without creating a focus on appearance. And the flip side of that – encouraging teens who are spending a lot of time, effort and energy on grooming to be a little less obsessive about maintaining their appearance.

It's hard to find the balance between appearing presentable, professional, and 'neat and tidy', and caring or focusing too much on the way we look. It's good to talk about the purpose or the motivation behind the things you might be doing with your appearance. What is the reason behind you wanting to dress and look a certain way? It's nice to look nice, but it depends whether we are doing it for ourselves or for other people. If we're comfortable in our own skin, that's okay. But if we feel our best when we've got our lashes on, and our eyebrows done or our nails painted, then I'm not saying there's anything wrong with that. But it's a hard one, because you are sort of conforming to the beauty ideal.

You just have to make sure that you're doing it for you, rather than for others.

AARAVI, MUM OF TWO, UK

FAQs

Q: How do I encourage my kids to look after themselves – to shower, clean their teeth, brush their hair and wear deodorant without making it about appearance?

It's pretty easy to get away without bathing your kids that much when they're young, but at that stage you can also just plonk them in the bath when you need to. Once puberty is in full swing, it's a little more complicated.

The main message here is to encourage personal grooming for health reasons rather than appearance, and to focus on the way that looking after their bodies might make them feel. You might like to talk about the changes in their body, how and why body odour is produced, and how often you shower and apply deodorant to keep your body healthy. You could talk through a schedule for what hygiene activities your kids will do when, and how often. Involving them in buying nice products that they would like to use can be helpful too. Talking about how nice and fresh you feel after a shower, or how they might feel after they shower can help to encourage self-care and give them a nice reason to do these activities for themselves rather than for you or anyone else. Using light-touch questioning like 'How many days has it been since we've washed your hair?', and 'Do you think it might be time for a shower?' can help rather than the more direct 'You stink!' Kids can get really self-conscious about their body odour, and any teasing about this from siblings can easily slide into teasing about appearance, so it's best to nip that in the bud wherever you can.

On the other side of the spectrum, teenage girls are often stereotyped as spending too long in the bathroom, and 'wasting time' on hair, beauty and makeup. Some of the parents we interviewed ask how to manage the balance between encouraging girls to care about their appearance enough, but not too much.

The way that Sara, mum of four (including three teenage girls) from Melbourne, talks about this makes us realise that while we think of it as 'caring about their appearance', it's about so much more than that: 'It's about them caring for their bodies and wanting them to be well and trying to give themselves what they need at a particular time. They love to do face masks and I'm just so conscious of affirming that what they're actually doing is looking after themselves and caring for themselves – it's not anything about beauty or looking any different afterwards, it's about investing that time and effort into yourself, and your own self-care. I grew up thinking that too much time looking in the mirror was vain or shallow. I never want them to doubt that looking after yourself, getting to know yourself and your body, and having that deeper knowing, is one of the best things you can do.'

While it may be partly about the way they look, it's more about giving themselves time to be with themselves, and treating them to the things that feel good, and make them feel good.

Action

Time for some reflection. Think back to your memories of your adolescent experiences in relation to:

☑ **Clothes shopping, fashion and modesty.**

☑ **Expressing sexuality and how sex education was delivered.**

☑ **Spending time on your personal hygiene and appearance.**

How might your experiences shape your responses and reactions to these concepts when they arise in your home? Consider your beliefs and values, and write about the sort of approach you would like to take with your kids.

16

Movement

AH, MOVEMENT. SOMETHING THAT KIDS seem to do so naturally for so long – to the point where you find yourself anchoring all furniture to the wall, searching Google for 'fully fenced playgrounds', and crossing the city for the chance to finally sit down while your cherubs burn off some energy. And then at some point, it changes. They get self-conscious. They start to worry about how they look while they are moving their bodies. They start to compare their sporting abilities and achievements to those of their peers. They sit down throughout lunchtime instead of tearing around the playground. And it takes a lot of convincing to get them to any sort of after-school sport or movement opportunity.

Physical activity is one of the things that most experts bang on about. We know it is good for us. We know it is good for our kids. But it's a complex thing, and there are many barriers to engaging in physical activity. Just knowing that it is good for us does very little to get us off our butts to do it.

It's hard, for one. Physically uncomfortable at times. Painful at others. Mostly involves sweating, which means we have to shower.

Most sports involve a certain level of showing up, saying 'I can do that' and putting our bodies on the line. Even if it is F grade hockey, or the swimming carnival at your regional high school – being active makes us vulnerable. There's a lot of reasons to avoid it, so why should we do it?

WHY SHOULD KIDS BE ACTIVE?

The short answer is that moving your body is good for you. It's good for you in all of the ways that have probably been repeated over and over again in public health messaging ever since that 'Norm' ad where he gets off the couch and starts running.

What Norm didn't tell you is that physical activity is also great for our kids' mental health. Studies around the world have confirmed it, and the evidence is stronger for adolescents than it is for children. Specifically, there are significant associations between physical activity and lower levels of psychological ill-health (i.e., depression, stress, negative affect, and distress) and greater psychological wellbeing (e.g., self-esteem, satisfaction with life and happiness).

Physical activity can also lead to improvements in body image. While research among adolescents has mostly just looked at the relationship between physical activity and body image, and concluded that the more active adolescents feel better about their bodies, studies with adults have found that even a thirty-minute session of riding on a stationary bike can make you feel better about your body.

Why? It turns out that these improvements in body image are

not due to any physical changes in the body that could happen as a result of being physically active. They happen because we feel a sense of achievement. We experience what it feels like for our body to be doing something, and not just being something to look at. We feel strong, competent and capable, and all of those things mean that we will be more likely to engage in physical activity again.

All of this research basically tells you what you already know. It's good for kids to be active. But this message can get a bit caught up in then specifying how much, what kind, and when and where this activity 'should' take place.

What we really need to aim for is kids moving and experiencing success with their bodies. If this looks like playing sport, great. If this happens incidentally as you force them to come with you on errands around town, perfect. If your kid loves yoga, they can do yoga. If they want to dance, let them dance. Not even in formal lessons. Just dance alone in your bedroom in the dark if that's where they feel most comfortable. The idea here is that they 'just do it' and no, we're not even sponsored by that major sporting goods brand. The advice still applies. Some kids will be more likely to move if you are doing it too; others will want to do their own thing. The key is to ask them more about what they want, try different things, and experiment.

Move for me – Ideas to get kids moving

1. Bike, scoot, do parkour or skate as active transport.
2. Find a nature trail or bushwalk. Try mountain biking or orienteering.

3. Turn up the music and dance. Put on a show.

4. Go ice skating, try a high ropes course, or laser tag.

5. Try some YouTube Yoga or Just Dance.

6. Slide down sand dunes (and run back up again!).

7. Practise soccer/basketball/netball in the park with parent or friends.

8. Play in a swimming pool.

9. Try circus, trampolining, Irish dancing, cheer sports, Ultimate Frisbee or martial arts.

10. Walk the dog. Race the dog. Carry the dog around.

GIRLS IN SPORT

So many research articles start off with the same old story: 'Girls are less active than boys. Girls drop out of sport, never to return. X per cent of girls don't meet the daily physical activity guidelines.' There are special sessions in conferences dedicated to girls in sport, and masses of research funding spent on programs to help reverse this situation.

One thing that is rarely considered in all of this outcry about physical activity is the fact that the way girls feel about their bodies might impact on their willingness to be active.

Girls often raise this in focus groups and interviews. They say that they don't want to get sweaty, they don't enjoy it, there are other things they would rather be doing, they are worried about how they look, and they don't feel comfortable in the uniforms.

And is it any wonder, when social, regional netball clubs require girls to wear skin-tight competition dresses to play in?

Is it any wonder that girls don't really feel like joining in because they have their period but have to wear white shorts to play? Has anyone thought about making girls feel more comfortable about what they are wearing so they feel more confident in putting their bodies on the line?

In the first ever Australian survey of adolescents' sports uniform preferences, it was found that only half of the adolescent girls (aged twelve to eighteen) indicated that they can 'forget about what I look like and focus on my performance', and a quarter agreed that 'When I wear my school uniform, it feels like people are judging me because my body is on display'. In open-ended comments, girls specifically requested sports uniforms that are designed to provide adequate coverage so they don't feel exposed in situations like 'sitting down' or 'going for the ball'. It all makes sense really, it makes so much sense, and yet some schools and clubs don't seem to think about this at all. It's been encouraging to see some of the excellent developments in elite sport with athletes wearing bodysuits and boycotting skimpy uniform requirements – let's extend this to kids' sport too. What is stopping clubs from just saying 'Here is the t-shirt [in a wide range of sizes] and you can wear whatever items you feel comfortable in on your bottom half'?

What girls want

1. Uniforms that fit their bodies (not the 'unisex' ones that are actually just the boys' uniforms).
2. Fabric that absorbs sweat. We've accepted that girls

> do a lot more than 'perspire' but they still don't feel like showing everyone that they do.
> 3. Not too tight, not too loose: just right.
> 4. Shorts, not skirts. There is nothing sporty that is easier to do in a skirt than shorts.
> 5. Dark-coloured shorts. They are already self-conscious enough about their period. Let's not make it worse with white shorts.

Professor Clare Hanlon, who led the research, thinks that providing girls with more choice around what they wear to play, and what they will feel comfortable in, could be a game changer in terms of increasing young girls' physical activity levels and sports participation: 'Findings from this study could enhance school and sport club uniform policies for girls when playing sport or being physically active to assist with their confidence, feeling comfortable and readiness to participate.'

Of course, some girls love playing sport, and it plays a really big part in their lives, as we heard from some parents:

My daughter is thirteen, enjoys soccer and volleyball, and playing these sports is a big part of her identity, they're a big part of how she spends her time and where she finds a lot of joy and pride – and she feels successful. Doing these sports activities is so empowering and such a good influence because she's using her body to do these amazing things, and to win, and it's all about the sport, and she is in an environment of supportive girls. I love the fact that she's getting joy from her body, that it has nothing to do with how it looks.

KELLIE, MUM OF TWO, BOSTON

Unfortunately, sport is another place where we can feel left out and vulnerable when we aren't picked for a team. If *Bring It On* has taught us anything, nowhere is more brutal than in cheerleading:

There's no I in team, but there's an I in rejection

My daughter really wanted to be a cheerleader. I think she loved the image of it all, and the Hollywood version of *Cheer* – it was all just so glamorous and exciting. So she joined the team – there weren't any tryouts, anyone could join the team. Then one night after practice she got an anonymous Snapchat that said: 'We don't want Poppy to join, because she's too fat.' She didn't tell me for about three days, and then she came into our room in the middle of the night and broke down and told me and, and I was – understandably – horrified. She was like: 'Please don't say anything – I don't want to get the girls in trouble.' I promised I wouldn't say anything, but of course, I did say something – I had to! It was too extreme just to let it go.

I called the coach, and said things like: 'Bullying leads to real consequences, and self-esteem issues, and I'm holding you guys responsible for this.' I'm not sure that Poppy realised what went on, but they definitely took it seriously. They met with the girls on the team, and took it to the board and everything. The coach really took Poppy in and protected her throughout the year. I don't know why she still wanted to do it, but she did! She wore the outfits and the big bows in her hair, and she had a great year.

So now she has started high school, and she tried out for cheerleading again, and she didn't get in. She says it's because she's too fat. So she's still feeling this horrible way. We've tried really hard to, you know, bolster her confidence and tell her how wonderful she is, but I'm not sure we can ever make up for what was done to her.

AMANDA, MUM OF TWO, USA

BODY SHAMING IN SPORT

There are so many benefits to being involved in sport: being part of a team, learning new skills and getting in some solid activity and movement. It should be something that every kid can be involved in without judgement – whether or not they are 'naturally talented', and no matter their size or shape. But unfortunately, some high-profile public cases, and quiet anonymous whispers from athletes at all levels, have alerted us to something else we need to be worried about. Some of the coaches and support staff involved in sport are making comments about athletes' bodies – both male and female – in various settings. Maybe this has been obvious all along, but what is concerning is the impact that it has on young people, as outlined in the following examples.

Body shaming from a soccer star

My oldest son Gus loves soccer. He is such a beautiful, respectful kid, and he just loved the sport, and had so much fun – he was actually quite good at it too. Gus had had a really good year playing with the under 10s and then the club brought over this big well-known Brazilian footballer who came to Australia and played in the A-League. Let's call him Francisco. Everyone was so excited about having Francisco – such a star – on the A-League team, and when he said he wanted to coach some of the junior teams, the club was delighted!

When Gus went to try out for the under 11s team, this superstar, Francisco, was there overseeing a training session. He pulled Gus aside and told him that he was heavy, he was unfit, and he needed to lose some weight. Gus is so polite, so apparently he just said 'Okay', but deep down he was actually quite devastated.

It took a while for him to tell us, but when he did, my husband was like: No, that's not right. He shouldn't make those comments to kids that age, it should be all about participation. You shouldn't have any focus on your ability, let alone how you look. We complained to the club, and the club didn't do anything about it, they had their superstar. So we left, and then there was this mass exit from the club. We found out that Francisco had spoken to probably about ten other players, and told them that they were too fat, or told their parents that the kids were too fat, they needed to lose weight. These were literally pre-pubescent kids who hadn't even started growing yet, let alone stopped. A lot of them gave up the sport because of that.

It doesn't sound like a huge incident, but I was just always completely outraged. It's obviously done some damage to Gus because he is very conscious of how he looks. He loves his food and he's quite active, but he still makes comments about his upper body and what he is eating. He is always making comments about wanting to be taller, slimmer, more toned. I do wonder if he would still be thinking this way and doing these things if Francisco hadn't body shamed him in that way.

DONNA, MUM OF THREE, ADELAIDE

An Olympian's perspective

I started Little Athletics when I was seven, and for the first few years, I can't recall anything about the way we talked or behaved or anything that indicated body dissatisfaction, or that it was even on people's minds. There were a range of different bodies and it was more of a 'function over form' headspace (which I'm trying to get back to now!). It was more like: 'Oh, that girl is good at throwing, and she's really strong, perhaps she's more muscular', and 'How fantastic that these girls find it easier to run further because they have that long, lean body shape.' Everyone had their superpowers and celebrated them, without comparing or attaching moral value to our different shapes.

I remember my first trip to a national athletics competition as a junior and recognising that all the senior athletes who I aspired to be like one day looked a particular way. I remember saying to Mum, 'They all have six-packs.' From that little glimpse, I had this idea of a cookie-cutter image of what a senior professional athlete should look like. I also (wrongly) assumed that the professional women athletes looked this way *all* year, as opposed to having normal healthy fluctuations in body composition. If I wanted to progress in this sport and become an Olympian one day, I'd have to look like them.

The current messaging from coaches can often take a very narrow, 'performance-based' focus, where smaller is better – at any cost. Male coaches in particular often said hurtful things, which have been imprinted in my mind ever since. There were comments that girls were looking 'a bit soft around the edges' or that someone 'was looking really fit', but even the positive comments were damaging. I wanted to say something and call them out, but I didn't know where to start. These influential figures in sport do come from a different generation, where commenting on female athletes' bodies was totally okay, if not necessary, for them to be doing a good job.

Rather than helpful support led by sports dietitians, I remember coaches and managers who were not educated in the food and body space giving unsolicited advice. On one international trip, a (female) manager sat us down on day one and told us a story about how, last year, some girls had gone a bit berserk at the buffet, and put on a few kilos before their competition, where they all performed really poorly. Her advice was to 'Go to every buffet with a plan, and be rigid so you don't make that silly mistake.' That has certainly ruined buffets for me.

From age fourteen onwards, we started to go on extended training camps and to international competitions where I started to pick up on little ideas that the other girls were putting out there. I think that many of these ideas were heavily influenced by social media influencers, and adult figures in their daily lives. Despite high training loads, these young women athletes would feel a pressure to copy celebrity 'Day On A Plate' diets because they were promised that this would lead to impossible body transformations to fit an ideal. Many of the young women in my sport were hesitant to get into the gym and build muscle that would elevate their sporting performance, because of the online pressure to be slim and 'fit.' These habits have been a slippery slope to long-term body dissatisfaction, disordered eating and simply a reduced enjoyment of life for lots of the girls I grew up training with.

The offhanded comments from these coaches, managers and parents, the casual chit chat between girlfriends in sport and toxic messaging from social media meant that eventually when I got to about seventeen, I could only associate sport with imposter syndrome. Feelings of pressure and nerves and not being right, like not quite fitting and not looking the right way, or feeling the right way. I was always taught that moving and sport was good for me, but the cons started to outweigh the pros. I just thought, 'This is crap – I don't want another minute of this! And that's when I really gave up on that idea of becoming an Olympian and pursuing it at the higher level for the ages of seventeen and eighteen.

It wasn't until school was finished and I was trying get back into the elite level training that I actually connected with a fantastic sports dietitian. She recognised pretty quickly that I was heading down the slippery slope with disordered eating behaviours and Relative Energy Deficiency in Sport [RED-S – see below for more information]. With this sports dietitian and a sports psychologist, I was able to shift the focus from form to function: could I be grateful for all that my body does for me and how it feels, rather than how it looks? My sports dietitian had some fantastic body acceptance cards with questions that prompted discussion in this space. Because of the culture we live in and the amount of unhelpful messaging out there, it does take ongoing work and awareness to come to the place I am now. I've just lived my dream of competing at the Olympic Games. I guess I can now recognise that in my sport, body composition is important from a performance point of view for those few weeks of the year where we're trying to perform at the Olympics. But I also understand that for most of the year, in order to be a happy, regular woman with a stable mood, I really need to unhook from a lot of those pressures. I've realised that I need to be careful of who I am following on social media, and recognise the sorts of conversations when they're happening with friends, and not only not allow myself to fall into them, but even try to point it out and help friends through it.

MELISSA, 23, ATHLETE

Relative Energy Deficiency in Sport (RED-S)

What used to be called the 'female athlete triad' when we were young is now called 'RED-S' – a broader, more comprehensive term as experts have realised that energy deficiency in sport affects men too. RED-S is a clinical syndrome where athletes do not consume enough energy to fuel their training and performance needs, resulting in impaired physiological functioning. Effects include impacts on their metabolism, bone health, immunity, cardiovascular health and menstrual function (in women). Psychological implications can either precede RED-S or occur as a result of low energy availability.

These stories make us sad. Actually, they make us angry. To think that adolescents, in the peak periods for physical growth and determining their identity, are so affected by these comments from people who are doing their best, but who don't have qualifications in nutrition or psychology is a very real concern. As parents, we put our kids into sport thinking that it will be good for them. Good for them to develop fitness, and an appreciation of what their bodies can do. Good for them to build character, work as a team, develop resilience.

Before we get too worried about the potential for negative experiences in sport and physical activity, Fiona Sutherland is here to reassure us: 'The research seems to indicate that involvement in sport is actually more protective than risky.' Fiona has done a lot of work with athletes and dancers as a sports dietitian, but also advises many sporting organisations about how to take an approach that will be protective of body image.

THE BODY CONFIDENT SPORT GUIDELINES

Over at the Body Confident Collective, Dr Georgie Buckley has put together the Body Confident Sport Guidelines, informed by the research from her PhD. This document is intended to inform sport policy and practice, and applies to athletes, parents, coaches and sports administrators. These five recommendations are designed to be relevant to all sports, to ensure that sporting environments are safe, welcoming and inclusive for all. You can access the full document through the Resources section, but the five guidelines in brief are as follows:

1. Use language that builds and sustains body confidence and avoids body shaming.
2. Prioritise mental and physical health and performance over weight and body composition. This means not weighing athletes or doing body composition tests like skinfold measurements.
3. Promote nourishing the body with food instead of supplements.
4. Provide a variety of uniforms that are size and access inclusive.
5. Create a sporting environment, team and club culture that is welcoming, safe and inclusive.

ENSURING THAT A CLUB OR CLASS IS BODY POSITIVE

Fiona Sutherland @themindfuldietitian gives us some things to look out for when finding a new class or club for your kids:

- Have a look at whether there is any size and body diversity in the older age groups. This will tell you a lot about how inclusive they are.
- Go to a class if you can, and listen to what they say about bodies.
- Ask the director or the teacher: What do you think about body inclusion?
- Check if they have a body image statement or a body positive statement.
- Ask about flexibility with uniform requirements.

Kids' sport and activity clubs should be safe places for all bodies. They should be spaces where the people in charge understand and appreciate that their bodies are still 'in progress'. They should be places where everyone feels included, and where bodies are respected because of what they can do, not what they look like. The only way we can make this a reality is by championing change from the ground up. If every parent can start to ask questions about body inclusivity, be aware of potential body shaming, and encourage clubs to take an inclusive approach, we will see change.

At the end of this chapter, we hope you now feel more aware of the broader reasons why moving our bodies is good for our kids and have some more ideas about how to get our kids moving with active transport, recreational family activities, classes, and more formalised sport in and out of school. We've talked a lot about the potential for body shaming in sporting contexts, and we think you will be pretty onto this now – hopefully you are feeling like you can influence change in terms of recommending broader uniform options, calling out body shaming, being aware that we shouldn't be weighing kids in sport, or recommending that they take supplements, and checking in to see if clubs and sports take a body confident approach.

FAQs

Q: What can you say when your child comes home saying they 'want a six-pack'?

We've heard that all eight-year-old boys are currently obsessed with six-packs – this seems to be related mostly to those who are into soccer (or football!) as they are looking up to their idols who all have six-packs, some of whom are spruiking expensive electronic devices that stimulate the muscles to contract with 'less effort', promising 'rock hard abs'.

It's important to try to dispel some associations between muscularity and masculinity, and some assumptions that everyone can (or should) have a six-pack.

Here are some things to talk through:

- Why do you want a six-pack? What does that mean? Where did you hear that from?
- Anatomy. We all have abdominal muscles in our stomach.

Some of us just have more fat over the top so you can't see the muscles as well.

- Functionality. What's the point in having the abs or the pecs like that? It won't really help you playing soccer/football.
- Time. Think about the amount of time those athletes put in to having a body like that. Is that how you want to spend your time? Would you rather spend time with friends instead of being in the gym to look like that?
- Health. In order for the muscles to show up like that, you need to have a very low percentage of body fat, lower than what is healthy for most people.
- Genetics. We all have different genes that decide how much fat we will have on our bodies and where it goes. Not everyone can have a six-pack.

Q: Are Fitbits and activity trackers a good idea to encourage kids to be active?

This is a really tough question. We know that physical activity has benefits for physical and mental health, so having a device that promotes that could be a good thing. However, there is always the possibility that kids might get obsessed with meeting certain goals, or tracking their data. We've seen girls at netball freak out when their parents take their Fitbit off, as per the rules of the game, because they want their movement during the game to 'count.'

Like most issues in parenting, it's not really about the activity tracker itself, it's about the conversations and teaching around the tracker. If it is introduced in a 'Wouldn't it be fun to see how much we can move in an enjoyable way each day' kind of challenge, it could be positive. If it is introduced as: 'You won't get dessert unless you've done 10,000 steps a day', it probably won't end well.

One research study among adult participants found that randomly assigned individuals who used a Fitbit for ten days didn't experience a negative impact on body dissatisfaction or disordered eating behaviours, but these are things that would likely emerge after longer than ten days.

Dr Beth Bell, who has a background in human–computer interaction, encourages parents to ensure that the devices and the interfaces are designed for children. 'I would always use caution in applying adults' technology to children, because they're not usually designed with kids' bodies in mind, or to be developmentally appropriate.'

Action

☑ **Now that you know what you know, start asking questions and observing what happens at your kids' sports clubs and sporting environments.**

- How do they talk about bodies?
- Do the uniform requirements have any flexibility to them?
- Are the coaches educated in relation to child growth and development?

☑ **If you need to refer your coaches, clubs, and sports organisations to some resources, give them a copy of this book to read, or direct them to the Body Confident Sport guidelines.**

17

Final word

AS WE TALKED TO EXPERTS from around the world, we were intrigued by how they applied their vast knowledge in their own homes. Here's a sneak peek inside the family life of some of the experts we spoke to for this book.

WHAT BODY IMAGE EXPERTS DO AT HOME

I want them to really appreciate their bodies for the way it functions. So I tell them that they are fast, strong, they did really well in the football game, or we talk about how our bodies do amazing things like digesting our food and healing. My son had this huge cut and his body was just amazing – you can't even tell that it was ever there now.

DR KRISTINA HOLMQVIST-GATTARIO

I tell them the way you look is wonderful and beautiful. You should be proud of it. But it's the least interesting thing about you, all of the other parts of you are so much more interesting and fantastic. And I want to see you invest in those parts, not the way you look. Because again, that's the least interesting part of this amazing package.

PROFESSOR LINDA LIN

In our home we didn't have any magazines, we didn't talk about our bodies, I never talked about going on a diet or anything like that. Yet both my daughters – despite all of my best intentions – both of them have said 'I'm fat' and they get caught up with what other people think about them.

DR JODY FORBES

I like to talk a lot about what we can do with our bodies and how amazing our bodies are for so many reasons. For example, what our different body parts do, even just in terms of eating or moving and sleeping and breathing – all those kinds of everyday things that we can do with our bodies and that our bodies are good for. I'm hoping this helps to reinforce the fact that our bodies are amazing and should be looked after and respected.

DR STEPHANIE DAMIANO

I try to praise the fact that they are listening to their bodies rather than the fact that they are doing what I want them to do. For example, saying 'You have been great at tuning in to what your tummy wants', rather than 'I'm so proud of you for eating the broccoli.' Or 'Well done for eating all of your dinner', or 'Great job for saving some of your lolly bag for tomorrow.' I'm trying to get them to internalise that they know what's right for them, that they really know that they need movement, or that they need some chill time or that they're full.

My oldest son is on the shorter side, I mean, we (his parents) aren't tall either. He gets really down about not being as tall as the other kids. I try to role model being accepting of my own body as I'm also short, as well as saying things like 'Well, you're very agile and you're a very fast runner.' Watching the Olympics was helpful too, because we could notice all of the things that bodies of all shapes and sizes could do.

DIETITIAN, TASMANIA

I try to weave in some social justice messages about privilege, respect and equity when it comes up in our day-to-day lives, and generally just questioning the cultural status quo, such as why someone at their school might be getting 'special treatment.' I am raising two white males after all, so they need to know this stuff! Hopefully it will help them to question the messages they're given (whether about food or otherwise), and hopefully they'll grow up to be respectful adults as a result. That's the plan, anyway. We talk a lot in our house about privilege. And we talk a lot about race, gender and sexuality, and that the world doesn't accommodate for everybody in the same way. So I do have to say, sometimes I get a little bit over-enthusiastic about the teaching moments – at which point in time, their eyes glaze over.

DIETITIAN, MELBOURNE

I walk around naked as often as I can in my home, because I like the opportunity to show my kids just how comfortable I am in my body. When the kids were younger, I'd often yell out, 'Nudey run' and do a lap through the house making it fun and silly. These days in a house full of teens and tweens I'm no longer announcing my nudey runs, or making a spectacle of myself, it just happens when situations occur like I forgot my towel after a shower, or my knickers are on the line!

TARYN

WHAT YOU KNOW NOW

You've just read a whole book about body image. You are kind of an expert now.

So, expert, we want you to have a look at the following case study and see what comes out for you.

This is a real story from an amazing mama, and our hearts broke for her as we listened to this story and saw her realise and connect things for the first time.

It's what you do and what you don't do . . .

My daughter Eloise has always been kind of bigger, from the age of about five or six. I have to admit, even though I want to be open-minded, I started to get a little anxious because I was worried that she would be left behind or teased. At eight she decided to become vegetarian – she loves animals so much – so I spoke with her doctor about my concerns about her growing BMI, and her dietary choices, and the doctor suggested that we see a nutritionist. We did that at eight, and then maybe again at around twelve, because her BMI wasn't categorised as obese, but definitely as overweight. I wanted her to learn, and I wanted to educate myself – to learn healthier ways of doing things, instead of dieting.

Nothing really came of it. She has lost a little weight lately, but her doctor said that is usual in a pandemic. Either way, we try not to focus on it now, and she seems really healthy and happy overall. Sometimes when I try to tell her how beautiful she is, she will bring it up and say 'But Mum, you took me to that nutritionist?' I thought I was doing the right thing, but now I'm not so sure. I think she knew why we were going, and maybe it just made things worse. I feel like I damaged her.

I was actually a little overweight myself as a teenager. My brother called me 'Tubby'. It wasn't until I was in college that I realised I didn't like my body. I wanted to get healthier because I wasn't eating well. I started making myself throw up. I can't remember how often but it was relatively consistent for about two years. I didn't lose any weight doing that. So I turned to my mum and I said, 'I want to get healthy. I want to lose some weight.' She said she would help me, and she did. I was home over summer, and she made lots of salad and I lost weight. I hate to admit this, but I felt like it gave me more confidence and then I started liking my body.

I remember my parents being quite critical. My dad said, 'I don't like those pants – your backside looks a little big.' My family was quite critical of other people too. If we ever saw somebody who was obese, my family would look down upon them. Actually, I remember my grandfather, who was a runner, we were watching some show, and the guy was talking about his struggle with weight and he's like: 'Well, you're just lazy – go to the gym!'

When I had my own kids, I did think more generally about our approach – I knew I didn't want to be critical with my children, and I didn't want to be judgemental about other people. I didn't want personal appearance comments. I've had to sit down and talk to my parents about that as well. And my brother. My husband and I are very different, but also very similar in the fact that we both didn't want that critical negative talk. We want to be open and accepting of everyone.

That kind of worked. They don't say anything to my kids directly. But a few years ago, my brother shared a photo that I'd put on Facebook of my husband and Eloise with my parents. My dad said, 'Eloise looks really heavy.' She was ten at the time. Dad, who was a surgeon, said, 'What you should do is buy a scale and have her get on it every day. And that way, she'll lose weight.' I didn't know what to say at the time, and so I called a friend who knows about body image things, and she was like: 'Umm, no.' So I called my parents back and I was just kind of firm. I had them on speaker phone and just said, 'Listen, if you want to give your grandchild an eating disorder, this is the way to do it. We're not going to talk about her body anymore. We're just going to help her be happy and find activities she's happy with and have healthy habits, but you just need to stop talking about her body, and talking about food.' To their credit, they shut up and they listened.

Now that I think about it, I've always associated being overweight with being rejected. Maybe that's what I was worried about with my daughter – that she was going to somehow get rejected from things, because I saw how my family would reject people who were overweight. Now I wish I hadn't got so worried about it. I wish I had just accepted her body, because now I think I've perpetuated some of her issues as well. I see her now being really protective over food, and I think it's because there were times when I was the 'food police' in our house. I wish I hadn't made food such a huge deal.

SABRINA, MUM OF TWO, USA

We are so grateful to be able to share this story, and for us, here are the main takeaways.

1. It's hard to see your child struggle. And it's even harder to watch that when it's something you might have been through, or when their body is a lot like your body.

2. You want to protect your child from everything that is mean and horrible in the world, and you can protect them from so much. But protecting them means you are constantly in a battle. Accepting them means that you get some peace.

Fiona Sutherland @themindfuldietitian says:

The number one thing that you can do to encourage your child to feel as good as possible in their body in this messed-up culture is to accept them, and validate them in whatever shape and size they come in. As soon as you take them to the doctor, take them to the dietitian, lead them to believe that there's something wrong with them, that's the moment stuff starts. A lot of parents, unfortunately, with the deepest of compassion are acting out their own trauma again, on their kids, but not knowing it – wanting to prevent the very thing that happened to them, and then just doing it all over again.

As crazy as it sounds, it's hard to have unconditional acceptance for your own child, particularly if you are scared for them, and if you have had some trauma around this yourself, it is so hard.

But you know what? When we all accept each other's bodies, no-one loses.

EDUCATING OTHERS

Unfortunately, the broader environments that we, and our children, interact with aren't always as evolved, enlightened and informed as we are. But now that you have read this book, you can start to create change in many ways, big and small.

How you can create change:

- Lend or suggest this book to others.

- Reframe conversations that become fixated on food.
- Advocate for more flexibility in school and sports uniforms.
- Stand up for people who are being body shamed.
- Ask questions about body inclusivity in sport and physical activity environments.
- Give positive feedback to brands that embody the principles in this book.
- Give feedback to brands that don't support body confidence.
- Make a pact with your friends to never discuss anyone's weight loss or weight gain ever again.

Whether it involves asking questions at your kids' sports club or prospective dance studio, questioning some of the worksheets that come home from your kids' school, or just talking to other parents about what you've learned, you have the power to create huge change. And just like a butterfly flapping its wings, those changes can ripple across the world. But how do we start these conversations without getting all 'preachy'? Some of the experts we spoke to are very used to educating others in big and small ways, like Danni Rowlands from the Butterfly Foundation, who is also a mum of two:

I always try to reframe and use language that is balanced – possibly in annoying ways – but if you're handing my kid a lolly bag and parents start to say 'Oh my goodness, they've already had so much sugar' or 'Sorry about the sugar.' I will reframe: 'Actually, they're lollies. It's okay, they've been at a party. It's all part of the fun.'

We need to start calling foods their names – what they are – rather than categorising foods (i.e., carbs, sugar, fat). Some people may have moved away from using 'good' and 'bad', but we need to move away from categorising foods as well. Simply call the food the name that it is – lollies, pasta, cake, an apple – as this can help to remove any moral judgement. The media and diet culture has really confused our understanding of what 'healthy eating' is. Helping your child to have a positive relationship with eating and food is such an important skill for them to learn and supports their body image too.

In gently reframing some of these situations, we can try to educate other parents in kind ways, as well as reducing the impact on our kids of what might be said.

Reframing weight bias and negative comments around weight can be just as subtle. Janine, a mum of two from Tasmania, adds:

Sometimes people will say something negative about food or bodies, and I know the kids have heard it, so I'll usually chat to them later about it. I'll say something like 'Did you hear when they said that food was bad? You know in our house we don't talk about food in that way. We enjoy all types of food.' Other times I might tackle it in the moment. For example, the other day a friend was telling me about going to the local pool with his children, and said, in 'that' tone, 'You should have seen some of the bodies there.' So I just said 'How great it is for kids to see bodies of all shapes and sizes, and good on them for not letting their body size stop them going to the pool.' I want my children to know that body shaming is not okay.

TAKING ACTION

At the start of this book, we told you that this wasn't a parenting book. We told you this was a book that wouldn't make you feel like a failure, a book that would help you reflect on your journey, do the work, and empower you with information for action. Now it's time for the action.

And here's where we get all excited.

You have the greatest capacity to make change right now. Not us. We've written down everything we could in this book, and talked to all of the experts and so many parents to get as many perspectives, stories and information as we could fit in one book.

So what are you going to do with that?

If you're going to do the work on yourself, that's great!

If you're going to stop saying things about people's bodies, amazing!

If you're going to go on a mission to change the sports uniforms at your kids' sports club and stop the coaches from talking badly about the kids' bodies, go for it!

If you're going to hand this book to another teacher, parent or friend, we love you!

If you're going to write your story, write a book, start a podcast, tell us about it!

If you're going to call your friends, get together and protest about social media, fashion or media companies, do it (and take pictures)!

If you're just going to think about doing some stuff because you're a bit tired right now? Rest, don't quit!

Literally, anything that you do as a result of reading this book makes us happy. Because all of the little things that we do can *change the world*. We know it sounds obvious, but it also makes us jump up and down on the spot, clapping our hands and grinning wildly. Because we are changing the world. Right now.

We are making the world a safer body image place for our kids to be in. And that's all we can hope for.

You deserve every inch of the space you need to take up.
You ARE unique.
You ARE special.
You have things that no one else has.
You have so much to offer the world.

LAURA MAZZA @ITSLAURAMAZZA

FINAL THOUGHTS FROM US

Taryn

The scariest part of writing a book for me is writing this part. It's the part where I question: did we do enough? Did we take you on the journey we promised we would and did we get you to the end in one piece without too much overwhelm? Did we fulfil our promise to make you feel seen and understood and give you a clear sense of direction on what to say and do next? Gosh, we hope so, because even though we can't see you, we know you, we are you, and we want nothing more than for you to put this book down and think 'Rightio, no matter what life throws my way, I've got this'. And got this you have.

It took me a really long time to back myself and my parenting (especially single parenting) and on occasions I feel I've wasted a lot of time comparing myself to others, their parenting styles, and mostly their really polite and utterly adorable kids with all the manners and trimmings. It's such a dichotomy that I've spent half of my parenting life being the world's proudest mum for all the amazing things that my kids have said and done and the other half thinking I'm a terrible mum for all the things my kids have said and done! Like the time my middle child was a toddler going through a biting phase and bit three out of four kids at Kindermusik, drawing blood on the last one. It was less than ideal.

The fact is, life is really gritty and when it comes to parenting, there is no black and white. It's an eclectic tapestry of contradictions that can live side-by-side. Forget fifty shades of grey, there's a million. I stand on stages talking to audiences about the importance of nourishing our bodies with foods blessed by the sun, in their most natural states and yet one of my kids sinks a Zinger burger from KFC every other week. My other son and I were at the gym the other day, moving our bodies, enjoying our bodies, feeling really good in our bodies, and at the end of the session he turns to me and says, 'Look at my abs.' I speak to my daughter endlessly about the loveliness of diversity and being unique but if you lined her up with all her friends, they'll all be wearing matching outfits and speak the same. Seriously, insert the head-slap emoji here!

But that is the reality of the ebb and flow of parenting. Some of it's good, some of it's a bit messy. And it's all okay, because we are doing our best. And as the saying goes: 'Do the best you can until you know better. Then when you know better you can do better.' So, this is your moment – you now know better, your body is and does incredible things. No-one was born into the world hating their body. It's a learned behaviour that can be unlearned. And the most exciting part is that we get to help embed this message into the hearts and minds of our kids now, rather than have them follow us down the path of body image misery that so many of us have been down.

The time to embrace your body is now. You can, and in the process you can be the hero that your child so desperately needs. And the good news is, it couldn't be easier. You've just got to enjoy your body and let them see you doing it. So, show them. Get on the dancefloor, jump off the jetty, slide down the waterslide, dive into the ocean and run through your house naked. Don't take what you have for granted; instead, exude appreciation for your body.

It's really so simple. Love yourself, just like you love your child and your child will be inspired to love themselves too.

> **The time to embrace your body is now. You can, and in the process you can be the hero that your child so desperately needs. And the good news is, it couldn't be easier. You've just got to enjoy your body and let them see you doing it.**
>
> TARYN

> **Our kids will have much better physical health, mental health, and body image, and maybe they will be happier and more successful too, if we just accept them.**
>
> ZALI

Zali

Science and research can make things overly complicated. And for the past fifteen years, I've been investigating risk factors and protective factors and intervention strategies and evaluating with numbers and data. And the advice that we would come up with for parents was always really complex. Even as the person who had come up with the advice, I still had to work hard to remember it.

But the process of speaking to parents, experts and experts who are parents for this book, really distilling the evidence but also being really curious about the reality of this situation for so many parents, has led me to realise that creating a body confident family and trying to boost your kids' body image can really come down to just one thing, summed up in one word.

And that word is . . .

Acceptance.

Okay, I'll be honest, it goes in a couple of different directions, but it all comes down to acceptance, and I'm pretty proud of myself for summing up this whole book into one word!

First: there's acceptance of your own body image journey, and acceptance of your own body. Accepting that your body is aging. Accepting that your weight will change over time.

Second: we accept our kids' bodies and *their selves* unconditionally too. I thought it was all about creating certain environments, having the right things to say when you're in all the situations and responding to things perfectly, like all of the questions that we've answered in this book. But what it comes down to is that children will have much better physical health, mental health and body image, and maybe they will be happy and more successful too, if we just accept them.

Before I had children, when I thought parenting was super easy, I really thought I would have ultimate control over the majority of situations, and that I'd be able to really know about and change what my kids were exposed to. Very quickly, I realised that I have so much less control than I think, and as they've grown older and older, that's become truer and truer. I don't have control; I can't control everything. What I can control is that I accept them as they are.

Once you learn to accept that that's the way they are, that they're going to be this way, whether you like it or not, that's when things feel easier. That's when there's an opportunity for connection rather than rejection.

It's the same thing with bodies. It's the exact same thing because when we show our kids we accept their bodies unconditionally, when we say 'There is nothing wrong with your body, there is nothing that you need to change', that gives them the permission to accept their bodies. And if we don't accept their bodies, they've got no chance.

So we accept our bodies, we accept their bodies, we show them this unconditional acceptance, that there are no good or bad bodies – no right or wrong, that everyone is worthy. And then we work to create almost a suit of armour against the world. To develop a shield so that shame can just bounce right off. That shield is made up of self-compassion and appreciation of body functionality.

In pursuing the answers to the questions we thought we needed answered, we went out, far and wide. We went directly to the experts, researchers and clinicians located all over the world. We talked to parents on (most) corners of the earth. But as we got further and further along, I started to realise how close to home some of the wisdom that I needed might be.

'You should interview us,' said my daughter, as we sat around the kitchen bench eating some delicious choc-chip cookies they had just baked with my mum. All of my kids have ~~interrupted~~ joined me in so many Zoom meetings, walking straight past the 'Mummy's in a meeting' Post-it note permanently stuck to the door of my home office. Like many during the pandemic, my work and my home life came together much more than ever before. I've introduced them to colleagues, experts I've barely known, people with interesting accents from all over the world. I don't think my kids realise that they have appeared in the transcripts of so many interviews for this book.

'Okay, what do you think we should tell parents, then?' I asked, not expecting much.

They jumped in right away, faces still covered in cookie crumbs:

Don't worry that you're not going to be a good mum. You don't have to be scared to do the things you want to do. Just do it, like I was scared to sing, but now it feels weird and amazing.

LUCY, AGE 6

Listen to your body, and don't worry about it, because you will always be safe and happy. Nothing can stop you from being who you want to be in the world.

EVIE, AGE 6

I looked over at my mum, and we both wiped the tears from our eyes.

I wonder what could have been different in her life, and in my life, if we had just known, or had we not forgotten, what my girls already have inside their hearts.

Resources

RESOURCES FOR ADULTS

Body image and acceptance
Books
Embrace Yourself by Taryn Brumfitt (Penguin Life Australia, Melbourne, 2018)

A Workbook of Acceptance-Based Approaches for Weight Concerns by Margit I. Berman (Routledge, New York, 2018)

Beautifully You: A daily guide to radical self-acceptance by Rosie Molinary (Seal Press, 2016)

Come As You Are by Dr Emily Nagoski (Simon & Schuster, 2021)

Embody: Learning to love your unique body by Connie Sobczak and Elizabeth Scott (Gurze Books, California, 2014)

More Than A Body: Your body is an instrument, not an ornament by Dr Lindsay Kite and Dr Lexie Kite (HarperCollins Publishers, US, 2021)

Pretty Unhealthy: Why our obsession with looking healthy is making us sick by Dr Nikki Stamp (Murdoch Books, Australia, 2019)

The Body Is Not An Apology: The power of radical self-love by Sonya Renee Taylor (Random House, US, 2021)

The Fat Studies Reader by Esther Rothblum and Sondra Solovay (NYU Press, New York, 2009)

The Yes Woman: How to reclaim your power by finally saying NO by Grace Jennings-Edquist (Affirm Press, Melbourne, 2021)

What We Don't Talk About When We Talk About Fat by Aubrey Gordon (Random House, US, 2021)

You Have the Right to Remain Fat by Virgie Tovar (The Feminist Press at CUNY, New York, 2018)

Websites
Embrace You online course
bodyimagemovement.com/resources/embrace-you/

More Than a Body blog and online courses
morethanabody.org/

Health At Every Size Australia
Contains comprehensive resources and listing of weight-neutral health professionals
haesaustralia.org.au/What-is-HAES

Body Confident Mums resources
Includes access to body functionality appreciation resources from
Dr Jessica Alleva
bodyconfidentcollective.org/bcm

Podcasts

Appearance Matters, from the Centre for Appearance Research
podcasts.apple.com/au/podcast/appearance-matters-the-podcast/
id1069856498

The Mindful Dietitian, hosted by Fiona Sutherland
themindfuldietitian.com.au/podcast

Self-compassion

Dr Kristin Neff's guided self-compassion meditations
self-compassion.org/guided-self-compassion-meditations-mp3-2/

Dr Kristin Neff's self-compassion writing exercises
self-compassion.org/exercise-3-exploring-self-compassion-writing/

The Compassionate Mind Foundation audios
compassionatemind.co.uk/resource/audio

Feelings

*Atlas of the Heart: Mapping meaningful connection and the language
of human experience* by Brené Brown (Vermillion, London, 2021)

Feelings Wheel by Dr Gloria Wilcox
gnyha.org/wp-content/uploads/2020/05/The-Feeling-Wheel-Positive-Psycology-Program.pdf

Narrative therapy

'How changing your story can change your life'
TED Talk by Lori Gottlieb
ted.com/talks/lori_gottlieb_how_changing_your_story_can_change_your_life

The Dulwich Centre
Australian organisation that compiles, creates and educates around narrative therapy. There are free resources and courses, and a bookshop that can help to educate and give examples of narrative practice.
dulwichcentre.com.au/

Motherhood

Books

Mama Rising: Discovering the new you through motherhood by Amy Taylor-Kabbaz (Hay House Australia Pty Ltd, Sydney, 2019)

Websites

Dear Mama Project with Nikki McCahon
dearmamaproject.com/

Podcasts and talks

The Good Enough Mother Podcast, hosted by Dr Sophie Brock
drsophiebrock.com/podcast

Happy Mama Movement Podcast, hosted by Amy Taylor Kabbaz
amytaylorkabbaz.com/podcast/

'Matrescence'
TED Talk by Alexandra Sacks
ted.com/talks/alexandra_sacks_a_new_way_to_think_about_the_transition_to_motherhood

Food

Intuitive Eating: A revolutionary anti-diet approach by Evelyn Tribole and Elyse Resch (St Martin's Essentials, US, 2020)

Vitamin A to Z: Your BS-free guide to wellbeing by Fiona Sutherland (ebook, Debut Books, Australia, 2021)
themindfuldietitian.com.au/vitamin-a-to-z-book

FOR PARENTS: ABOUT KIDS

Body image

Butterfly Foundation Body Kind Families
butterfly.org.au/get-involved/campaigns/bodykindfamilies/

Butterfly Body Bright Program for primary schools
butterflybodybright.org.au/

Dove National Schools Partnership
'Uniquely Me: A parent's guide to building body confidence'
dove.nationalschoolspartnership.com/_files/ugd/7704f1_6c-1d1065e0f641088222831115ab38a6.pdf

National Association for Media Literacy Education (NAMLE)
'Parent's Guide to Media Literacy'
medialiteracyweek.us/resources/parents/

Puberty

Books

Untangled: Guiding teenage girls through the seven transitions into adulthood by Lisa Damour (Ballantine Books, US, 2017)

Under Pressure: Confronting the epidemic of stress and anxiety in girls by Lisa Damour (Ballantine Books, US, 2019)

Websites

Downloadable bookmarks by Dr Lisa Damour
Offering free practical guidance to manage a variety of common situations
drlisadamour.com/resources/guide/

Reporting image-based abuse to the eSafety Commissioner
esafety.gov.au/key-issues/image-based-abuse/take-action/report-to-esafety-commissioner

Sexting: A parent's guide
International Centre for Missing and Exploited Children
icmec.org/wp-content/uploads/2018/11/a-parents-guide-to-dealing
-with-sexting.pdf

Sexting and the impacts on young people
Kids Helpline
kidshelpline.com.au/parents/issues/sexting-and-impacts-young
-people

Podcasts and talks

Ask Lisa: The psychology of parenting, hosted by Dr Lisa Damour
drlisadamour.com/resources/podcast/

The Puberty Podcast, hosted by Dr Cara Natterson and Vanessa
Kroll Bennett

Raising Good Humans, hosted by Dr Aliza Pressman
draliza.com/episodes/

Raising Teens, hosted by Collet Smart and Ben McEachen
raisingteenagers.com.au/media-library/podcasts/

*Know Them, Be Them, Raise Them: Helping Moms to Be and Raise
Strong Women,* with Carmelita Tiu
podcasts.apple.com/us/podcast/know-them-be-them-raise-them/
id1581581645

Gender and sexuality

Books

Helping Your Transgender Teen: A guide for parents, 2nd ed by Irwin Krieger (Jessica Kingsley Publishers, US, 2018).

TV

Australian Story: About A Girl
ABC iview
iview.abc.net.au/show/australian-story/series/2016

Websites

Emerging Minds (based in Australia)
Supporting trans and gender diverse children and their families
emergingminds.com.au/resources/supporting-trans-and-gender-diverse-children-and-their-families/

Strong Family Alliance (based in the US)
strongfamilyalliance.org/

Talks

'Toilets, bowties, gender and me'
TED Talk by Aud Mason-Hyde
youtube.com/watch?v=NCLoNwVJA-o

Nutrition

Confident Body Confident Child
For parents of 2–6 year olds
bodyconfidentcollective.org/cbcc

Ellyn Satter Institute
ellynsatterinstitute.org

Fiona Sutherland – The Mindful Dietitian blog
themindfuldietitian.com.au/blog

Sunny Side Up Nutrition (USA)
Free resources for schools
sunnysideupnutrition.com/diet-free-resources-for-schools/

The Full Bloom Podcast, hosted by Zoë Bisbing
fullbloomproject.com/podcast

Eating Disorders
The Butterfly Foundation
butterfly.org.au/get-support/how-we-help/
Body Kind Families resources: butterfly.org.au/get-involved/
campaigns/bodykindfamilies/
Red flags: butterfly.org.au/eating-disorders/risks-and-warning-signs/

Eating Disorders Victoria
Eating disorders explained
eatingdisorders.org.au/eating-disorders-a-z/eating-disorders-
explained/

Sport
Websites
Body Confident Sport guidelines
bodyconfidentcollective.org/sport

Informed Sport
Supplement safety
sport.wetestyoutrust.com/

Goodform Traffic Light Poster
bodyconfidentcollective.org/goodform

Apps
Informed Sport
sport.wetestyoutrust.com/news/informed-sport-introduces-mobile-app

Sport Integrity app (by Sport Integrity Australia)
sportintegrity.gov.au/what-we-do/education

FOR KIDS

Body image
Kids' picture books for ages 2–8
Embrace Your Body by Taryn Brumfitt (Puffin, Melbourne, 2020)

Be Your Own Man by Jessica Sanders (Five Mile, Braeside, 2020)

Little Miss Jessica Goes to School by Jessica Smith (Jessica Smith, 2016)

The Magnificent Toby Plum by Deirdre Ryan and Deirdre Colman (Magnificently U, Waterford, 2011)

Minnie and Max Are OK!: A story to help children develop a positive body image by Chris Calland and Nicky Hutchinson (Jessica Kingsley Publishers, UK, 2017)

My Shadow is Pink by Scott Stuart (Larrikin House, Dandenong South, 2020)

Shapesville by Andy Mills and Becky Osborn (Gurze Books, Carisbad, 2003)

Sparrowlegs by Anupa Roper (Sparrowlegs, UK, 2021)

Your Body is Brilliant: Body respect for children by Sigrun Danielsdottir (Singing Dragon, UK, 2014)

Books for teens
Young adult fiction featuring characters in larger bodies:
My Eyes Are Up Here by Laura Zimmermann (Dutton Books, New York, 2020)

Leah on the Offbeat by Becky Albertalli (Balzer + Bray, New York, 2018)

The Learning Curves of Vanessa Partridge by Clare Strahan (Allen & Unwin Children's, Sydney, 2018)

Love Is A Revolution by Renée Watson (Bloomsbury YA, New York, 2021)

The Upside of Unrequited by Becky Albertalli (Balzer + Bray, New York, 2017)

What I Like About Me by Jenna Guillaume (Pan Australia, 2019)

Non-fiction:

Being You: The body image book for boys by Charlotte Markey, Daniel Hart and Douglas N Zacher (Cambridge University Press, Cambridge, 2022)

Body Image Book for Girls by Charlotte Markey (Cambridge University Press, Cambridge, 2020) – for 14+ year-old girls who have some body image concerns

Fat Girls In Black Bodies: Creating communities of our own by Joy Arlene Renee Cox (North Atlantic Books, Berkeley, 2020)

Girl Stuff 8–12 by Kaz Cooke (Viking, Sydney, 2016)

Girl Stuff 13+ by Kaz Cooke (Viking, Sydney, 2013)

The (Other) F Word: A celebration of the fat and fierce, edited by Angie Manfredi (Amulet Books, New York, 2019)

Love Your Body: Your body can do amazing things by Jessica Sanders (Frances Lincoln Ltd, 2020) – for younger teens

Welcome To Your Period! by Yumi Stynes and Dr Melissa Kang (Hardie Grant Children's Publishing, 2019)

Other resources for teens

Dove Self-Esteem Project and Steven Universe collaboration videos
dove.com/uk/dove-self-esteem-project/our-mission/steven
-universe.html

eSafety Guides (from the eSafety Commissioner)
esafety.gov.au/young-people

Big Life Journal
biglifejournal.com.au

Body confidence playlist

These songs have lyrics that have a good message, or might spark
a conversation about body image. (Note that the music videos for
these are not always appropriate. Safe videos are marked with an *.)

'Embrace' by Pevan & Sarah, Taryn Brumfitt*
'Beautiful' by Christina Aguilera
'The Body Positivity Song' by Holly & Georgie
'Brave' by Sara Bareilles*
'Confident' by Demi Lovato
'Fight Song' by Rachel Platten*
'My Skin' by Lizzo*
'Perfect' (clean version) by Pink
'Who You Are' by Jessie J*
'Video' by India Arie

For older kids (12+):
'Good as Hell' by Lizzo*
'Kiss My Fat Ass' by Sheppard

*'Safe' music videos don't focus on idealised bodies and appearance – they are hard to find!

If anything in this book has raised any issues for you, or you've realised that your concerns might be deeper than you thought, make sure that you talk to your GP, or call the Butterfly Foundation Helpline on 1800 334 673 for more guidance around referrals.

We have created The Embrace Hub to bring together and link to a wide range of body image resources for parents, young people, schools, and community organisations, including most of the below resources.

Visit: theembracehub.com

List of selected references

CHAPTER 2: HOW WE FEEL ABOUT OUR BODIES (AND WHY)

Andrew, R., Tiggemann, M., & Clark, L. (2016). Positive body image and young women's health: Implications for sun protection, cancer screening, weight loss and alcohol consumption behaviours. *Journal of Health Psychology*, 21(1), 28–39.

Arroyo, A., & Harwood, J. (2012). Exploring the causes and consequences of engaging in fat talk. *Journal of Applied Communication Research*, 40(2), 167–87.

Bornioli, A., Lewis-Smith, H., Slater, A., & Bray, I. (2021). Body dissatisfaction predicts the onset of depression among adolescent females and males: a prospective study. *Journal of Epidemiology and Community Health*, 75(4), 343–48.

Buss, D. M., & Schmitt, D. P. (1993). Sexual strategies theory: an evolutionary perspective on human mating. *Psychological Review*, 100(2), 204.

Chan, C. Y., Lee, A. M., Koh, Y. W., Lam, S. K., Lee, C. P., Leung, K. Y., & Tang, C. S. K. (2020). Associations of body dissatisfaction with anxiety and depression in the pregnancy and postpartum periods: A longitudinal study. *Journal of Affective Disorders*, 263, 582–92.

Clay, S., & Brickell, C. (2021). The Dad Bod: An impossible body? *The Journal of Men's Studies*, 30(1), 70–86.

Crawford, D., & Campbell, K. (1999). Lay definitions of ideal weight and overweight. *International Journal of Obesity*, 23(7), 738–45.

Festinger, L. (1957). Social comparison theory. *Selective Exposure Theory*, 16.

Fiske, L., Fallon, E. A., Blissmer, B., & Redding, C. A. (2014). Prevalence of body dissatisfaction among United States adults: Review and recommendations for future research. *Eating Behaviors, 15*(3), 357–65.

Fuller-Tyszkiewicz, M., Broadbent, J., Richardson, B., Watson, B., Klas, A., & Skouteris, H. (2020). A network analysis comparison of central determinants of body dissatisfaction among pregnant and non-pregnant women. *Body Image, 32,* 111–20.

He, J., Sun, S., Zickgraf, H. F., Lin, Z., & Fan, X. (2020). Meta-analysis of gender differences in body appreciation. *Body Image, 33,* 90–100.

Hodgkinson, E. L., Smith, D. M., & Wittkowski, A. (2014). Women's experiences of their pregnancy and postpartum body image: A systematic review and meta-synthesis. *BMC Pregnancy and Childbirth, 14*(1), 1–11.

Huang, Q., Peng, W., & Ahn, S. (2021). When media become the mirror: A meta-analysis on media and body image. *Media Psychology, 24*(4), 437–89.

Ingram, G. P., Enciso, M. I., Eraso, N., García, M. J., & Olivera-La Rosa, A. (2019). Looking for the right swipe: Gender differences in self-presentation on Tinder profiles. *Annual Review of CyberTherapy and Telemedicine,* 149.

Lovering, M. E., Rodgers, R. F., George, J. E., & Franko, D. L. (2018). Exploring the tripartite influence model of body dissatisfaction in postpartum women. *Body Image, 24,* 44–54.

MacBeth, A., & Gumley, A. (2012). Exploring compassion: A meta-analysis of the association between self-compassion and psychopathology. *Clinical Psychology Review, 32*(6), 545–52.

McKay, K., Ross, L. E., & Goldberg, A. E. (2010). Adaptation to parenthood during the post-adoption period: A review of the literature. *Adoption Quarterly, 13*(2), 125–44.

Milton, A., Hambleton, A., Roberts, A., Davenport, T., Flego, A., Burns, J., & Hickie, I. (2021). Body image distress and its associations from an international sample of men and women across the adult life span: Web-based survey study. *JMIR Formative Research, 5*(11), doi: 10.2196/25329

Puhl, R. M., Wall, M. M., Chen, C., Austin, S. B., Eisenberg, M. E., & Neumark-Sztainer, D. (2017). Experiences of weight teasing in adolescence and weight-related outcomes in adulthood: A 15-year longitudinal study. *Preventive Medicine, 100,* 173–79.

Rallis, S., Skouteris, H., Wertheim, E. H., & Paxton, S. J. (2007). Predictors of body image during the first year postpartum: A prospective study. *Women & Health*, 45(1), 87–104.

Riquin, E., Lamas, C., Nicolas, I., Lebigre, C. D., Curt, F., Cohen, H., ... & Godart, N. (2019). A key for perinatal depression early diagnosis: The body dissatisfaction. *Journal of Affective Disorders*, 245, 340–47.

Rodin, J., Silberstein, L., and Striegel-Moore, R. (1984). Women and weight: A normative discontent. *Nebraska Symposium on Motivation*. University of Nebraska Press.

Roth, H., Homer, C., & Fenwick, J. (2012). 'Bouncing back': How Australia's leading women's magazines portray the postpartum body. *Women and Birth*, 25(3), 128–34.

Rubin, L. R., & Steinberg, J. R. (2011). Self-objectification and pregnancy: Are body functionality dimensions protective?. *Sex Roles*, 65(7), 606–18.

Runfola, C. D., Von Holle, A., Trace, S. E., Brownley, K. A., Hofmeier, S. M., Gagne, D. A., & Bulik, C. M. (2013). Body dissatisfaction in women across the lifespan: Results of the UNC-SELF and gender and body image (GABI) studies. *European Eating Disorders Review*, 21(1), 52–9.

Salk, R. H., & Engeln-Maddox, R. (2012). Fat talk among college women is both contagious and harmful. *Sex Roles*, 66(9), 636–45.

Thompson, K. A., & Bardone-Cone, A. M. (2022). Self-oriented body comparison and self-compassion: Interactive models of disordered eating behaviors among postpartum women. *Behavior Therapy*.

Tiggemann, M., & McCourt, A. (2013). Body appreciation in adult women: Relationships with age and body satisfaction. *Body Image*, 10(4), 624–27.

Vartanian, L. R., & Dey, S. (2013). Self-concept clarity, thin-ideal internalization, and appearance-related social comparison as predictors of body dissatisfaction. *Body Image*, 10(4), 495–500.

CHAPTER 3: WHAT THE WORLD TELLS US ABOUT OUR BODIES

Becker, C. B., Diedrichs, P. C., Jankowski, G., & Werchan, C. (2013). I'm not just fat, I'm old: has the study of body image overlooked 'old talk'? *Journal of Eating Disorders*, 1(1), 1–12.

Bellard, A. M., Cornelissen, P. L., Mian, E., & Cazzato, V. (2021). The ageing body: Contributing attitudinal factors towards perceptual body size estimates in younger and middle-aged women. *Archives of Women's Mental Health*, 24(1), 93–105.

Calogero, R. M., Boroughs, M., & Thompson, J. K. (2007). The impact of Western beauty ideals on the lives of women and men: A sociocultural perspective. In: V. Swami & and A. Furnham (Eds.), *Body beautiful: Evolutionary and sociocultural perspectives* (pp. 259–98). Palgrave Macmillan.

Cunningham, J., & Roberts, P. (2021). *Brandsplaining: Why marketing is (still) sexist and how to fix it.* Penguin UK.

CHAPTER 4: UNLEARNING WHAT WE THOUGHT WE KNEW ABOUT WEIGHT

Adab, P., Pallan, M., & Whincup, P. H. (2018). Is BMI the best measure of obesity? *BMJ*, 360, doi: 10.1136/bmj.k2293

Andrew, R., Tiggemann, M., & Clark, L. (2016). Positive body image and young women's health: Implications for sun protection, cancer screening, weight loss and alcohol consumption behaviours. *Journal of Health Psychology*, 21(1), 28–39.

Blackburn, H., & Jacobs Jr, D. (2014). Commentary: Origins and evolution of body mass index (BMI): Continuing saga. *International Journal of Epidemiology*, 43(3), 665–69.

Bucchianeri, M. M., Arikian, A. J., Hannan, P. J., Eisenberg, M. E., & Neumark-Sztainer, D. (2013). Body dissatisfaction from adolescence to young adulthood: Findings from a 10-year longitudinal study. *Body Image*, 10(1), 1–7.

Daly, M., Sutin, A. R., & Robinson, E. (2019). Perceived weight discrimination mediates the prospective association between obesity and physiological dysregulation: Evidence from a population-based cohort. *Psychological Science*, 30(7), 1030–39.

Fothergill, E., Guo, J., Howard, L., Kerns, J. C., Knuth, N. D., Brychta, R., ... & Hall, K. D. (2016). Persistent metabolic adaptation 6 years after 'The Biggest Loser' competition. *Obesity*, 24(8), 1612–19.

Gillen, M. M. (2015). Associations between positive body image and indicators of men's and women's mental and physical health. *Body Image*, 13, 67–74.

Gutin, I. (2018). In BMI we trust: Reframing the body mass index as a measure of health. *Social Theory & Health*, 16(3), 256–71.

Hardy, L. L., Jin, K., Mihrshahi, S., & Ding, D. (2019). Trends in overweight, obesity, and waist-to-height ratio among Australian children from linguistically diverse backgrounds, 1997 to 2015. *International Journal of Obesity*, 43(1), 116–24.

Hatzenbuehler, M.L., Keyes, K.M., & Hasin, D.S. (2009). Associations between perceived weight discrimination and the prevalence of psychiatric disorders in the general population. *Obesity*, 17(11), 2033–9.

Hunger, J. M., & Tomiyama, A. J. (2014). Weight labeling and obesity: A longitudinal study of girls aged 10 to 19 years. *JAMA Pediatrics*, 168(6), 579–80.

Keys, A. (1946). Human Starvation and Its Consequences1. *Journal of the American Dietetic Association*, 22(7), 582–87.

Keys, A., Brozek, J., Henschel, A., Mickelsen, O., Taylor, H. L., Simonson, E., & Wells, S. (1945). *Experimental starvation in man*. Air Force Office Of Scientific Research Arlington VA.

Leibel, R.L., & Hirsch, J. (1984). Diminished energy requirements in reduced-obese patients. *Metabolism*, 33(2), 164–70.

Major, B., Hunger, J. M., Bunyan, D. P., & Miller, C. T. (2014). The ironic effects of weight stigma. *Journal of Experimental Social Psychology*, 51, 74–80.

Ogden, C. L., Carroll, M. D., Fryar, C. D., & Flegal, K. M. (2015). Prevalence of obesity among adults and youth: United States, 2011–2014. *NCHS Data Brief*, (219), 1–8.

Puhl, R. M., Himmelstein, M. S., & Pearl, R. L. (2020). Weight stigma as a psychosocial contributor to obesity. *American Psychologist*, 75(2), 274.

Rose, K. L., Evans, E. W., Sonneville, K. R., & Richmond, T. (2021). The set point: weight destiny established before adulthood? *Current Opinion in Pediatrics*, 33(4), 368–72.

Silventoinen, K., Rokholm, B., Kaprio, J., & Sørensen, T. I. (2010). The genetic and environmental influences on childhood obesity: a systematic review of twin and adoption studies. *International Journal of Obesity*, 34(1), 29–40.

Sonneville, K. R., Thurston, I. B., Milliren, C. E., Kamody, R. C., Gooding, H. C., & Richmond, T. K. (2016). Helpful or harmful? Prospective association between weight misperception and weight gain among overweight and obese adolescents and young adults. *International Journal of Obesity*, 40(2), 328–32.

Sutin, A.R., Stephan, Y., & Terracciano, A. (2015). Weight discrimination and risk of mortality. *Psychological Science*, 26(11), 1803–11.

Sutin, A. R., & Terracciano, A. (2013). Perceived weight discrimination and obesity. *PLoS one*, 8(7), e70048.

Tomiyama, A. J. (2014). Weight stigma is stressful: A review of evidence for the Cyclic Obesity/Weight-Based Stigma model. *Appetite*, 82, 8–15.

CHAPTER 5: BE KIND TO YOURSELF

Albertson, E. R., Neff, K. D., & Dill-Shackleford, K. E. (2015). Self-compassion and body dissatisfaction in women: A randomized controlled trial of a brief meditation intervention. *Mindfulness*, 6(3), 444–54.

Ferrari, M., Hunt, C., Harrysunker, A., Abbott, M. J., Beath, A. P., & Einstein, D. A. (2019). Self-compassion interventions and psychosocial outcomes: A meta-analysis of RCTs. *Mindfulness*, 10(8), 1455–73.

Hewitt, P. L., Flett, G. L., & Ediger, E. (1995). Perfectionism traits and perfectionistic self-presentation in eating disorder attitudes, characteristics, and symptoms. *International Journal of Eating Disorders*, 18(4), 317–26.

Hill, A. P., & Curran, T. (2016). Multidimensional perfectionism and burnout: A meta-analysis. *Personality and Social Psychology Review*, 20(3), 269–88.

Jefferson, F. A., Shires, A., & McAloon, J. (2020). Parenting self-compassion: A systematic review and meta-analysis. *Mindfulness*, 11(9), 2067–88.

Linardon, J., Anderson, C., Messer, M., Rodgers, R. F., & Fuller-Tyszkiewicz, M. (2021). Body image flexibility and its correlates: A meta-analysis. *Body Image*, 37, 188–203.

MacBeth, A., & Gumley, A. (2012). Exploring compassion: A meta-analysis of the association between self-compassion and psychopathology. *Clinical Psychology Review*, 32(6), 545–52.

Marsh, I. C., Chan, S. W., & MacBeth, A. (2018). Self-compassion and psychological distress in adolescents: A meta-analysis. *Mindfulness*, 9(4), 1011–27.

Neff, K. D., & Germer, C. K. (2013). A pilot study and randomized controlled trial of the mindful self-compassion program. *Journal of Clinical Psychology*, 69(1), 28–44.

Phillips, W. J., & Hine, D. W. (2021). Self-compassion, physical health, and health behaviour: A meta-analysis. *Health Psychology Review, 15*(1), 113–39

Rahimi-Ardabili, H., Reynolds, R., Vartanian, L. R., McLeod, L. V. D., & Zwar, N. (2018). A systematic review of the efficacy of interventions that aim to increase self-compassion on nutrition habits, eating behaviours, body weight and body image. *Mindfulness, 9*(2), 388–400.

Stern, N. G., & Engeln, R. (2018). Self-compassionate writing exercises increase college women's body satisfaction. *Psychology of Women Quarterly, 42*(3), 326–41.

Tobin, R., & Dunkley, D. M. (2021). Self-critical perfectionism and lower mindfulness and self-compassion predict anxious and depressive symptoms over two years. *Behaviour Research and Therapy, 136*, 103780.

Zessin, U., Dickhäuser, O., & Garbade, S. (2015). The relationship between self-compassion and well-being: A meta-analysis. *Applied Psychology: Health and Well-Being, 7*(3), 340–64.

CHAPTER 6: APPRECIATING YOUR BODY: ACTION!

Alleva, J. M., Martijn, C., Van Breukelen, G. J., Jansen, A., & Karos, K. (2015). Expand Your Horizon: A programme that improves body image and reduces self-objectification by training women to focus on body functionality. *Body Image, 15*, 81–9.

Alleva, J. M., Tylka, T. L., van Oorsouw, K., Montanaro, E., Perey, I., Bolle, C., ... & Webb, J. B. (2020). The effects of yoga on functionality appreciation and additional facets of positive body image. *Body Image, 34*, 184–95.

Alleva, J. M., Veldhuis, J., & Martijn, C. (2016). A pilot study investigating whether focusing on body functionality can protect women from the potential negative effects of viewing thin-ideal media images. *Body Image, 17*, 10–13.

Aniulis, E., Sharp, G., & Thomas, N. A. (2021). The ever-changing ideal: The body you want depends on who else you're looking at. *Body Image, 36*, 218–29.

Campbell, A., & Hausenblas, H. A. (2009). Effects of exercise interventions on body image: A meta-analysis. *Journal of Health Psychology, 14*(6), 780–93.

Danthinne, E. S., Giorgianni, F. E., & Rodgers, R. F. (2020). Labels to prevent the detrimental effects of media on body image: A systematic review and meta-analysis. *International Journal of Eating Disorders*, 53(5), 647–61.

Diedrichs, P. C., & Lee, C. (2010). GI Joe or Average Joe? The impact of average-size and muscular male fashion models on men's and women's body image and advertisement effectiveness. *Body Image*, 7(3), 218-226.

Diedrichs, P. C., & Lee, C. (2011). Waif goodbye! Average-size female models promote positive body image and appeal to consumers. *Psychology & Health*, 26(10), 1273–91.

Engeln, R., Loach, R., Imundo, M. N., & Zola, A. (2020). Compared to Facebook, Instagram use causes more appearance comparison and lower body satisfaction in college women. *Body Image*, 34, 38–45.

Hazzard, V. M., Telke, S. E., Simone, M., Anderson, L. M., Larson, N. I., & Neumark-Sztainer, D. (2020). Intuitive eating longitudinally predicts better psychological health and lower use of disordered eating behaviors: Findings from EAT 2010–2018. *Eating and Weight Disorders: EWD*, 26(1), 287–94.

Homan, K. J., & Tylka, T. L. (2014). Appearance-based exercise motivation moderates the relationship between exercise frequency and positive body image. *Body Image*, 11(2), 101–8.

Lee, M. F., Williams, S. L., & Burke, K. J. (2019). Striving for the thin ideal post-pregnancy: A cross-sectional study of intuitive eating in postpartum women, *Journal of Reproductive and Infant Psychology*, 38(2), 127–38.

McIntosh-Dalmedo, S., Nicholls, W., Devonport, T., & Friesen, A. P. (2018). Examining the effects of sport and exercise interventions on body image among adolescent girls: A systematic review. *Journal of Sport Behavior*, 41(3), 1–37.

Mulgrew, K. E., McCulloch, K., Farren, E., Prichard, I., & Lim, M. S. (2018). This girl can #jointhemovement: Effectiveness of physical functionality-focused campaigns for women's body satisfaction and exercise intent. *Body Image*, 24, 26–35.

Prichard, I., McLachlan, A. C., Lavis, T., & Tiggemann, M. (2018). The impact of different forms of #fitspiration imagery on body image, mood, and self-objectification among young women. *Sex Roles*, 78(11), 789–98.

Rebar, A. L., Stanton, R., Geard, D., Short, C., Duncan, M. J., & Vandelanotte, C. (2015). A meta-meta-analysis of the effect of physical activity on depression and anxiety in non-clinical adult populations. *Health Psychology Review*, 9(3), 366–78.

Stewart, S. J., & Ogden, J. (2021). The impact of body diversity vs thin-idealistic media messaging on health outcomes: An experimental study. *Psychology, Health & Medicine*, 26(5), 631–43.

Tiggemann, M., & Anderberg, I. (2020). Muscles and bare chests on Instagram: The effect of influencers' fashion and fitspiration images on men's body image. *Body Image*, 35, 237–44.

Tylka, T. L., Calogero, R. M., & Daníelsdóttir, S. (2020). Intuitive eating is connected to self-reported weight stability in community women and men. *Eating Disorders*, 28(3), 256–64.

Van Dyke, N., & Drinkwater, E. J. (2014). Review article relationships between intuitive eating and health indicators: Literature review. *Public Health Nutrition*, 17(8), 1757–66.

Yager, Z., Prichard, I., & Hart, L. M. (2020). #Ihaveembraced: A pilot cross-sectional naturalistic evaluation of the documentary film *Embrace* and its potential associations with body image in adult women. *BMC Women's Health*, 20(1), 1–9.

CHAPTER 7: ROLE MODELLING BODY CONFIDENCE

Bandura, A. (1986). *Social foundation of thought and action: A social cognitive theory*. Prentice-Hall, Inc.

Becker, C., Bull, S., Smith, L. M., & Ciao, A. C. (2008). Effects of being a peer-leader in an eating disorder prevention program: Can we further reduce eating disorder risk factors? *Eating Disorders*, 16(5), 444–59.

Damiano, S. R., Yager, Z., Prichard, I., & Hart, L. M. (2019). Leading by example: Development of a maternal modelling of positive body image scale and relationships to body image attitudes. *Body Image*, 29, 132–39.

Gorman, G. (2021, 25 May). 'How do you teach kids body positivity when you don't have it?' *ABC Everyday*.

Miller, K. (2021). Displays of Adaptive Body Image by Others: Examining Their Influence on College Women's Body Image. [PhD thesis, University of Waterloo]. UWSpace.

Scaglioni, S., Salvioni, M., & Galimberti, C. (2008). Influence of parental attitudes in the development of children eating behaviour. *British Journal of Nutrition*, 99(S1), S22–S25.

Tylka, T. L., & Wood-Barcalow, N. L. (2015). What is and what is not positive body image? Conceptual foundations and construct definition. *Body Image*, 14, 118–29.

CHAPTER 8: KEY MESSAGES FOR BODY CONFIDENCE

Gillen, M. M., & Markey, C. H. (2021). Body image, weight management behavior, and women's interest in cosmetic surgery. *Psychology, Health & Medicine*, 26(5), 621–30.

Gouveia, M. J., Frontini, R., Canavarro, M. C., & Moreira, H. (2014). Quality of life and psychological functioning in pediatric obesity: the role of body image dissatisfaction between girls and boys of different ages. *Quality of Life Research*, 23(9), 2629–38.

Hahn, S. L., Borton, K. A., & Sonneville, K. R. (2018). Cross-sectional associations between weight-related health behaviors and weight misperception among US adolescents with overweight/obesity. *BMC Public Health*, 18(1), 1-8.

Hsu, Y. W., Liou, T. H., Liou, Y. M., Chen, H. J., & Chien, L. Y. (2016). Measurements and profiles of body weight misperceptions among Taiwanese teenagers: A national survey. *Asia Pacific Journal of Clinical Nutrition*, 25(1), 108–17.

Jankauskiene, R., & Baceviciene, M. (2019). Body image concerns and body weight overestimation do not promote healthy behaviour: Evidence from adolescents in Lithuania. *International Journal of Environmental Research and Public Health*, 16(5), 864.

Jones, B. A., Haycraft, E., Murjan, S., & Arcelus, J. (2016). Body dissatisfaction and disordered eating in trans people: A systematic review of the literature. *International Review of Psychiatry*, 28(1), 81–94.

Mustapic, J., Marcinko, D., & Vargek, P. (2017). Body shame and disordered eating in adolescents. *Current Psychology*, 36(3), 447–52.

Nechita, D. M., Bud, S., & David, D. (2021). Shame and eating disorders symptoms: A meta-analysis. *International Journal of Eating Disorders*, 54(11), 1899–1945.

Neumark-Sztainer, D., Paxton, S. J., Hannan, P. J., Haines, J., & Story, M. (2006). Does body satisfaction matter? Five-year longitudinal associations between body satisfaction and health behaviors in adolescent females and males. *Journal of Adolescent Health*, 39(2), 244–51.

Neumark-Sztainer, D., Wall, M., Story, M., & Standish, A. R. (2012). Dieting and unhealthy weight control behaviors during adolescence: Associations with 10-year changes in body mass index. *Journal of Adolescent Health*, 50(1), 80–86.

Rohrich, R. J., & Cho, M. J. (2018). When is teenage plastic surgery versus cosmetic surgery okay? Reality versus hype: A systematic review. *Plastic and Reconstructive Surgery*, 142(3), 293e–302e.

Schaefer, L. M., Burke, N. L., Calogero, R. M., Menzel, J. E., Krawczyk, R., & Thompson, J. K. (2018). Self-objectification, body shame, and disordered eating: Testing a core mediational model of objectification theory among White, Black, and Hispanic women. *Body Image*, 24, 5–12.

Sonneville, K. R., Thurston, I. B., Milliren, C. E., Kamody, R. C., Gooding, H. C., & Richmond, T. K. (2016). Helpful or harmful? Prospective association between weight misperception and weight gain among overweight and obese adolescents and young adults. *International Journal of Obesity*, 40(2), 328–32.

Stice, E., & Shaw, H. E. (2002). Role of body dissatisfaction in the onset and maintenance of eating pathology: A synthesis of research findings. *Journal of Psychosomatic Research*, 53(5), 985–93.

Wawrzyniak, A., Myszkowska-Ryciak, J., Harton, A., Lange, E., Laskowski, W., Hamulka, J., & Gajewska, D. (2020). Dissatisfaction with body weight among Polish adolescents is related to unhealthy dietary behaviors. *Nutrients*, 12(9), 2658.

CHAPTER 9: BODY IMAGE DEVELOPMENT IN CHILDREN AND ADOLESCENTS

Becker, I., Auer, M., Barkmann, C., Fuss, J., Möller, B., Nieder, T. O., ... & Richter-Appelt, H. (2018). A cross-sectional multicenter study of multidimensional body image in adolescents and adults with gender dysphoria before and after transition-related medical interventions. *Archives of Sexual Behavior*, 47(8), 2335–47.

Bornioli, A., Lewis-Smith, H., Slater, A., & Bray, I. (2021). Body dissatisfaction predicts the onset of depression among adolescent females and males: a prospective study. *Journal of Epidemiology and Community Health*, 75(4), 343–8.

Burrows 1, A., & Johnson, S. (2005). Girls' experiences of menarche and menstruation. *Journal of Reproductive and Infant Psychology*, 23(3), 235–49.

Enright, R. D., Shukla, D. G., & Lapsley, D. K. (1980) Adolescent egocentrism-sociocentrism and self-consciousness. *Journal of Youth and Adolescence*, 9(2), 101–16.

Evans, E. H., Tovée, M. J., Boothroyd, L. G., & Drewett, R. F. (2013). Body dissatisfaction and disordered eating attitudes in 7- to 11-year-old girls: Testing a sociocultural model. *Body Image*, 10(1), 8–15.

Fahs, B. (2020). There will be blood: Women's positive and negative experiences with menstruation. *Women's Reproductive Health*, 7(1), 1–16.

Frankel, L. (2002). 'I've never thought about it': Contradictions and taboos surrounding American males' experiences of first ejaculation (semenarche). *The Journal of Men's Studies*, 11(1), 37–54.

Garza, R., Clauss, N., & Byrd-Craven, J. (2021). Do BMI and Sex Hormones Influence Visual Attention to Food Stimuli in Women? Tracking Eye Movements Across the Menstrual Cycle. *Evolutionary Psychological Science*, 7(3), 304–14.

Hughes, E. K., & Gullone, E. (2011). Emotion regulation moderates relationships between body image concerns and psychological symptomatology. *Body Image*, 8(3), 224–31.

Malina, R. M. (2006). Weight training in youth-growth, maturation, and safety: An evidence-based review. *Clinical Journal of Sport Medicine*, 16(6), 478–87.

McCabe, M. P., & Ricciardelli, L. A. (2003). Body image and strategies to lose weight and increase muscle among boys and girls. *Health Psychology*, 22(1), 39.

Milton, A., Hambleton, A., Roberts, A., Davenport, T., Flego, A., Burns, J., & Hickie, I. (2021). Body image distress and its associations from an international sample of men and women across the adult life span: Web-based survey study. *JMIR Formative Research*, 5(11), doi: 10.2196/25329

Romito, M., Salk, R. H., Roberts, S. R., Thoma, B. C., Levine, M. D., & Choukas-Bradley, S. (2021). Exploring transgender adolescents' body image concerns and disordered eating: Semi-structured interviews with nine gender minority youth. *Body Image, 37*, 50–62.

Russell, S. T., Pollitt, A. M., Li, G., & Grossman, A. H. (2018). Chosen name use is linked to reduced depressive symptoms, suicidal ideation, and suicidal behavior among transgender youth. *Journal of Adolescent Health, 63*(4), 503–5.

Spiel, E. C., Paxton, S. J., & Yager, Z. (2012). Weight attitudes in 3- to 5-year-old children: Age differences and cross-sectional predictors. *Body Image, 9*(4), 524–7.

Stein, J. H., & Reiser, L. W. (1994). A study of white middle-class adolescent boys' responses to 'semenarche' (the first ejaculation). *Journal of Youth and Adolescence, 23*(3), 373–84.

Tiller, E., Greenland, N., Christie, R., Kos, A., Brennan, N., & Di Nicola, K. (2021). *Youth survey report 2021*. Mission Australia.

Yager, Z., & McLean, S. (2020). Muscle building supplement use in Australian adolescent boys: relationships with body image, weight lifting, and sports engagement. *BMC Pediatrics, 20*(1), 1–9.

CHAPTER 10: FEELINGS

Brown, B. (2021). *Atlas of the heart: Mapping meaningful connection and the language of human experience*. Random House.

Ekman, P. (2022). *Universal emotions*. paulekman.com/universal-emotions

Gilbert, P. (2010). *Compassion focused therapy: Distinctive features*. Routledge.

Haynos, A. F., Roberto, C. A., Martinez, M. A., Attia, E., & Fruzzetti, A. E. (2014). Emotion regulation difficulties in anorexia nervosa before and after inpatient weight restoration. *International Journal of Eating Disorders, 47*(8), 888–91.

Prefit, A. B., Cândea, D. M., & Szentagotai-Tătar, A. (2019). Emotion regulation across eating pathology: A meta-analysis. *Appetite, 143*, 104438.

Russell, J. (2003). Core affect and the psychological construction of emotion. *Psychological Review, 110*(1), 145–72.

Wakelin, K. E., Perman, G., & Simonds, L. M. (2022). Effectiveness of self-compassion-related interventions for reducing self-criticism: A systematic review and meta-analysis. *Clinical Psychology & Psychotherapy, 29*(1), 1–25.

Willcox, G. (1982). The feeling wheel: A tool for expanding awareness of emotions and increasing spontaneity and intimacy. *Transactional Analysis Journal*, 12(4), 274–76.

Wilcox, G. (2021). *The feeling wheel, positive psychology practitioner's toolkit.* blossomandberry.com/wp-content/uploads/2021/09/Feeling-Wheel.pdf

CHAPTER 11: FOOD

Christoph, M., Järvelä-Reijonen, E., Hooper, L., Larson, N., Mason, S. M., & Neumark-Sztainer, D. (2021). Longitudinal associations between intuitive eating and weight-related behaviors in a population-based sample of young adults. *Appetite*, 160, 105093.

Damiano, S. R., Hart, L., Paxton, S. J., Cornell, C., & Sutherland, F. (2014). Are body image and eating attitudes, behaviours, and knowledge of parents of pre-schoolers associated with parent feeding practices? *Journal of Eating Disorders*, 2(1), 1-1.

Fuentes Artiles, R., Staub, K., Aldakak, L., Eppenberger, P., Rühli, F., & Bender, N. (2019). Mindful eating and common diet programs lower body weight similarly: Systematic review and meta-analysis. *Obesity reviews*, 20(11), 1619–27.

Gattario, K. H., & Frisén, A. (2019). From negative to positive body image: Men's and women's journeys from early adolescence to emerging adulthood. *Body Image*, 28, 53–65. doi: dx.doi.org/10.1016/j.bodyim.2018.12.002

Hart, L. M., Damiano, S. R., Chittleborough, P., Paxton, S. J., & Jorm, A. F. (2014). Parenting to prevent body dissatisfaction and unhealthy eating patterns in preschool children: A Delphi consensus study. *Body Image*, 11(4), 418–25.

Hart, L. M., Damiano, S. R., Li-Wai-Suen, C. S., & Paxton, S. J. (2019). Confident body, confident child: Evaluation of a universal parenting resource promoting healthy body image and eating patterns in early childhood – 6- and 12-month outcomes from a randomized controlled trial. *International Journal of Eating Disorders*, 52(2), 121–31.

Hazzard, V. M., Telke, S. E., Simone, M., Anderson, L. M., Larson, N. I., & Neumark-Sztainer, D. (2021). Intuitive eating longitudinally predicts better psychological health and lower use of disordered eating behaviors:

Findings from EAT 2010–2018. *Eating and Weight Disorders – Studies on Anorexia, Bulimia and Obesity*, 26(1), 287–94.

Linardon, J., Tylka, T. L., & Fuller-Tyszkiewicz, M. (2021). Intuitive eating and its psychological correlates: A meta-analysis. *International Journal of Eating Disorders*, 54(7), 1073–98.

The Original Intuitive Eating Pros. (2007–2019). *10 principles of intuitive eating*. intuitiveeating.org/10-principles-of-intuitive-eating/

Therapeutic Goods Administration. (2020, 24 September). *Changes to the regulation of sports supplements in Australia*. tga.gov.au/changes-regulation-sports-supplements-australia

Tucker, J., Fischer, T., Upjohn, L., Mazzera, D., & Kumar, M. (2018). Unapproved pharmaceutical ingredients included in dietary supplements associated with US Food and Drug Administration warnings. *JAMA Network Open*, 1(6): e183337.

Tylka, T. L., Calogero, R. M., & Daníelsdóttir, S. (2020). Intuitive eating is connected to self-reported weight stability in community women and men. *Eating Disorders*, 28(3), 256–64.

Van Dyke, N., & Drinkwater, E. J. (2014). Review article relationships between intuitive eating and health indicators: Literature review. *Public Health Nutrition*, 17(8), 1757–66.

CHAPTER 12: MEDIA

Bell, B. T., Taylor, C., Paddock, D., & Bates, A. (2021). Digital Bodies: A controlled evaluation of a brief classroom-based intervention for reducing negative body image among adolescents in the digital age. *British Journal of Educational Psychology*, e12449.

Casale, S., Gemelli, G., Calosi, C., Giangrasso, B., & Fioravanti, G. (2021). Multiple exposure to appearance-focused real accounts on Instagram: Effects on body image among both genders. *Current Psychology*, 40(6), 2877–86.

Cohen, R., Newton-John, T., & Slater, A. (2021). The case for body positivity on social media: Perspectives on current advances and future directions. *Journal of Health Psychology*, 26(13), 2365–73.

Coyne, S. M., Davis, E. J., Warburton, W., Stockdale, L., Abba, I., & Busby, D. M. (2021). Mirror, mirror on the wall: The effect of listening to body positive music on implicit and explicit body esteem. *Psychology of Popular Media*, 10(1), 2.

Coyne, S. M., Linder, J. R., Booth, M., Keenan-Kroff, S., Shawcroft, J. E., & Yang, C. (2021). Princess power: Longitudinal associations between engagement with princess culture in preschool and gender stereotypical behavior, body esteem, and hegemonic masculinity in early adolescence. *Child Development*, 92(6), 2413–30.

Danthinne, E. S., Giorgianni, F. E., & Rodgers, R. F. (2020). Labels to prevent the detrimental effects of media on body image: A systematic review and meta-analysis. *International Journal of Eating Disorders*, 53(5), 647–61.

Dohnt, H. K., & Tiggemann, M. (2008). Promoting positive body image in young girls: An evaluation of 'Shapesville'. *European Eating Disorders Review: The Professional Journal of the Eating Disorders Association*, 16(3), 222–33.

Gillen, M. M., & Markey, C. H. (2021). Body image, weight management behavior, and women's interest in cosmetic surgery. *Psychology, Health & Medicine*, 26(5), 621–30.

Giorgianni, F., Danthinne, E., & Rodgers, R. F. (2020). Consumer warning versus systemic change: The effects of including disclaimer labels on images that have or have not been digitally modified on body image. *Body Image*, 34, 249–58.

Huang, Q., Peng, W., & Ahn, S. (2021). When media become the mirror: A meta-analysis on media and body image. *Media Psychology*, 24(4), 437–89.

Jarman, H. K., Marques, M. D., McLean, S. A., Slater, A., & Paxton, S. J. (2021). Social media, body satisfaction and well-being among adolescents: A mediation model of appearance-ideal internalization and comparison. *Body Image*, 36, 139–48.

Lee, M., & Lee, H. H. (2021). Social media photo activity, internalization, appearance comparison, and body satisfaction: The moderating role of photo-editing behavior. *Computers in Human Behavior*, 114, 106579.

López-Guimerà, G., Levine, M. P., Sánchez-Carracedo, D., & Fauquet, J. (2010). Influence of mass media on body image and eating disordered attitudes and behaviors in females: A review of effects and processes. *Media Psychology*, 13(4), 387–416.

McArthur, B.A., Racine, N., Browne, D., McDonald, S., Tough, S.,

Madigan, S. (2021). Recreational screen time before and during COVID-19 in school-aged children. *Acta Paediatrica*, doi: 10.1111/apa.15966

McLean, S. A., Paxton, S. J., Wertheim, E. H., & Masters, J. (2015). Photoshopping the selfie: Self photo editing and photo investment are associated with body dissatisfaction in adolescent girls. *International Journal of Eating Disorders*, 48(8), 1132–40.

National Association for Media Literacy Education. (2022). Key questions. namle.net/resources/key-questions-for-analyzing-media/

Politte-Corn, M., & Fardouly, J. (2020). #nomakeupselfie: The impact of natural no-makeup images and positive appearance comments on young women's body image. *Body Image*, 34, 233–41.

Rice, K., Prichard, I., Tiggemann, M., & Slater, A. (2016). Exposure to Barbie: Effects on thin-ideal internalisation, body esteem, and body dissatisfaction among young girls. *Body Image*, 19, 142–49.

Robinson, L., Prichard, I., Nikolaidis, A., Drummond, C., Drummond, M., & Tiggemann, M. (2017). Idealised media images: The effect of fitspiration imagery on body satisfaction and exercise behaviour. *Body Image*, 22, 65–71.

Rodgers, R. F., Paxton, S. J., & Wertheim, E. H. (2021). #Take idealized bodies out of the picture: A scoping review of social media content aiming to protect and promote positive body image. *Body Image*, 38, 10–36.

CHAPTER 13: FRIENDS

Ata, R. N., Ludden, A. B., & Lally, M. M. (2007). The effects of gender and family, friend, and media influences on eating behaviors and body image during adolescence. *Journal of Youth and Adolescence*, 36(8), 1024–37.

Hutchinson, D. M., & Rapee, R. M. (2007). Do friends share similar body image and eating problems? The role of social networks and peer influences in early adolescence. *Behaviour Research and Therapy*, 45(7), 1557–77.

Jones, D. C., & Crawford, J. K. (2006). The peer appearance culture during adolescence: Gender and body mass variations. *Journal of Youth and Adolescence*, 35(2), 243–55.

Lawlor, M., & Nixon, E. (2011). Body dissatisfaction among adolescent boys and girls: The effects of body mass, peer appearance culture and internalization of appearance ideals. *Journal of Youth and Adolescence*, 40(1), 59–71.

Lieberman, M., Gauvin, L., Bukowski, W. M., & White, D. R. (2001). Interpersonal influence and disordered eating behaviors in adolescent girls the role of peer modeling, social reinforcement, and body-related teasing. *Eating Behaviors, 2*, 215–36.

Mills, J., & Fuller-Tyszkiewicz, M. (2017). Fat talk and body image disturbance: A systematic review and meta-analysis. *Psychology of Women Quarterly*, 41(1), 114–29.

Paddock, D. L., & Bell, B. T. (2021). 'It's better saying I look fat instead of saying you look fat': A qualitative study of UK adolescents' understanding of appearance-related interactions on social media. *Journal of Adolescent Research*, doi.org/10.1177/07435584211034875.

Rodgers, R. F., Simone, M., Franko, D. L., Eisenberg, M. E., Loth, K., & Neumark-Sztainer, D. (2021). The longitudinal relationship between family and peer teasing in young adulthood and later unhealthy weight control behaviors: The mediating role of body image. *International Journal of Eating Disorders*, 54(5), 831–40.

Sutherland, F. (2018). *Help! My kid has been sent home with a serve of diet culture.* themindfuldietitian.com.au/blog/help-my-kid-has-been-sent-home-with -a-serve-of-diet-culture-your-guide-to-keeping-your-sht-together-and-taking-effective-action

Tompkins, K. B., Martz, D. M., Rocheleau, C. A., & Bazzini, D. G. (2009). Social likeability, conformity, and body talk: Does fat talk have a normative rival in female body image conversations? *Body Image*, 6(4), 292–98.

CHAPTER 14: FAMILIES

Al Sabbah, H., Vereecken, C. A., Elgar, F. J., Nansel, T., Aasvee, K., Abdeen, Z., ... & Maes, L. (2009). Body weight dissatisfaction and communication with parents among adolescents in 24 countries: international cross-sectional survey. *BMC public health*, 9(1), 1–10.

Keery, H., Boutelle, K., Van Den Berg, P., & Thompson, J. K. (2005). The impact of appearance-related teasing by family members. *Journal of Adolescent Health*, 37(2), 120–7.

Neumark-Sztainer, D., Bauer, K. W., Friend, S., Hannan, P. J., Story, M., & Berge, J. M. (2010). Family weight talk and dieting: how much do they matter for body dissatisfaction and disordered eating behaviors in adolescent girls? *Journal of Adolescent Health*, 47(3), 270-276.

CHAPTER 15: SEXY TIME

Burén, J., Holmqvist Gattario, K., & Lunde, C. (2021). What do peers think about sexting? Adolescents' views of the norms guiding sexting behavior. *Journal of Adolescent Research*, 37(2), 221–49.

Damour, L. (2019, 14 November). My 13-year-old likes sexy clothes. What can I say that won't shame her? *New York Times*.

Mori, C., Cooke, J. E., Temple, J. R., Ly, A., Lu, Y., Anderson, N., ... & Madigan, S. (2020). The prevalence of sexting behaviors among emerging adults: A meta-analysis. *Archives of Sexual Behavior*, 49(4), 1103–19.

CHAPTER 16: MOVEMENT

Campbell, A., & Hausenblas, H. A. (2009). Effects of exercise interventions on body image: A meta-analysis. *Journal of Health Psychology*, 14(6), 780–93.

Gittus, M., Fuller-Tyszkiewicz, M., Brown, H. E., Richardson, B., Fassnacht, D. B., Lennard, G. R., ... & Krug, I. (2020). Are Fitbits implicated in body image concerns and disordered eating in women?. *Health Psychology*, 39(10), 900.

Hanlon, C., Yager, Z., Flowers, E., & Dadswell, K. (2021). *What girls want from sport uniforms*. changeourgame.vic.gov.au/__data/assets/pdf_file/0018/160353/Final-Sport-uniforms.pdf

Homan, K. J., & Tylka, T. L. (2014). Appearance-based exercise motivation moderates the relationship between exercise frequency and positive body image. *Body Image*, 11(2), 101–8.

Lessard, L. M., Puhl, R. M., Larson, N., Simone, M., Eisenberg, M. E., & Neumark-Sztainer, D. (2021). Parental contributors to the prevalence and long-term health risks of family weight teasing in adolescence. *Journal of Adolescent Health*, 69(1), 74–81.

Lucibello, K. M., Koulanova, A., Pila, E., Brunet, J., & Sabiston, C. M. (2021). Exploring adolescent girls' experiences of body talk in non-aesthetic sport. *Journal of Adolescence*, 89, 63–73.

Mountjoy, M., Sundgot-Borgen, J., Burke, L., Carter, S., Constantini, N., Lebrun, C., ... & Ljungqvist, A. (2014). The IOC consensus statement:

beyond the female athlete triad – relative energy deficiency in sport (RED-S). *British Journal of Sports Medicine, 48*(7), 491–7.

Rodriguez-Ayllon, M., Cadenas-Sánchez, C., Estévez-López, F., Muñoz, N. E., Mora-Gonzalez, J., Migueles, J. H., ... & Esteban-Cornejo, I. (2019). Role of physical activity and sedentary behavior in the mental health of preschoolers, children and adolescents: a systematic review and meta-analysis. *Sports Medicine, 49*(9), 1383–1410.

Salci, L. E., & Ginis, K. A. M. (2017). Acute effects of exercise on women with pre-existing body image concerns: A test of potential mediators. *Psychology of Sport and Exercise, 31*, 113–22.

Slater, A., & Tiggemann, M. (2011). Gender differences in adolescent sport participation, teasing, self-objectification and body image concerns. *Journal of Adolescence, 34*(3), 455–63.

Victoria University, Institute for Health and Sport, S-Trend. (2021). *What girls want in sport uniforms to make them feel comfortable and confident to participate in sport: A national study.* vu.edu.au/sites/default/files/girl-sport-uniforms-national-study.pdf

Willson, E., & Kerr, G. (2021). Body shaming as a form of emotional abuse in sport. *International Journal of Sport and Exercise Psychology,* 1–19.

Acknowledgements

HUMANS LEARN THROUGH STORIES. We thank you for your time and vulnerability in sharing your stories so we can learn from them.

Thanks to the amazing parents from around the world who contributed their stories and wisdom.

And the incredible professionals who gave up their time and expertise so generously: Dr Beth Bell, Zoë Bisbing, Dr Georgie Buckley, Dr Stephanie Damiano, Dr Jody Forbes, Ginger Gorman, Denise Hamburger, Professor Clare Hanlon, Dr Laura Hart, Dr Kristina Holmqvist-Gattario, Sara Ibrahim, Dr Megan Lee, Professor Linda Lin, Dr Carolina Lunde, Carole MacGregor, Laura Mazza, Danielle Paddock, Dr Ivanka Prichard, Anupa Roper, Danni Rowlands, Dr Veya Seekis, Amy Sheppard, Fiona Sutherland, Dr Kendrin Sonneville, Amy Taylor-Kabbaz, Carmelita Tiu, Chevese Turner, Dr Danielle Wagstaff, Dr Jennifer Webb and Dr Robert Wood.

From Taryn

To my children, Oliver, Cruz and Mikaela, thanks for sparking the magic in me . . . I love you more than dumplings. To Tim, thanks for holding space for the magic to exist. To my mum and dad, Justine and friends, the magic is meaningful because of you.

From Zali

Huge thanks to my family for their support in making this happen, most of all to Tom, my love, and my three: Jack, Evie and Lucy, as well as all of my parents, siblings, in-laws and out-laws who got excited about, and supported me in, this work.